Textual Authority in Classical Indian Thought

Theistic Vedānta originated with Rāmānuja (1077–1157), who was one of the foremost theologians of Viśiṣṭādvaita Vedānta and also an initiate of the Śrīvaiṣṇava sectarian tradition in South India. As devotees of the God Viṣṇu and his consort Śrī, the Śrīvaiṣṇavas established themselves through various processes of legitimation as a powerful sectarian tradition. One of the processes by which the authority of the Śrīvaiṣṇavas was consolidated was Rāmānuja's synthesis of popular Hindu devotionalism with the philosophy of Vedānta.

This book demonstrates that by incorporating a text often thought to be of secondary importance—the Viṣṇu Purāṇa (first to fourth century CE)—into his reading of the Upaniṣads, which were the standard of orthodoxy for Vedānta philosophy, Rāmānuja was able to interpret Vedānta within the theistic context of Śrīvaiṣṇavism. Rāmānuja was the first Brahmin thinker to incorporate devotional purāṇas into Vedānta philosophy and his synthetic theology called Viśiṣṭādvaita (unity-of-the-differenced) wielded tremendous influence over the expansion of Viṣṇu devotionalism in South India. In this book, the exploration of the exegetical function of the Viṣṇu Purāṇa in arguments salient to Rāmānuja's Vedānta facilitates our understanding of the processes of textual accommodation and reformulation that allow the incorporation of divergent doctrinal claims.

Expanding on and reassessing current views on Rāmānuja's theology, the book contributes new insights to broader issues in religious studies such as canon expansion, commentarial interpretation, tradition-building, and the comparative study of scripture. It will be of interest to students and scholars of Indian philosophy and Religious Studies.

Sucharita Adluri is Assistant Professor in the Department of Philosophy and Comparative Religion at Cleveland State University. Her research interests include the History of Religions of South India, Sanskrit Commentary and Intellectual History.

Routledge Hindu Studies Series

Series Editor: Gavin Flood, Oxford Centre for Hindu Studies

A RECOGNISED INDEPENDENT CENTRE OF THE UNIVERSITY OF OXFORD

The *Routledge Hindu Studies Series*, in association with the Oxford Centre for Hindu Studies, intends the publication of constructive Hindu theological, philosophical and ethical projects aimed at bringing Hindu traditions into dialogue with contemporary trends in scholarship and contemporary society. The series invites original, high quality, research level work on religion, culture and society of Hindus living in India and abroad. Proposals for annotated translations of important primary sources and studies in the history of the Hindu religious traditions will also be considered.

Epistemologies and the Limitations of Philosophical Inquiry
Doctrine in Madhva Vedanta
Deepak Sarma

A Hindu Critique of Buddhist Epistemology
Kumarila on perception The "Determination of Perception" chapter of Kumarilabhatta's *Slokarvarttika* translation and commentary
John Taber

Samkara's Advaita Vedanta
A way of teaching
Jacqueline Hirst

Attending Krishna's Image
Chaitanya Vaishnava Murti-seva as Devotional Truth
Kenneth Russell Valpey

Advaita Vedanta and Vaisnavism
The Philosophy of Madhusudana Sarasvati
Sanjukta Gupta

Classical Samkhya and Yoga
An Indian metaphysics of experience
Mikel Burley

Self-Surrender (prapatti) to God in Shrivaishnavism
Tamil cats and Sanskrit monkeys
Srilata Raman

The Chaitanya Vaishnava Vedanta of Jiva Gosvami
When knowledge meets devotion
Ravi M. Gupta

Gender and Narrative in the Mahabharata
Edited by Simon Brodbeck and Brian Black

Yoga in the Modern World
Contemporary perspectives
Edited By Mark Singleton and Jean Byrne

Consciousness in Indian Philosophy
The Advaita doctrine of 'awareness only'
Sthaneshwar Timalsina

Desire and Motivation in Indian Philosophy
Christopher G. Framarin

Women in the Hindu Tradition
Rules, roles and exceptions
Mandakranta Bose

Religion, Narrative and Public Imagination in South Asia
Past and place in the Sanskrit Mahabharata
James Hegarty

Interpreting Devotion
The poetry and legacy of a female Bhakti saint of India
Karen Pechilis

Hindu Perspectives on Evolution
Darwin, dharma, and design
C. Mackenzie Brown

Pilgrimage in the Hindu Tradition
Salvific space
Knut A. Jacobsen

A Woman's Ramayana
Candravati's Bengali Epic
Mandakranta Bose and Sarika Priyadarshini Bose

Classical Vaisesika in Indian Philosophy
On Knowing and What is to be Known
Shashiprabha Kumar

Re-figuring the Ramayana as Theology
A History of Reception in Premodern India
Ajay R Rao

Hinduism and Environmental Ethics
Law, Literature and Philosophy
Christopher G. Framarin

Hindu Pilgrimage
Shifting Patterns of Worldview of Srisailam in South India
Prabhavati C.Reddy

The Death and Afterlife of Mahatma Gandhi
Makarand R. Paranjape

Bhakti and Embodiment
Fashioning Divine Bodies and Devotional Bodies in Kṛṣṇa Bhakti
Barbara A. Holdrege

Textual Authority in Classical Hindu Thought
Rāmānuja and the Viṣṇu Purāṇa
Sucharita Adluri

Indian Thought and Western Theism
The Vedānta of Rāmānuja
Martin Ganeri

Debating "Conversion" in Hinduism and Christianity
Ankur Barua

Textual Authority in Classical Indian Thought

Rāmānuja and the Viṣṇu Purāṇa

Sucharita Adluri

Routledge
Taylor & Francis Group
LONDON AND NEW YORK

First published 2015
by Routledge
2 Park Square, Milton Park, Abingdon, Oxon OX14 4RN

and by Routledge
711 Third Avenue, New York, NY 10017

First issued in paperback 2017

Routledge is an imprint of the Taylor & Francis Group, an informa business

British Library Cataloguing in Publication Data
A catalogue record for this book is available from the British Library

Library of Congress Cataloging in Publication Data
A catalog record for this book has been requested

ISBN 13: 978-1-138-49156-4 (pbk)
ISBN 13: 978-0-415-69575-6 (hbk)

Typeset in Times New Roman
by Taylor & Francis Books

For my teachers

Contents

List of tables xi
Acknowledgements xii
Abbreviations xiii

1 **Introduction** 1
Rāmānuja's exegetical method 2
Viṣṇu Purāṇa 5
VP 1.1 7
VP 1.2 8
VP 1.3 8
VP 1.22 9
VP 2.7 9
VP 2.12 9
VP 2.14 10
VP 6.4 and VP 6.5 10
VP 6.7 10
Outline of chapters 10
Editorial notes 12

2 **The individual self, cosmology, and the divine body in the *Vedārthasaṃgraha*** 14
The individual self 15
Śruti on the individual self 15
Viṣṇu Purāṇa on the individual self 18
Viṣṇu Purāṇa on the embodied self 21
Brahman's originative causality 25
*Brahman as the material cause as a whole (*aviśeṣaṇakāraṇa*)* 26
Śruti support 26
Bhagavadgītā support 28
Viṣṇu Purāṇa support 30
*Causality as an aspect of the essential nature of Brahman (*brahmsvarūpaviśeṣa*)* 31

The divine body of Brahman *39*
Structure of Rāmānuja's argument *40*
The first description of Brahman's divine form *41*
Śruti support *43*
Smṛti support *46*
The second description of Brahman's divine form *50*
Conclusion *54*

3 Brahman, the individual self, and ignorance in the *Śrībhāṣya* 64
The nature of Brahman *67*
Śruti support *69*
Bhagavadgītā support *72*
Viṣṇu Purāṇa support *74*
The nature of the individual self *81*
The essential nature of the individual self *81*
Plurality of individual selves *85*
The liberated self is distinct from Brahman *89*
Defining ignorance *93*
Śruti support *93*
VP (2.12.36–46) support *96*
Conclusion *102*

4 Sāṃkhya-Yoga, Kṛṣṇa, and the foremost devotee in the *Bhagavadgītābhāṣya* 113
Defining Sāṃkhya and Yoga *114*
*Being (*sat*) and Non-being (*asat*)* *114*
*Realization of Brahman (*samyagdarśana*) and realization of the individual self (*ātmadarśana*)* *120*
Kṛṣṇa's nature *123*
*The two natures (*prakṛti*) of Kṛṣṇa* *124*
*The field (*kṣetra*) and the field-knower (*kṣetrajña*)* *128*
Bondage and liberation *134*
Kṛṣṇa's māyā *135*
The foremost devotee (jñānin) *137*
Conclusion *140*

Bibliography 150
Index 155

Table

Acknowledgements

This book is based on ideas developed in my doctoral dissertation at the University of Pennsylvania, and I owe a deep gratitude to my advisors, Frank Clooney (Harvard University), E. Ann Matter, and Ludo Rocher. In the initial stages, I worked extensively with Ludo and Frank and I thank them for all their helpful feedback. I am also grateful to Ann for her unflagging support and encouragement.

My initial research in India was supported by the Fulbright Program and I would also like to thank Cleveland State University for additional funding. I am grateful to the late Dr. M. Narasimhachary (University of Madras), K.S. Varadachary of Mysore, and Dr. S. Padmanabhan (University of Madras) for working with me on the commentaries of Rāmānuja. My thanks also, to the folks at Kuppuswami Sastri Research Institute, Chennai for all their help.

Friends and family have cheered me on during this work – Sunita Adluri, Ashish Agrawal, Signe Cohen, Leah Comeau, Benjamin Fleming, Amruta Inamdar, Mrs. Vasantha Parthasarthy, Annette Reed, Valerie Stoker, Mrs. Vishalam Ramanathan, and Kate Zubko—and I am grateful for their support. My thanks, also to Gavin Flood, Dorothea Schaefter, Jillian Morrison, and Rebecca Lawrence at Routledege. Last but not least, I would like to thank my colleagues in the Department of Philosophy and Comparative Religion at Cleveland State University for all their encouragement and support.

Abbreviations

Adhyātma Upaniṣad	Adhy Up
Aitareya Upaniṣad	Ait Up
Brahma Sūtras	Br Sū
Bhagavadgītā	BhG
Bhāgavatapurāṇa	BhP
Bṛhadāraṇyaka Upaniṣad	Bṛ Up
Bṛhadāraṇyaka Upaniṣad (Mādhyandina recension)	Bṛ Up Mādh
Chāndogya Upaniṣad	Ch Up
Kaṭha Upaniṣad	Kaṭh Up
Kena Upaniṣad	Kena Up
Mahābhārata	MBh
Mahānārāyaṇa Upaniṣad	Mahā Nār Up
Maitrī Upaniṣad	Maitrī Up
Māṇḍūkya Upaniṣad	Māṇḍ Up
Muṇḍaka Upaniṣad	Muṇḍ Up
Rāmānuja's Bhagavadgītābhāṣya	RBhGBh
Ṛg Veda	RV
Śaṅkara's Bhagavadgītābhāṣya	ŚBhGBh
Śaṅkara's Brahmasūtrabhāṣya	ŚBrSuBh
Śrībhāṣya	ŚBh
Śrutaprakāśikā	ŚP
Stotraratna	SR
Subāla Upaniṣad	Sub Up
Śvetāśvatara Upaniṣad	Śvet Up
Taittirīya Āraṇyaka	Taitt Ār
Taittirīya Saṃhitā	Taitt Saṃhitā
Taittirīya Upaniṣad	Taitt Up
Tātparyacandrikā	TC
Tātparyadīpikā	TD
Vedārthasaṃgraha	VS
Viṣṇu Purāṇa	VP
Viṣṇudharmottara Purāṇa	Viṣṇu Dharm

1 Introduction

Rāmānuja (1077–1157), one of the foremost proponents of systematic theistic Vedānta[1] was not only a Vedānta philosopher but also an initiate of the Śrīvaiṣṇava sectarian tradition in Tamilnadu.[2] As devotees of the God Viṣṇu and his consort Śrī, the Śrīvaiṣṇavas established themselves through various processes of legitimation as a powerful sectarian tradition in South India. One of the ways by which the authority of the Śrīvaiṣṇavas was consolidated was Rāmānuja's synthesis of popular Hindu devotionalism with the philosophy of Vedānta.[3] This theology, that came to be known as Viśiṣṭādvaita (unity-of-the-differenced), wielded tremendous influence over the expansion of Viṣṇu devotionalism in South India and beyond. By incorporating more popular religious texts such as the *Viṣṇu Purāṇa* (VP) into his reading of the Vedānta texts, which were the standard of orthodoxy for Vedānta philosophy, Rāmānuja legitimized identification of the absolute principle, Brahman, in the upaniṣads, with the supreme deity Viṣṇu. While he was certainly not the first Brahmin thinker to be influenced by the devotional purāṇas, he was the first to incorporate such traditions into Vedānta philosophy.

Broadly speaking this study investigates Rāmānuja's use of the VP to accommodate, within Vedānta, the doctrinal claims of the Śrīvaiṣṇava sectarian tradition. Though it has been noted by many scholars that he is one of the first Vedānta commentators to identify the supreme reality of the upaniṣads, Brahman, with the deity Viṣṇu, there are not many sources that investigate how Rāmānuja manages this. I suggest that the use of the *Viṣṇu Purāṇa* as a valid means of knowledge (*śabdapramāṇa*) of Brahman is one such strategy.

In Vedānta philosophy, the application of the authority of scripture as a valid means of knowledge in the domain of extra-sensory matters is a common convention. Known as verbal testimony (*śabdapramāṇa*), scriptures are the basis of authentication of specific ontological frameworks and are important in constructing the legitimacy of various systems of thought. In this scheme, philosophical and theological concepts are substantiated with evidence first from śruti and then from smṛti.[4] In the Vedānta system it is primarily the upaniṣads, the later portions of the Vedic texts, and to a certain extent the earlier sections of the Veda that qualify as śruti. Though smṛti was acknowledged as of secondary importance, its use in Vedānta philosophy was negligible, except for the *Bhagavadgītā*.[5] As a smṛti text, the importance of the VP in Rāmānuja's writings is considerable and unique.

Lott (1980: 47) notes that "Rāmānuja's polemic takes two forms: some arguments are aimed at the logical structure of the absolute position, while others are based more on theological affirmation or scriptural interpretation." Though, these two aspects cannot be entirely divorced, this study will only be concerned with the latter in that it only takes into account arguments relevant to scripture as a valid means of knowledge. As such it is not solely devoted to the Vedānta of Rāmānuja, but does address philosophical contexts in which scriptural citations, specifically those of the VP are embedded. This book evaluates Vedānta as both a philosophical and a commentarial enterprise, but does not attempt a comprehensive treatment of Rāmānuja's vast exegetical project (Clooney 1992: 47–68). I only examine distinct sections utilizing the use of the VP to demarcate the limits of my exegetical analysis.

Each of the core chapters (2–4) on Rāmānuja's three key writings evaluates the role of the *Viṣṇu Purāṇa* as valid means of knowledge (*śabdapramāṇa*). In so doing, I draw out structures in the purāṇa conducive to Rāmānuja's argument, underscore its function in interpretive maneuvers that counter rival doctrines such as Advaita, and evaluate some of these strategies. The *Viṣṇu Purāṇa* cannot be said to espouse Viśiṣṭādvaita Vedānta systematically. Rāmānuja, however, taking citations from diverse sections of this purāṇa arranges them thematically and in a coherent fashion and in so doing incorporates the *Viṣṇu Purāṇa* into his sectarian theological vision.

In evaluating the various exegetical uses of the *Viṣṇu Purāṇa* in Rāmānuja's Vedānta this study also contributes to the understanding of inter-textuality in the Indian context. For the purposes of this study, I define inter-textuality as an awareness of other texts, whether this is explicitly mentioned or is alluded to (Rocher 1994; Olivelle 2004). This notion of inter-textuality is built into the Vedānta commentarial tradition in the form of *śabdapramāṇa* (scripture as a valid means of knowledge), which allows for the interplay of various interpretations and contexts. An examination of the *Viṣṇu Purāṇa*'s use as scriptural evidence in Vedānta commentaries reveals the fluidity of this purāṇa as a text that exists at the nexus of inter-textual exegesis, in some ways similar to texts such as the *Bhagavadgītā*.

Rāmānuja's exegetical method

In his commentaries, Rāmānuja does not explicitly describe his method of exegesis as far as the use of scripture as a valid means of knowledge is concerned. Though it is generally noted that Rāmānuja accords equal importance to śruti and authoritative smṛti, how this "equality" manifests in his exegesis of Vedānta is not a primary concern of most scholarly works on Viśiṣṭādvaita (van Buitenen 1956: 48ff; Lipner 1986; Bartley 2002). On the topic of the authority and function of smṛti, Rāmānuja has much to say. I have addressed this issue elsewhere and only discuss it briefly here (Adluri 2006).

Rāmānuja does use the traditional exegetical principles of corroboration (*upabṛṃhaṇa*), harmonization of scripture (*samanvaya*), and so on, to validate his use of the *Viṣṇu Purāṇa*. He claims that he follows the Pūrvamīmāṃsā understanding of corroboration as augmentation that is not contrary to the Veda. That is, smṛti that does not contradict the Veda is deemed authoritative. The primary function of smṛti then is to augment the Veda as stated in his commentary on BhG 16.24:

> [t]herefore *śāstra* alone is your authority to determine what is to be done and what is not to be done, that is, what is acceptable and what is not acceptable. The Vedas augmented (*upabṛṃhita*) by the dharmaśāstras, itihāsas, and purāṇas, teach only the highest reality called Puruṣottama, His pleasing form, and the actions that are the means to attain Him.[6]

The term *upabṛṃhita* used to denote smṛti's function is a derivative of the verbal root *bṛh*, meaning to "expand", "grow", "increase", "raise" and so on; together with the prefix "*upa*" it denotes "the act of making strong, invigorating, promoting, nourishing" and so on. According to Rāmānuja, only by knowing both the Veda and smṛti is one to perform one's duties, which are not Vedic sacrifices but acts of devotion to Viṣṇu. This inseparability of śruti from smṛti[7] and the latter's amplificatory function is also discussed in the *Śrī bhāṣya* 2.1.1. In commenting on *Brahma Sūtra* 1.1.1, Rāmānuja explores further, the corroborative function of smṛti:

> *The Veda should be amplified by the itihāsas and purāṇas.*
> *The Veda fears that he of little learning will do me wrong.*
>
> (MBh 1.1.264)
>
> This is what is taught by scripture 'the act of amplifying', is the meaning of epics (itihāsa) and purāṇa. To amplify means to gain a clear perception of the meaning of Vedic passages known to oneself, by means of the statements of those who know the entire Veda and its meaning and those who have directly perceived the essential nature of the Veda and its meaning, by means of the great power of their yoga. Indeed, amplification of Veda ought to be done, because without it one cannot reach a settled conclusion, since the knowledge of all the branches (of the Veda) is not comprehensible from listening to a small portion.[8]

The *purāṇas* and *itihāsas* are correctives to the misuse of the Veda. But what corroboration can mean is open to interpretation. Scholarship's unanimous declaration of the function of smṛti as strictly corroborative in Rāmānuja's commentaries is not entirely helpful. In the context of justifying the use of smṛti texts, it has been noted that "Rāmānuja's citations of the VP are illustrative and corroborative. His justification of these citations shows clearly that he was anxious not to introduce any evidence that would be unacceptable to his fellow Vedāntins" (van Buitenen 1956: 35). That Rāmānuja occasionally utilizes smṛti such as the BhG to interpret śruti has been noted, but this has not led to closer examinations of the use of scripture as a valid means of knowledge (Lott 1976: 28). Another explanation for Rāmānuja's use of smṛti is that he took his scripture literally, unlike other Vedāntins (Lott 1976: 28; Lipner 1986: 83). While all these claims are valid, they do not offer enough insight into the exegetical practices that exemplify corroboration.

Corroboration by smṛti of an argument already established by śruti meant that, exegetically speaking, the śruti passages would be cited followed by smṛti. However, this is not always Rāmānuja's method, as we see in the following chapters. Some of the patterns of usage of the VP he employs are the following. First, there is the more traditional usage of citing śruti and then the VP. Second, the VP sometimes is used to interpret śruti. Third, a valid smṛti is used to validate another smṛti whose authority may be in question. Fourth, only smṛti (VP) is used as valid means of proof. Each of these categories is represented in the discussion of Rāmānuja's commentaries in the subsequent chapters.

Though in a traditional sense, Rāmānuja maintains the canonical status of the Vedic texts, he also expands their boundaries without, however, admitting to such a change (Smith 1982: 48–49). He constructs a Vedānta canon of religiously meaningful texts that includes not only the canonical Vedas, but also a purāṇa, the *Viṣṇu Purāṇa*, in order to maximize legitimation for his philosophy without altering the Vedānta canon in the process. As a Vedānta exegete, Rāmānuja actively participated in the making and remaking of the world in which these texts were embedded and recovers the "true" meaning of the upaniṣads relevant for 12th century South India, by manipulating the scriptural categories of śruti and smṛti (Inden, Ali and Waters 2000). The rest of this chapter considers the sources for this study, followed by an introduction to the provenance and content of the VP and concludes with an outline of chapters.

The primary sources for this study are Rāmānuja's expositions on the three foundational texts of Vedānta, the upaniṣads, the *Brahmasūtras* (Br Sū), and the *Bhagavadgītā* (BhG) called the *Vedārthasaṃgraha* (VS), the *Śrībhāṣya* (ŚBh), and the *Bhagavadgītābhāṣya* (RBhGBh) respectively.[9] I also utilize commentaries on the VS and ŚBh titled the *Tātparyadīpikā* (TD) and the *Śrutaprakāśikā* (ŚP) by Sudarśanasūri (thirteenth century CE), as well as the *Tātparyacandrikā* (TC), the commentary on RBhGBh by Vedānta Deśika (fourteenth century CE). In addition to these Śrīvaiṣṇava sources, I also consider the Advaita commentaries of Śaṅkara (seventh century CE), the *Brahmasūtrabhāṣya* (ŚBrSuBh) and *Bhagavadgītābhāṣya* (ŚBhGBh) on the *Brahma Sūtras* (Br Sū) and the *Bhagavadgītā* (BhG) respectively. I juxtapose these rival interpretations with those of Rāmānuja to clarify the importance of the VP in his interpretation of Vedānta texts and this is especially evident in the RBhGBh.

Viṣṇu Purāṇa

As one of the most important purāṇas, the *Viṣṇu Purāṇa* comes closest to the *pañcalakṣaṇa* characteristic that is thought to be the hallmark of purāṇic literature (Rocher 1986: 29). Wilson's theory that the VP contains the five components characteristic of the purāṇa genre—details regarding cosmogony, dissolution and the recreation of the universe, genealogical lists of gods and patriarchs, different periods of Manu, and dynastic history—is said to be one of the reasons he chose to translate this particular purāṇa (Rocher 1986: 26, 29). Although the significance of this theory of *pañcalakṣaṇa* as regards the study of purāṇas is debated, it is still considered one of the defining characteristics of purāṇic literature (Rocher 1986: 24–30).

The provenance of the VP is between the first and the fourth century CE and it is considered a Pāñcarātra[10] document by some scholars (Farquhar 1920: 145; Rocher 1986: 248; Pathak 1997: 20). Its geographic area of composition is not known, however, a theory as to its origins in Andhra has been advanced (Vaidya 1921–26: 1.352). The VP is one of the shorter purāṇas comprising six books with 22, 16, 18, 24, 38, and 8 chapters respectively. All of Rāmānuja's citations from the VP are to be found in the critical edition of this purāṇa (Pathak 1997).[11]

Several commentaries on the VP are extant as printed editions or manuscripts: Viṣṇucitta's *Vyākhyā*/*Viṣṇucittīya* (twelfth century CE), Śrīdhara's *Ātmaprakāśa*/*Svaprakāśa* (1276 CE), Gangādhara's *Saṅketa* (1383 CE), Ratnagarbha's *Vaiṣṇavākūtacandrikā* (1811 CE) and others such as the commentaries of Nṛhari, and Kumāra Yogin's *Viṣṇu Vallabhā* (Pathak 1997: 16; Rocher 1986: 249). Wilson, in his translation of the VP notes that Śrīdhara at the beginning of his commentary mentions a commentator by the name of Chitsukhayoni, who, however, is not readily identifiable (Wilson 2003: LXXII). Both the commentaries of Śrīdhara and Ratnagarbha are written from an Advaita perspective; the work of Viṣṇucitta is the only Viśiṣṭādvaita commentary to date in Sanskrit.

Presented as a dialogue between the sage Parāśara and his disciple Maitreya, the VP's main endeavor is the elucidation of the true nature of the universe. According to the VP, the universe arises out of Viṣṇu, is entirely dependent on Him, and is reabsorbed into Him during dissolution.[12] In addition to identifying Viṣṇu with the entire universe, the VP also identifies Him with the Brahman of the upaniṣads (VP 1.2.12–13). In comparison to the *Mahābhārata*, which also makes an identification between Brahman and Viṣṇu, the VP is unique in that this identity is "not simply one strand of theology, but a deliberate and consistent redactional emphasis" throughout the entire purāṇa (Matchett 2001: 69).

The VP, then, alternates between the transcendent and immanent aspects of Viṣṇu. In this sense, it is similar to the upaniṣad theology of Brahman. However, even as it declares the transcendence and the immanence of Viṣṇu with the world, the VP also uses proto-Sāṃkhyan[13] language to describe the evolution of creation from Viṣṇu. Rāmānuja finds such cosmological detail useful in clarifying his soul–body (*śarīraśarīribhāva*) paradigm. It is this type of detail that he finds lacking in the upaniṣads.

Scholarship on the VP is limited to the examination of the concept of incarnation (*avatāra*) in comparison to other Vaiṣṇava texts such as *Bhāgavatapurāṇa* (BhP) and the *Harivaṃśa*, or to the study of the divinity of Kṛṣṇa, which on the whole is relegated to Book V of the VP (Sheth 1985; Matchett 2001). The devotion (*bhakti*) embodied in the VP narratives such as the Prahlāda story and its counterpart in the BhP, have been explored. According to Hacker, the VP on the whole exemplifies an intellectual devotion in contrast to the emotional Kṛṣṇa devotion of the *Bhāgavatapurāṇa*; the latter being identified as the first purāṇa in Sanskrit to epitomize emotionalism (Hacker 1959; Hirst 1993: 117–46). Hardy, too, notes that though the source of its emotionalism is the Tamil Vaiṣṇava tradition of the Āḻvārs, the VP served as a literary model for the BhP (Hardy 2001). Some research explores the linguistic dimensions of the VP through specific concepts such as cosmogony or the nature of time (Penner 1965; Salomon 1986; Wessler 1995). However, there has been no scholarly work on the VP as it relates to Rāmānuja.[14]

The VP was an important text for Yāmuna (eleventh century CE), Rāmānuja's predecessor who in his hymn, the *Stotra Ratna* (SR) praises the VP as a gem among purāṇas:

> Salutations to Parāśara, who is the best among sages, who composed the gem among purāṇas wishing to show correctly the sentient, insentient entities, and Īśvara, along with their true nature,the enjoyment of entities in the world, their liberation and the means to attain this freedom.[15]
>
> (SR 4)

In light of this high praise, it is not surprising that Rāmānuja utilizes this purāṇa in his commentaries to construct the "right" relationship between individual selves (*cit*), matter (*acit*), and Brahman (Venkatachari 1994: 203–6). The importance of the VP is also evident in the later Śrīvaiṣṇava tradition as it serves as the model for the first commentary on Piḷḷāṉ's (twelfth century CE) commentary on the *Tiruvāymoḻi* of Nammāḻvār (tenth century CE) called the *Āṛāyirappaṭi* (*Six Thousand Paṭis*) and is numerically modeled on the VP. A paṭi is a metrical unit consisting of 32 syllables. The *Āṛāyirappaṭi* is 32 x 6000 syllables, the same length as the VP (Carman and Narayanan 1989: 10). It is highly probable that the reason for such emulation of the VP is due to Rāmānuja's high regard for this purāṇa, which is reflected in its use in his commentaries.

Another characteristic of the VP useful for Rāmānuja's purposes is that certain sections of this purāṇa clearly articulate the distinction between Brahman/Viṣṇu, individual selves (*jīva/ātman*), and matter (*prakṛti/pradhāna*). The VP's declaration of the different forms of Viṣṇu, such as the principle of consciousness (*puruṣa*), manifest and unmanifest universe (*pradhāna/prakṛti*), and time expressed in Sāṃkhyan terms is the kind of differentiation that Rāmānuja utilizes to affirm his theology of the unity-of-the-differenced (*Viśiṣṭādvaita*). Again, these details are difficult to find in the upaniṣads that Rāmānuja cites in his commentaries: it is the VP that provides Rāmānuja pertinent information while maintaining a connection to the upaniṣad theology of Brahman.

It has been noted that the reason for Rāmānuja's use of this purāṇa may be that "[i]n comparison with the [s]mṛtis that were generally accepted as authoritative, the epics among which the *Bhagavadgītā* has a privileged position, and *Manu*, the smārta authority of the [p]urāṇas was not so widely and completely recognized before Rāmānuja's age" (van Buitenen 1956: 34). Rāmānuja found in the VP not only a description of Brahman/Viṣṇu that coincides with his own sectarian views, but he also utilizes the cosmological details not found in the upaniṣads that bring coherence to his interpretation of Vedānta. Indeed, it is this last reason that is the most compelling.

Rāmānuja was the first Vedāntin to quote profusely from a purāṇa. Śaṅkara utilizes the VP as well, but not as frequently as Rāmānuja.[16] Śaṅkara's *Brahmasūtrabhāṣya* utilizes *Mārkaṇḍeya Purāṇa* and other puranas in eight instances (Deussen 1990: 34). Three passages from the VP are used in Śaṅkara's commentary on Br Sū 1.3.28 and 1.3.30; however, these passages are also said to be found in the MBh (Raghavan 1975: 294–95). It has been noted that in Śaṅkara's commentaries, especially the BhG, the perceptible theistic background is of the Vaiṣṇava religion rather than the Śaiva tradition (Hacker 1965: 147–54; Hirst 1993).[17] In the ŚBh, Rāmānuja has the Advaitin quote the VP in several instances to support the *prima facie* (*pūrvapakṣa*) view; he then goes to great lengths to refute the Advaita interpretation. One reason might be that this purāṇa was esteemed in Advaita circles, but it is also possible that the objector's (*pūrvapakṣin*) utilization of the VP rhetorically necessitates Rāmānuja's own use later in his conclusion (*siddhānta*). That the Advaitins were interested in the VP is known by the existence of the two commentaries of Śrīdhara and Ratnagarbha. Even as late as the twentieth century Advaita scholars such as Rāma Rāya (1875–1914) in his *Śaṅkarāśaṅkarabhāṣyavimarṣa*, establish the Advaitic nature of the VP (Datta 1978: 193–94). It is probable that the VP enjoyed a special status not only among the budding Śrīvaiṣṇava sect, but also among other groups, such as the smārta Brahmins of medieval South India who were mostly Advaitins.

The rest of this section addresses the content of the VP. Since several synopses of the chapters of the various books (*aṃśa*) of the VP are available, I will examine in detail only those chapters that are important for Rāmānuja as reflected by their use in his commentaries (Rocher 1986; Pathak 1997; Matchett 2001; Wilson 2003). As a result of this focus, certain sections and interpretations relevant to other concepts in this purāṇa will not be addressed.

VP 1.1

In the first chapter of Book I, the sage Maitreya, well-versed in the Vedic sciences and dharma, questions his teacher, the sage Parāśara on the nature of the universe. Parāśara first explains the boon that has been bestowed upon him that enables him to compose this purāṇa. As a result of the clemency Parāśara shows the demons (*rākśasa*) in not avenging the death of his father at their hands, Pulastya the progenitor of demons grants Parāśara two boons—that he would be well-versed in all scripture (*śāstra*) and that he would compose a summary of all the purāṇas (i.e., the VP).

What is important for Rāmānuja here is Maitreya's query (1.1.4–5) into the workings of the universe; specifically Maitreya's questions as to the state of this world in the past and in the future, the substantial nature of the universe, and its source at the time of creation and dissolution. More importantly, Parāśara's detailed answer to these questions (1.1.31)—that the world evolves from Viṣṇu, that it exists in him, and that it dissolves into him, and the identity of the world with Viṣṇu—is one of the most important passages for Rāmānuja. Though the VP distinguishes the world as distinct from Brahman, it also argues for an identity between the two that is similar to the upaniṣad descriptions of Brahman. However, on the topic of matter, individual selves, and karma as powers (*śakti*) of Viṣṇu, (VP 1.2) the purāṇa is unique and offers Rāmānuja adequate detail to support his soul–body paradigm.

VP 1.2

This chapter begins with a lengthy glorification of Viṣṇu, and describes the chain of transmission of the VP. The god Brahmā imparts the VP to Dakṣa[18] and other sages before it is transmitted to the king Purukutsa, reigning on the banks of the river Narmada. He then imparts it to Sarasvata who in turn repeats it to Parāśara. Following this is the description of Brahman as Vāsudeva and his different forms (*rūpa*) and powers (*śakti*), such as individual selves (*puruṣa*), matter (*pradhāna/prakṛti*) both manifest and unmanifest, and time (*kāla*). Through the playful action (*līlā*) of Viṣṇu, these forms are the cause of creation. Rāmānuja turns to this conception of the world as a form or power of Viṣṇu in arguing a much closer and positive connection between Brahman and the world. The association between individual selves and matter leads to the various evolutes, which ultimately form the cosmic egg, the abode of the god Brahmā. Viṣṇu, as the inner self of both Rudra and Brahmā, participates in this creation. The transcendence of Viṣṇu is underscored by the discussion of the three dispositions (*bhāvana*) inherent in all creatures but the Supreme Being. The cosmological details of this chapter are very important for Rāmānuja, since they allow him to introduce information he feels is lacking in the śruti passages.

VP 1.3

The major portion of this chapter concerns the different divisions of time. The first section is the most important for Rāmānuja. Interrupting Parāśara, who had just explained elemental creation (1.2), Maitreya asks how it is that creative agency is attributed to Brahman who is pure, eternal, and infinite. In Parāśara's response Rāmānuja finds much detail to support his theology. Parāśara explains that this aspect of Brahman, as the creator who remains unsullied by the process, is something that is peculiar to Him alone, just as heat is a unique quality of fire. Rāmānuja takes these passages as illustrative of his soul–body perspective and depends on them significantly in his commentaries.

VP 1.22

Though VP 1.22 is the last chapter of Book I, it continues to address the questions posed by Maitreya in VP 1.3, in regard to the nature of Brahman's relation to the world. Begun in the previous chapters, the conclusion of the creation of different beings such as demons (*rākṣasa*), gods (*daitya*), anti-gods (*dānava*), and so on, forms this chapter's primary topic. Parāśara further declares the universality of Viṣṇu with all these beings. He utilizes concepts such as: 1) the world as Viṣṇu's lordly manifestation (*vibhūti*); 2) the world as a portion or part (*aṃśa*) of Viṣṇu; 3) the world as the body (*vapu*) of Brahman; 4) the world as the essential nature (*svarūpa*) of Viṣṇu; and 5) the individual selves and matter as powers (*śakti*) of Viṣṇu. Additionally, two forms of Viṣṇu are described—one that is perishable and is identified as the world of matter, and the other which is imperishable and inherent in all beings as the individual self. Using the above-mentioned terminology to deliberate on creation, Parāśara affirms the world as interwoven with Brahman, even as it is distinct from Him. He concludes this chapter with a description of the ornaments and weapons of Viṣṇu which are identified with different aspects of creation.

VP 2.7

Having heard the geographic descriptions of the various regions on earth, Maitreya questions Parāśara about the celestial worlds. The majority of the chapter enumerates the planets, constellations, and their relation to each other. It also includes a listing of the material evolutes and their relation to Viṣṇu. What is important for Rāmānuja in this chapter is the description of matter and individual selves as dependent on Brahman and as encompassed by Him, even as He brings about their association and disassociation.

VP 2.12

The function of celestial bodies such as the sun begun in 2.11 extends into 2.12 and ends with an exploration of the world's relation to Brahman. In the ŚBh, both the Advaitin and Rāmānuja utilize about ten passages from this chapter to establish their respective views. While for Śaṅkara these passages elucidate ultimate reality from an Advaita point of view, for Rāmānuja the purāṇa affirms the metaphysical reality of the individual self as distinct from

Brahman. The passages on the whole seem to support the Advaita view, but Rāmānuja spends a considerable amount of time reinterpreting these passages according to his theology as we see in Chapter 3 of this study.

VP 2.14

The narrative of Bharata is covered in 2.13 and 2.14. Even though a devout worshipper of Vāsudeva, he fails to attain liberation because of excessive attachment to a fawn. After successive births on earth, he finally reaches his goal. The highest truth of life, namely, the highest reality is defined as eternal, immutable, imperishable, and essentially different from the rest of the created world. Whereas the Advaitin interprets this highest reality as Brahman which is pure knowledge, without attributes (*nirguṇa*), Rāmānuja interprets this as the individual self in its essential nature. I discuss Rāmānuja's use of passages from this section in Chapters 3 and 4.

VP 6.4 and VP 6.5

These two chapters detail the dissolution of the universe and the absorption of creation into Viṣṇu. The description of the resolution of matter and spirit into Brahman is important for Rāmānuja. His refutation of Advaita doctrine that posits the world as unreal compared to Brahman relies on these chapters. In 6.5, the exegesis of the word *bhagavān* is connected to the causal nature of Viṣṇu and He is proclaimed as the self of all, residing in all beings. For this reason, all beings are said to dwell in Him. Much of the information from these chapters Rāmānuja utilizes to establish his theology.

VP 6.7

Parāśara's teaching in 6.5 is said to have been first taught by Keśidhvaja to his brother Khāndikhya, also known as Janaka. For Rāmānuja this chapter offers support on the reality of the individual self and on the divine form (*divyarūpa*) of Viṣṇu. The description of Viṣṇu's divine form as the auspicious object of meditation (*śubhāśraya*) includes a head-to-toe description of the deity adorned with ornaments. Though this chapter contains the passage (6.7.53) quoted by the Advaitin in ŚBh 1.1.1 to support his view that Brahman is attribute-less and pure knowledge, Rāmānuja once again reinterprets it to refer to the individual soul, in its essential nature. Rāmānuja relies on this very important section of the purāṇa in both the VS and the ŚBh, which I evaluate in Chapters 2 and 3.

Outline of chapters

Chapter 2 of this book evaluates the exegetical role of the VP in the VS. Rāmānuja turns to this purāṇa to support some salient doctrines of his theology, such as the metaphysical reality of the individual self, Brahman's originative causality, and Brahman's divine form. As valid means of knowledge of Brahman (*śabdapramāṇa*), the VP is indispensable in the details it provides on the essential nature of individual selves and their embodied condition while bound in the cycle of birth-and-rebirth (*saṃsāra*). This purāṇa is also a source text for the nature of ignorance (*avidyā*), which Rāmānuja defines as karma and its effects on the individual self. In these discussions, the VP is the only scripture utilized for support, and the importance of this purāṇa is also borne out by the commentator, Sudarśanasūri (thirteenth century CE), in his commentary on the VS, the *Tātparyadīpikā* (TD).

In the second section of Chapter 2 I examine the implications of Brahman's material causality. The concepts of Brahman as a cause as a whole (*aviśeṣṇakāraṇa*) and causality as a unique quality of Brahman's essential nature (*brahmasvarūpaviśeṣa*) are unique aspects of Viśiṣṭādvaita. Rāmānuja relies on the VP in developing these doctrinal positions that differentiate his Vedānta from that of his rivals.

In the last section of Chapter 2, I focus on the scriptural evidence that supports a divine body (*divyarūpa*) for Brahman. Contrary to his Vedānta predecessors such as Śaṅkara and Bhāskara, Rāmānuja articulates a divine transcendent body for Brahman, for which he utilizes the VP. In addition to an essential nature (*svarūpa*), support for which is abundant in the upaniṣads, Rāmānuja envisions Brahman as Viṣṇu possessing an anthropomorphic form unique to the deity. An examination of the śruti passages quoted as evidence for Brahman's divine form are inadequate and Rāmānuja owes much to the VP to consolidate his perspective on this issue.

Chapter 3 explores the importance of the VP in *Śrībhāṣya* (ŚBh) 1.1.1, Rāmānuja's commentary on *Brahma Sūtra* 1.1.1. The nature of Brahman, the metaphysical reality of the individual self, its relationship to Brahman, in both the embodied and liberated states, are the topics for which he relies on the VP. In these sections, the VP allows Rāmānuja to overcome certain ambiguities inherent in śruti passages in regard to the distinction between the individual self and Brahman. Both Rāmānuja in the ŚBh and his commentator Sudarśanasūri (thirteenth century CE), in the *Śrutaprakāśikā* (ŚP) are indebted to the VP in according the individual self a real metaphysical status.

An interesting feature of the use of the VP in the ŚBh is that Rāmānuja has the objector (Advaitin) quote generously from the VP as well, in order to establish the non-dual (Advaita) point of view. Rāmānuja then reinterprets the same VP passages and numerous additional VP citations to establish his Vedānta of the unity-of-the-differenced (Viśiṣṭādvaita). Such use of the VP to support the objector's point of view is not evident in Rāmānuja's other commentaries. There is a sense of a deliberate re-reading, reclaiming of the VP as a Viśiṣṭādvaita text that is not seen in his other commentaries. This suggests that perhaps the VP was also an important text for the Advaitins or that Rāmānuja has the Advaitin utilize the VP for rhetorical purposes.

Chapter 4 identifies the role of the VP in the reinterpretation of key BhG doctrines such as Sāṃkhya Yoga, the nature of Kṛṣṇa, and the concepts of bondage and liberation. Rāmānuja's task in his commentary on the BhG is to not only interpret Kṛṣṇa's teaching, but to also refute Śaṅkara's interpretation of the very same BhG passages. I show in this chapter how, both in his *Bhagavadgītābhāṣya* (RBhGBh) and in his commentator Vedānta Deśika's *Tātparyadīpikā* (TD), the importance of this purāṇa in recasting the BhG as a Viśiṣṭādvaita exposition contra-Advaita is significant.

Editorial notes

Reference to all *Viṣṇu Purāṇa* passages is from the critical edition (Pathak 1997). Where relevant, I note any discrepencies found in content between the critical edition and Rāmānuja's *Viṣṇu Purāṇa* quotations. All citations of the *Śrī Bhāṣya* refer to Abhyankar's (1916) critical edition, while I also indicate the corresponding page numbers in George Thibaut's (1996) translation.

Notes

1 Rāmānuja was the first to comment on all the foundational texts of Vedānta and differs from his predecessor, Yāmuna (10th century CE), who also contributed to theistic Vedānta. For more on Yāmuna's philosophy and his importance within the Śrīvaiṣṇava tradition see van Buitenen 1971; Neeval 1977; Mesquita 1990; Narasimhachary 1998.

2 See Carman 1974: 24–64 for Rāmānuja's life and writings.

3 Nayar 1992: 9 notes that "Rāmānuja set the stage, even if selectively, for a more complete blending of the Tamil and Sanskrit scriptures by creating the 'scope' for several salient features of Southern Religiosity ... he provided certain theological openings for several features of Āḻvār spirituality – including the worship of God in his iconic incarnations in the temple ... the aesthetic appreciation of the loveliness of God's form, and emotional bhakti – themes that occupy a prominent place in the Āḻvārs' verses." For more on Āḻvār devotion and the interaction of Tamil and Sanskrit traditions within Śrīvaiṣṇavism see Narayanan 1987 and 1992.

4 This categorization of scripture as it concerns Rāmānuja is discussed in Adluri 2006.

5 The BhG is considered one of the foundational texts of Vedānta philosophy. Its status within the Hindu scriptural hierarchy is unique (van Buitenen 1981: 6–13).

6 tasmāt kāryākāryavyavasthitau upādeyānupādeyavyavasthāyāṃ śāstrameva tava pramāṇam. dharmaśāstretihāsapurāṇādiyupabṛmhitā vedā yadeva puruṣottamākhyaṃ paraṃ tattvaṃ tatprīṇarūpaṃ tatprāptyupāyabhūtaṃ ca karmāvabodhayanti (RBhGBh 16.24).

7 For more on this see Pollock 2011.

8 itihāsapurāṇābhyāṃ vedaṃ samupabṛmhayet. bibhety alpaśrutād vedo māṃ ayaṃ pratariṣyati (MBh 1.1.264) iti śāstreṇāsyārthasyetihāsapurāṇābhyām upabṛṃhaṇaṃ kāryamiti jñāyate. upabṛmhaṇaṃ nāma viditasakalavedatadarthānāṃ svayogamahimasākṣātkṛtavedatattvārthānāṃ vākyaiḥ svāvagatavedavākyārthavyaktīkaraṇam. sakalaśākhānugatasya vākyārthasyālpabhāgaśravaṇād duravagamatvena tena vinā niścayāyogād upabṛṃhaṇaṃ hi kāryameva (ŚBh 72; cf Thibaut 1996: 91).

9 I do not include Rāmānuja's *Vedāntadīpa* and *Vedāntasāra* in this study. Both these works are shorter commentaries on the Br Sū and are summary texts of his Vedānta and as such, they are not detailed and are rather unpersuasive in their argumentation (Carman 1974: 58). Moreover, there is not much use of the VP in these works.

10 Pāñcarātra is an extra-Vedic tradition that is incorporated into Śrīvaiṣṇavism. Yāmuna in his *Āgamaprāmāṇyam* argues for the validity of these texts as Vedic, and so does Rāmānuja in ŚBh 2.2.40–43.

11 Although the numbering of these passages may be a little different, all passages utilized by Rāmānuja are found in the critical edition.

12 The beginning verses such as VP 1.1.31 and the concluding passages such as VP 6.8.27 lend a cohesive wholeness to the purāṇa.

13 This is classified as Sāṃkhya prior to its systematization in the *Sāṃkhyakārikā* of Īśvarakṛṣṇa (Larson 1979).

14 Exceptions to this are the MA thesis of Menzies (1991) and the Ph.D dissertation of Ranganayaki (1999). Menzies explores the importance of the VP for Rāmānuja's conception of god only in a cursory manner. His thesis title, *The Viṣṇu Purāṇa as Śruti*, suggests the importance of the VP for Rāmānuja. He notes a few instances where Rāmānuja uses the VP exclusively, such as the qualities of god (Menzies 1991: 152), but does not thoroughly evaluate the importance of the VP in regards to the Vedānta texts used. I demonstrate, analyzing both the Vedānta passages and the VP verses, that the VP is crucial in establishing Rāmānuja's argument. Ranganayaki has examined the commentary on the VP by Rāmānuja's disciple, Viṣṇucitta to demonstrate the latter's reliance on Rāmānuja's Vedānta to comment on the VP. Additionally, Viṣṇucitta seems to borrow Rāmānuja's interpetation of the VP from commentaries such as the VS and ŚBh in commenting on the purāṇa (Ranganayaki 1999: 264–72).

15 tattvena yaścidacidīśvaratatsvabhāvabhogāpavārgatadupāyagatīr udāraḥ sandarśyan niramimīta purāṇaratnaṃ tasmai namo munivarāya parāśarāya (SR 4).

16 For instance, in ŚBhGBh 3.37, VP 6.7.74 and 78 are cited.

17 Also, on the role of divine grace in Śaṅkara's soteriology, see Malkovsky 2001.

18 VP 1.7.5 describes Dakṣa as one of nine mind-born sons of god Brahmā.

2 The individual self, cosmology, and the divine body in the *Vedārthasaṃgraha*

The *Vedārthasaṃgraha* (VS) "summary of the meaning of the Veda" is the earliest exposition of Rāmānuja's philosophical oeuvre (van Buitenen 1956: 30; Carman 1974: 50–51). While the *Bhagavadgītābhāṣya* (RBhGBh) and the *Śrībhāṣya* (ŚBh) are commentaries on primary texts, the *Bhagavadgītā* (BhG) and the *Brahma Sūtras* (Br Sū) respectively, the VS is not a commentary on a single text, but rather is Rāmānuja's interpretation of the philosophy of all upaniṣads. In this chapter, I examine the exegetical use of the *Viṣṇu Purāṇa* (VP) in discussions on three topics, the individual self, Brahman's causal nature, and the divine form. Rāmānuja often relies solely on the VP to further his argument on these key issues and even when he does use śruti it is his interpretation of the VP that is decisive. At times, he even uses the VP to interpret śruti itself.

The first section of this chapter addresses Rāmānuja's indebtedness to the VP in his discussion of the individual self (*jīvātman*), both in its essential nature (*svarūpa*), when liberated from matter, and in its embodied state (*kṣetrajña*). Brahman's originative causality is the second theme for which the *Viṣṇu Purāṇa* is essential. Though all Vedāntins affirm the causal nature of Brahman, none discuss it as an aspect of the essential nature (*svarūpaviśeṣa*) of Brahman.[1] Rāmānuja, in contrast claims that the created world of individual selves and matter is not an illusion (*māyā*) and that the exact relationship between matter, selves, and Brahman, in no way compromises the unity, eternity, and infinity of Brahman as defined by the upaniṣads. In addition to causality as an aspect of Brahman's essential nature, Rāmānuja also affirms Brahman as the material cause as a whole (*aviśeṣaṇakāraṇa*) to establish creation as a positive manifestation of a causal Brahman that is eternally differentiated. To support both these salient doctrines of Viśiṣṭādvaita Vedānta, on Brahman's causality, he turns to the VP. The proto-Sāṃkhyan evolution of matter and the conception of the world as Brahman's power (*śakti*), discussed in the VP, aid Rāmānuja significantly in differentiating his own perspective from that of his rivals. This purāṇa, then, is the defining text that separates his interpretation of Brahman's causality from that of other Vedāntins.

A third issue for which the VP is utilized is the discussion of the divine form of Brahman. The concept of a divine body (*divyarūpa*) for Brahman is not accepted by Rāmānuja's Vedāntic predecessors. He however argues that the upaniṣads not only declare Brahman as possessing a form but that they enjoin worship and devotion to a specific divine form, that of Viṣṇu. Rāmānuja's description of the divine form relies solely on the VP. This chapter also takes the commentary on the *Vedārthasaṃgraha*, the *Tātparyadīpikā* (TD) by his disciple Sudarśanasūri (~thirteenth century CE), into consideration as a guide to further evaluate the importance of the VP.

The individual self

Unlike Advaita, which denies the metaphysical reality of the individual self, Rāmānuja affirms the metaphysical reality of the individual self, both in its essential nature (*svarūpa*) and as an embodied entity. For Rāmānuja, since consciousness is both the essential nature and a defining property of the self it cannot be sublated. Instead, it is only the attributive quality of the individual self that is obscured during embodiment. This is in contrast to the Advaita view that, "the absolute Self must be identified with consciousness, *is* consciousness, and the distinctions between the individual knower, object known, and the act of knowing cease to apply" from the ultimate point of view (Lipner 1986: 56). The next two sections examine VP's role as evidence for the essential nature of the individual self as consciousness and its embodied manifestation. Rāmānuja first quotes śruti and then the VP. However a closer examination, of his argument and the commentary, the *Tātparyadīpikā* (TD) of his disciple reveals that through some ingenious exegetical moves, the corroborative function of the VP is amplified considerably.

Śruti on the individual self

Immediately after the two invocatory verses, in the VS, Rāmānuja states that Vedānta teaches:

> 1) the essential nature (*svarūpa*) of the individual self as different from the body; 2) the attributes (*svabhāva*)[2] of the individual self; 3) the essential nature (*svarūpa*) of Brahman as the inner ruler; 4) the attributes (*svabhāva*) of Brahman; 5) the worship (*upāsana*) of Brahman; 6) and the goal of such worship: liberation (*mokṣa*).[3]

He then cites the following śruti texts as support:

> 1 And that's how you are
>
> (Ch Up 6.9.4)
>
> 2 Brahman is this self
>
> (Māṇḍ Up 2)

3 He who, although residing in the soul, is different from that soul, whom the self does not know, whose body is the soul, and who directs the soul from within, He is the immortal inner ruler of thy soul.

(Bṛ Up, Mād 3.7.22)

4 He is the inner self of all beings, free from all evil, the divine, and sole god Nārāyaṇa.

(Sub Up 7)

5 It is he that Brahmins seek to know by means of Vedic recitation, sacrifice, gift-giving, austerity, and fasting

(Bṛ Up 4.4.22)

6 A man who knows brahman obtains the highest there is.

(Taitt Up 2.1)

7 Only when a man knows him does he pass beyond death; there is no other path for getting there.

(Śve Up 3.8)[4]

One inconsistency is that for the six-fold teaching of Vedānta, Rāmānuja cites seven upaniṣad examples. To justify the anomaly, the TD explains that the first upaniṣad passage (Ch Up 6.9.4) is a summation of all of the six teachings, whereas the rest correspond to each of the six topics.[5] If that is the case, then evidence for the essential nature of the individual self as different from the body and its attributive nature is provided by Māṇḍ Up 2 and the Bṛ Up 3.7.22 (*Mādhyandina* recension) respectively. These citations correspond to the first two of the six topics that Vedānta is said to address:

the essential nature of the self is different from the body	Brahman is this self (Māṇḍ Up 2)
the attributive nature of the self	He who, although residing in the soul, is different from that soul, whom the self does not know, whose body is the soul, and who directs the soul from within, He is the immortal inner ruler of thy soul (Bṛ Up, Mādhy, 3.7.22)

The essential nature of the self as different from the body, but as of the nature of Brahman is supported by *this self is brahman* (Māṇḍ Up 2). The TD explains that this upaniṣad passage demonstrates the similarity of the self with Brahman, in the sense that only the individual self has the same nature as Brahman characterized as consciousness and bliss and is unlike the physical body.[6] However, the individual self in its essential nature, lacks the creative ability and other auspicious qualities that constitute the essential nature of Brahman. The śruti passage is vague enough that it leaves open the possibility of an Advaita interpretation—that the individual self is ultimately Brahman. To counter this, Rāmānuja indicates the individal self's relationship to Brahman with a second example (Bṛ Up 3.7.22), which declares the attributive nature of the self as an accessory of Brahman as He is its inner self. Commenting on Māṇḍ Up 2 given as support for the essential nature of the self, the TD states that "[t]he essential nature (*svarūpa*) of the self is that it is solely characterized by consciousness and bliss and its attributive quality (*svabhāva*) is to be an accessory (*śeṣa*) to the Lord."[7]

The attributive quality of the individual self as an accessory of Brahman is conveyed here. Neither Rāmānuja, nor the śruti passages he cites, offer adequate information on the nature of the individual self itself, though the commentator does try to rectify this. The upaniṣads, which Rāmānuja has quoted, clarify the self's relation to Brahman, an important distinction, as we cannot speak of the self existing outside such a relationship. Yet they do not convey the individual self's essential characteristics. The emphasis in the upaniṣad examples is on Brahman, and the individual self is defined in relation to it.

Thus, śruti's support for Rāmānuja's views on the essential nature of the individual self is incomplete. Attentive to this deficiency the commentator goes on to say that:

> [i]f the doubt arises as to how in these passages the essential nature of the individual self alone is obtained, Rāmānuja wishes to show that the essential nature of these two (self and Brahman) is obtained from śruti which is supported by corroboration.[8]

What does corroboration mean here? The commentator refers to Rāmānuja's method of citing śruti along with smṛti/VP passages as support. An examination of the two śruti passages, Māṇḍ Up 2 and Bṛ Up Mādh, 3.7.22 in no way intimate any information on the individual self only its relationship to Brahman. They do provide information that the self has Brahman for its inner self; this relational definition, though important, does not speak of the self's essential nature directly.

The interpretation of the universe as the body of Brahman (*śarīraśarīribhāva*) was "primarily a theological application", where "the more purely philosophical aspects of Rāmānuja's thought—such as his position on the self (*jīvātman*) as conscious and embodied … enter into the model's theological comprehension only indirectly" (Lipner 1986: 120–21). This "indirectness" is mirrored in the types of scripture that Rāmānuja needs to utilize to support his views. In the several instances throughout the VS where Rāmānuja discusses the individual self and supports his assertions with scripture, he relies only on the VP, instead of the upaniṣad passages, as means of proof (*pramāṇa*).[9] The description of the real nature of the individual self, taken from the VP and outlined later, is said to be indescribable, self-knowing, and so on, and speaks of the self in a direct sense than in its relation to Brahman, such as an accessory of Brahman and so on, although this relationship cannot be denied or trivialized. In other words, the scriptural evidence for the essential nature of the individual self as Rāmānuja envisions it is not from śruti.

Viṣṇu Purāṇa on the individual self

Having evaluated the scriptural evidence from śruti we now examine VP's contribution to Rāmānuja's exposition of the essential nature of the individual self. In the very beginning of the VS after Rāmānuja gives a succinct account of his Vedānta, he elaborates on the essential nature of the self, but does not provide any scriptural evidence:

> The essential nature of the self is devoid of the differences, of distinctive myriad forms such as gods, men and so on, which are a result of the evolution of matter (*prakṛti*). It is solely characterized by consciousness and bliss (*jñānānandaikaguṇa*). Once these differences of form such as gods, which are a result of the workings of karma, are removed, the self's essential individuality is indescribable (*vācām agocara*), known only by itself (*svasaṃvedya*), and can only be defined as of the nature of consciousness (*jñānasvarūpa*). And this essential nature is common to all individual selves.[10]

Several concepts in regard to the essential nature of the individual selves are presented here: first, when separated from matter the essential nature of the self is "solely characterized by consciousness and bliss" (*jñānānandāikaguṇa*); second that their essential individuality is "indescribable" (*vācām agocara*) third, that the essential nature of the self is "known only by itself" (*svasaṃvedya*) and fourth, the essential nature of the self is of the nature of consciousness (*jñānasvarūpa*). The scriptural source for all these terms is the VP.

According to the commentary on the VS, the term that conveys the individual self's "essential nature as consciousness" (*jñānasvarūpa*) is a reference to VP 1.4.40:

> consciousness (*jñānasvarūpa*) is the nature of this whole world, those who are ignorant
> erroneously perceive it as of the nature of the world and are lost in the ocean of ignorance.[11]
>
> (VP 1.4.40)

Chapter 1.4 of the VP, from which the description of the essential nature of the self as consciousness is taken, is a discussion of Viṣṇu as the boar (Varāha) incarnation. Beholding the body of Viṣṇu as the boar, the sages praise him as pervading all existence and then declare the essential nature of this majestic form as of the nature of consciousness (*jñānātman*). Subsequently in 1.4.40, the world is affirmed as comprised of consciousness as well. Those who in ignorance see the world as an object of perception rather than of the nature of consciousness are mired in the cycle of birth and rebirth. In 1.4.41, the world is defined as of the nature of consciousness (*jñānātman*) and as a form of Viṣṇu. Both Rāmānuja and the commentator take the individual self to be the topic of discussion of this VP section. Such an interpretation is possible through the imposition of the soul–body paradigm; however, what is important for us here is that the essential nature of the individual self is seen as rooted in the VP according to Rāmānuja and his followers.

As mentioned earlier, the connection of Rāmānuja's description of the individual self to the VP does not end with VP 1.4.40. Previously, we identified several terms that were used to describe the essential nature of the self by Rāmānuja, which are also from the VP: *devādibhede' apadhvaste* (once differences such as gods and so on are removed) is from VP 2.14.33, *vācām agocara* (indescribable) is from VP 6.7.53, and *svasaṃvedya* (self-knowing) is borrowed from VP 6.7.53.[12] Neither Rāmānuja nor his commentator Sudarśanasūri, use any śruti passages to support this view of the essential nature of the individual self. Thus, even though we may doubt the commentator's assertion that the term *jñānasvarūpa* refers to VP 1.4.40, the fact that the rest of the individual self's description is taken from VP 2.14.33 and 6.7.53, suggests that Rāmānuja has the VP in mind.

Amplifying Rāmānuja's definition of the self as different from matter, and also to illustrate that he does indeed rely on the VP, the commentary cites additional passages from this purāṇa.

> Also, when the soul is associated with matter, it is defiled by I-ness
> The self assumes the qualities of matter, although it is distinct from them and immutable
>
> (VP 6.7.24)

> A living being is neither god, nor human, nor animal, nor a tree.
> These different bodily forms are due to the effects of karma.[13]
>
> (VP 2.13.94)

These verses clarify that the self takes on different physical forms due to karma and that these embodiments are not due to the inherent nature of the self which is essentially consciousness. The commentator does not cite any śruti at this juncture. Chapter 6.7 of the VP, which is the context of 6.7.24 stated above, is a dialogue between the brothers Keśidhvaja and Khāṇḍikya. The latter entreats the former to divulge the nature of discriminative knowledge. Keśidhvaja then proceeds to declare the distinction between the self/soul (*ātman*) and the body that is comprised of matter (*prakṛti*). In this context, it is difficult to interpret the term *ātman* in terms of Advaita, because Keśidhvaja in VP 6.7.30 distinguishes liberation utilizing the metaphor of a magnet (Brahman) and pieces of iron (individual selves). Just as the pieces of iron drawn to the magnet will never become magnets in their essential nature, so also, the individual self at liberation is drawn to Brahman, but does not become Brahman. Thus the commentator's interpretation of the term "self" as the individual self and not Brahman, in VP 6.7.24, is accurate. So also is the case with the context of VP 2.13.94, taken from a discussion on the distinction between the self and the body.

To support the term that Rāmānuja uses to describe the real nature of the self, *jñānānandāikaguṇa*, the TD once again cites the relevant VP passage:

> By means of *jñānadāikaguṇa* the meaning of the following verse is aimed at:
> The self is by itself solely blissful, conscious (*jñānadaikaguṇa*) and pure
> The qualities(dharma) of suffering, ignorance, and impurity are those of matter and not the individual self.[14]
>
> (VP 6.7.22)

In other words, the TD makes it clear that the VP is the source of the vocabulary utilized to discuss the essential nature of the individual self. The purāṇa is the only scripture cited thus far, that gives the specifics of the self's essential nature (*svarūpa*). Furthermore, Rāmānuja's use of the term for "once differences such as gods and so on are removed" (*devādibhede' padhvaste*) is explained by the commentary as a reference to another VP verse:

> By means of *karmakṛtadevadibhede' padhavaste*, the meaning of the following verse is aimed at:
> The differentiation of this one nature is brought about by the consequences of outward actions
> When differences such as gods are removed (*devādibhede' padvaste*) there is absolutely no distinction.[15]
>
> (VP 2.14.33)[16]

The context of VP 2.14 is the discussion of the difference between the self and the body. The commentator, Sudarśanasūri, like Rāmānuja turns to the VP to characterize the essential nature of the self when unassociated with matter, as indescribable (*vācām agocara*) and self-knowing or self-congnizant (*svasaṃvedya*):

> By means of the phrase "the essential individuality indescribable and self-conscious" Rāmānuja explains the following verse:
> That consciousness which does not recognize distinctions, is pure being, and is indescribable (*vacasām agocaram*)
> The self is cognizant of itself (*svasaṃvedya*), that consciousness is called Brahman.[17]
>
> (VP 6.7.53)

This purāṇa, according to Rāmānuja, offers a distinction between the supreme self (Brahman), the individual self (*ātman*), and matter (*prakṛti*) that is not an interpretation accessible through reading śruti that has been utilized as support. In fact, the vocabulary for Rāmānuja's definition of the essential nature of the self as *jñānandaikaguṇa, devādibhede' padhvaste, vacasām agocara, and svasamvedya* is taken from the VP.

It is worth noting that the TD elaborates on VP 6.7.53 stated above, to reach another conclusion regarding the nature of the individual self:

> The VP says that the self is self-conscious (6.7.53) in order to exclude that it is empty (*tuccha*);[18] and that the self has this consciousness as an essential nature (*svarūpa*) and as an attribute (*dharma*).[19]

The distinction between consciousness as the substrate and as an attribute of the individual self is rooted in the purāṇa. The importance of the distinction between consciousness as both substrate and attribute of the individual self, I address in the section on the embodied nature of the self.

In conclusion, in all the instances in the VS where Rāmānuja speaks of the essential nature of the individual self, he always cites evidence from the VP, not from the upaniṣads.[20] To prove that the essential nature of the individual self is of the nature of consciousness and bliss he cites passages such as VP 6.7.22:

> This self is made up of bliss, is conscious, and pure
> Sorrow, ignorance, and impurity are the properties of matter, not the self.[21]
> (VP 6.7.22)

The VP alone is used as scriptural support to establish that the individual self is different from the body, which is comprised of matter, and that the individual self in its essential nature is consciousness and bliss. Furthermore, the distinctions in various embodiments such as gods, and men, do not represent the real nature of the individual self. Both Rāmānuja and his commentator cite VP passages 1.4.40, 6.7.24, 2.13.94, 6.7.10, 2.14.33, and 6.7.53 as proof for these assertions.

Viṣṇu Purāṇa on the embodied self

In addition to the use of VP to articulate the essential nature of the self, Rāmānuja utilizes it again to support his assertion that the individual self has consciousness, both for its essential nature (*svarūpa*) and as its essential attribute (*dharma/svabhāva*). This distinction has important implications for the refutation of the Advaitin discussed below, as it allows him to distinguish between the liberated self, the self in its essential nature and the embodied individual self. Here he does not quote from śruti at all, but utilizes only the VP as scriptural support.

The concept of consciousness functioning as both substrate and quality is an important aspect of Rāmānuja's thought, and is illustrated with the metaphor of the lamp or flame. Just as "the stuff of the flame (*tejas*) may be spoken of as functioning both as substance and as quality … because it has the flame as substrate, but it also possesses illumining-power and colour as its properties" so also the "*ātman*, like the lamp—strictly speaking, the flame—is the substrate of consciousness while consciousness may be likened to light. Just as light and its substrate are the dual form of the one *tejas* stuff, so also consciousness and its substrate (the *ātman* or knowing self) are essentially of the same stuff" (Lipner 1986: 51–52).The implication of consciousness that exists both as the substrate of the self and as its attribute is that during embodiment, in *saṃsāra*, it is only the attributive consciousness that is affected. Consciousness as the substrate, which is the self's essential nature remains unchanged.

In the VS, Rāmānuja's refutation of the Advaita doctrine of the concealment of Brahman leads the latter to pose the following question:

> However, you too (Rāmānuja), must hold that the essential nature of the *ātman* is discriminative consciousness (*vijñānasvarūpa*) and that it is self-luminous/self-cognizant (*svayaṃprakāśa*). Now, when the self is wrongly identified with the body, as gods and so on, it must be assumed that its essential nature is obscured (*tirodāna*); because if the essential nature of an entity is known, it is not possible to wrongly attribute to it, characteristics that do not belong to it. Therefore, the error you (Rāmānuja) pointed out applies to you also.[22]

Both Rāmānuja and the Advaitin agree that embodiment involves concealment, how it operates, and what is concealed is a different matter. When the Advaitin refers to the essential nature of the self he means Brahman, whereas Rāmānuja's reply assumes the topic of discussion to be the individual self. However, the issue here is not what is being concealed, but rather how the concept of concealment functions. The Advaitin's view is that the Self/Brahman's essential nature, which is conscious and self-conscious, wrongly identifies itself with the body, due to concealment by adjuncts. Rāmānuja replies:

> Our acceptance of the following view refutes your (Advaitin's) entire objection—that consciousness, which is an inherent attribute (*svabhāva*) of the individual self, is really existent, and contracts (*saṅkoca*) and expands (*vikāsa*) due to karma. However, for you (the Advaitin) illumination (consciousness) is not a quality (*dharma*), but rather the essential nature (*svarūpa*) itself, whose contraction or expansion cannot be admitted. Factors that obscure the essential nature such as karma, restrict the unimpeded spread of illumination (consciousness).[23]
>
> If ignorance (*avidyā*) obscures, that is, if ignorance is the concealing factor, then it destroys the illumination (consciousness) which is the essential nature itself, as stated before. However, according to us, the eternal attribute (*dharma*) of the self's essential nature (*svarūpa*)

> contracts. By this contraction, the identification of the self with forms such as gods and so on, comes about; this is the difference between our views.[24]

The important distinction Rāmānuja makes here is between consciousness as the individual self's essential nature (substrate) and consciousness as an essential attribute. Consciousness that is an attribute (*dharmabhūtajñāna*) can be obscured; it can contract and expand due to karma, which is real. When consciousness itself is the essential attribute (*svarūpa*), as the Advaitin claims, any change must lead to the destruction of the eternal nature of the self; this idea runs counter to the upaniṣad teaching of a permanent, unchanging self. Whereas the Advaitin subscribes to the concept of concealment of consciousness, Rāmānuja prefers the model of contraction and expansion of attributive consciousness. In this way the essential nature of the self remains unchanged (Lacombe 1966: 184–88).

While for Śaṅkara the Self is neither an agent nor an enjoyer of actions and any reference to such a process is strictly within the realm of the empirical experience or illusion (*māyā*) for Rāmānuja, the individual soul when embodied is subject to the viccisistudes of karma, as a performer of actions and so on, but remains unaffected in its essential nature. This very real experience of the embodied self in the cycle of birth and rebirth occurs without the essential nature of the self being affected but only its attributive consciousness (Lipner 1986: 66–74). For scriptural support of the concept of attributive consciousness, Rāmānuja turns not to śruti, but to the VP:

> It has been said that:
>
> Viṣṇu's power (*śakti*) is said to be supreme; when it is called the *kṣetrajña*[25] it is not supreme,
> the third power is ignorance (*avidyā*) called karma.[26]
>
> (VP 6.7.61)
>
> O' King, with karma the power called the *kṣetrajña* is enclosed (*veṣṭita*) and suffers all the torment of repeated eternal worldly existence.
>
> (VP 6.7.62)
>
> O' King, concealed by that (illusion) the power called *kṣetrajña*
> exists in all beings in different degress (*tāratamya*).[27]
>
> (VP 6.7.63)

According to the first passage, VP 6.7.61, Brahman/Viṣṇu has complete power over ignorance (*avidyā*) as it belongs to Him, in contrast to the Advaitin, for whom ignorance conceals Brahman. Rāmānuja has shown earlier that if concealment affects the essential nature of the self, the inevitable implication would be that the self as it succumbs to changes in its essential nature, is no longer the imperishable entity described in the upaniṣads. He circumvents this issue by arguing for a differentiation between consciousness as an attribute and consciousness as constituting the essential nature of the self. He declares ignorance in the form of karma as the obscuring factor, based on VP 6.7.72, albeit a factor that is real (*pāramārthika*). Both of these perspectives find direct support in the VP verses cited above. Karma is real because it is a power of Viṣṇu, just as the individual self as a power of Viṣṇu is also real, and because the individual self is one of the three distinct realities (the supreme Brahman, the individual self, and karma) according to the VP.[28]

Rāmānuja takes his proof for the concept of contraction and expansion from VP 6.7.63, where the embodied self is said to exist in all beings, but in different degrees. Though the VP mentions the concept of *tāratamya*, it does not mention it in association with attributive consciousness. The TD comments on this concept of gradation (*tāratamya*) of the embodied self:

> with the phrase "in different degrees", the contraction and expansion of consciousness is established. Indeed, it cannot be the gradation of the essential nature of the individual self, which has the size of only an atom (*aṇumātra*).[29] Therefore there is gradation of the individual self only by means of consciousness which is the property (*dharmabhūta*) of the self. That consciousness is an attribute of the self is expressed by the following verses:
>
> > in the inanimate it is minute, it is more in the sentient but immovable things.[30]
> >
> > (VP 6.7.64 ab)

According to the TD, the term "gradation" refers to consciousness as the attribute of the individual self rather than its essential nature. The individual self is constant in its essential nature, and it is only its attributive consciousness that is concealed to various extents depending on one's karma. The concept of gradation of karma as the means of contraction and expansion of attributive consciousness is an important characteristic that distinguishes Rāmānuja's Vedānta from that of his predecessors and the VP's support on this perspective is significant.

VP 6.7.64 ab quoted by the commentator, states that the power called consciousness exists in a minute degree in things without life and in an ascending degree from men to gods and other semi-divine beings. In Viṣṇu, however, attributive consciousness is never impaired, as in the case of the embodied self. Although the TD only quotes VP 6.7.64 ab, it states "by the following verses", which would mean at least three other passages (i.e. VP 6.7.64 to VP 6.7.67). These passages describe how the energy of Viṣṇu, called the individual self, is present to a small degree in insects and to a higher degree in divine beings. In the VS then, on the topic of the individual self, the VP is invaluable as the source text for the essential and embodied natures of the individual self.

Brahman's originative causality

A second exegetical instance where the VP serves more than a corroborative function in the VS is in support of the doctrine of Brahman's causality. For Śaṅkara, the true intention of śruti discussions on causality are meant to deny the absolute as an effect, to affirm the non-difference of the cause and effect, to reject the universe as self-caused, and to deny the world an independent nature. Then finally, the true nature of Brahman is conveyed by denying that Brahman can be a cause either. This method of "false attribution followed by retraction" is one of the hallmarks of Śaṅkara's methodology (Sarasvati 1989: 41, 76) and is ultimately meant to lead the mind of the meditator beyond the realm of causality and empirical reality altogether. In marked contrast to Advaita, Brahman's causality "is central to Rāmānuja's theology to affirm the relatedness of his God to finite being" (Lipner 1986: 82). Thus, in all his works he spends considerable time detailing this relationship and the VS is no exception.

According to Rāmānuja, Brahman himself is the material and efficient cause of creation, but does not himself, undergo any modification. To uphold such a view, Brahman's causality is addressed in two ways, for which the VP is utilized. First, Rāmānuja illustrates that cause and effect are both different conditions (*avasthā*) of Brahman and that Brahman, which is eternally differentiated into individual selves and matter, is the material cause as a whole (*aviśeṣaṇakāraṇa*). Creation then is not so much a coming into being of something new but simply a change from a causal state (*kāraṇāvasthā*) to the effected state (*kāryāvasthā*) of this complex whole. For support, Rāmānuja turns to the Proto-Sāṃkhyan concepts of the VP. As we shall see, he is unable to comprehensively support the claim that the effect (world) is simply a change in condition of a differentiated Brahman with content from the upaniṣads alone.

Second, Rāmānuja understands causality as a specific characteristic of Brahman's essential nature (*brahmasvarūpaviśeṣa*). If in some ways the discussion of Brahman as the material cause as a whole (*aviśeṣakāraṇa*) is about the mechanics of creation, the concept of causality as an aspect of Brahman essential nature (*brahmasvarūpaviśeṣa*) argues against the non-illusory nature of the world since it is Brahman itself:

> Rāmānuja in particular took seriously the many scriptural images and utterances which seemed naturally to imply that finite being emerges from or issues out of Brahman, its permanent ground or substratum and the fund into which it is reabsorbed in dissolution. Philosophically-theologically, this meant that the 'creational gap', i.e., the ontological chasm between infinite and finite being, represented by the *ex-nihilo* of the *creatio* doctrine was eschewed, and that instead an existential 'umbilical cord', i.e., a continuous existential relation between the originative cause (Brahman) and the finite order was posited.
>
> (Lipner 1986: 83)

Both concepts of *aviśeṣaṇakāraṇa* and *brahmasvarūpaviśeṣa* allow Rāmānuja to posit such a "continuous existential relation" between Brahman and the world. At the same time, he is able to refute many of the objections that result from upholding the eternal, unchanging Brahman as both the creator and the created. These two concepts are uniquely Viśiṣṭādvaitic, and Rāmānuja finds support in the VP. We begin with the discussion of Brahman as the material cause as a whole (*aviśeṣaṇakāraṇa*) and then address causality as an aspect of Brahman's essential nature (*brahmasvarūpaviśeṣa*).

Brahman as the material cause as a whole (*aviśeṣaṇakāraṇa*)

Van Buitenen (1956: 39) describes Rāmānuja's apparent disinterest in the mechanics of world evolution as follows: "Rāmānuja's and indeed Vedānta's main concern is with ontology: only when the ontological relation between the supreme cause and the phenomenal effect has been established cosmology and cosmogony can proceed." In the case of Rāmānuja, the cosmological details of the continuous existential link between Brahman and the world, is vital to his overall ontology. Although the fundamental paradigm of Rāmānuja's theology is the soul–body relationship, still scriptural support is needed to explain the specifics of creative evolution within the framework of Viśiṣṭādvaita. Thus "cosmology and cosmogony" are very much relevant and the role of the VP in this matter is significant.

Śaṅkara, Bhāskara, Yādavaprakāśa, and Rāmānuja all subscribe to the theory of causality called *satkāryavāda*, which states that the effect itself is present in the cause. But, exactly how this immanent causality manifests as the effect and the relation of this effect to the cause is a point of contention. Rāmānuja needs to show that Brahman eternally constituted of matter and individual selves is the cause as a whole (*aviśeṣaṇakāraṇa*). Furthermore, he must provide scriptural support that Brahman is eternally differentiated into matter and individual selves, that these are inseparable from him, and that it is only these modes as the body of Brahman that undergo transformation. Only then can the claim that the causal state (*kāraṇāvasthā*) transforms into the effected state (*kāryāvasthā*) is intelligible. Though in the upaniṣads that Rāmānuja utilizes there may be evidence of Brahman differentiated into matter and selves, they lack a coherent framework to articulate *kāraṇāvasthā* and *kāryāvasthā* as fundamental to the conception of Brahman as the cause as a whole (*aviśeṣaṇakāraṇa*). First we examine the śruti passages provided as support for the conception of Brahman as the material cause as a whole comparing their contribution to evidence from the *Bhagavadgītā* and the *Viṣṇu Purāṇa*.

Śruti support

In the *siddhānta* section of the VS,[31] Rāmānuja summarizes his position regarding Brahman and creation:

> What has been said so far is that in the phrase 'Brahman alone exists thus' (*brahmaivam avasthitam*), the reality which is the phenomenal world composed of myriad sentient and insentient entities in their subtle (*sthūla*) and gross (*sūkṣma*) state is a mode (*prakāra*) denoted by words such as 'thus'.[32]

Contrary to Advaita, where God (*Īśvara*) is the cause (*kāraṇa*) and effect (*kārya*) only provisionally, from the level of empirical truth, for Rāmānuja, ultimate reality itself is Brahman comprised of selves and matter as his modes. This whole complex of Brahman and his modes is denoted here by the term "thus"; it is a single entity and is in line with Rāmānuja's assertion that Brahman is eternally differentiated. He goes on to say that it is only from such an understanding that even śruti such as *may I become many, may I grow forth* (Ch Up 6.2.3) are meaningful.[33] Rāmānuja elaborates further on what he understands to be Brahman as the material cause as a whole:

> Therefore, Brahman himself is also all effects, since he has the generic structure of being modified by all things—*prakṛti, puruṣa, mahat, ahaṃkāra, tanmātra*, elements, and the senses, the egg of Brahmā consisting of fourteen worlds that derive from the above entities and the gods, men, demons, plants etc. that live within the universe. So by knowing solely that Brahman is the reason we know all. In this manner it is established very well that knowledge of all can be had from knowledge of the one (Ch Up 6.1). At the same time it is stated on the strength of the causal relation etc established hereby, that the sum-total of sentient and insentient entities is ensouled by the supreme Brahman in as much as it modifies him.[34]

Brahman comprised of *puruṣa* and *prakṛti* is the cause as a whole and is identical to Brahman as the effect comprised of matter and selves. Rāmānuja notes that "the sum-total of sentient and insentient entities" are "ensouled by Brahman (*tadātmaka*)." It is in this sense that Rāmānuja understands identity (*tādātmya*) between cause and effect, which is in marked contrast to that of the Advaitin. Śaṅkara takes *tādātmya* as essential identity in a substantial sense. (Lacombe 1966: 51–52). To support the claim that Brahman is the material cause as a whole, first matter (*prakṛti*) and individual selves (*puruṣa*) must be established as eternal. Second, Brahman must be eternally differentiated into matter and individual selves. Third, such a Brahman must be a cause as a whole. Rāmānuja utilizes śruti, BhG and the VP to support these claims.

To support *puruṣa* and *prakṛti* as eternal entities he turns to Śvet Up 4.5 and 4.9–10:

> with the one uncreated (matter) that has form and that produces various effects of various kinds, one uncreated (soul) joins itself to enjoy it, whereas another uncreated (soul) goes free from it when it has ceased to enjoy it.[35]
>
> (Śvet Up 4.5)

One of the major precoccupations of this upaniṣad is "to establish that the God who creates and from whom one expects salvation is *one*" (Olivelle 1998: 413). It begins by stating that creation proceeds from Brahman and then dissolves into him: *in whom the universe comes together at the beginning and dissolves in the end* (4.1). Śvet Up 4.5 according to Rāmānuja confirms that matter, embodied selves and liberated selves are all eternal. It is the embodied soul in association with matter that is the enjoyer of karma and it is the latter that undergoes transformation. *Śvetāśvatara Upaniṣad* 4.9–10 that Rāmānuja subsequently cites, affirms further that it is matter (*prakṛti*), by its essential nature, which is the substratum of transformation:

> from that the illusionist creates this whole world and in it the other remains confined by the illusory power (*māyā*).
>
> (Śvet Up 4.9)

> one should recognize the illusory power (*māyā*) as primal matter (*prakṛti*), and the illusionist, as the great Lord.[36]
>
> (Śvet Up 4.10)

These passages clarify the eternal relationship between Brahman, matter, and individual selves; Brahman as the controller of matter, which is his *māyā* that confines individual selves. However, there is no mention of the exact relationship of these as eternal modes of Brahman. More clarification is needed to articulate Brahman as the material cause as a whole. Also problematic is the use of the term *māyā* to denote *prakṛti*, which can color any discussion of the world as an illusion. As Śaṅkara notes in Br Sū 1.4.3, matter which the upaniṣads define as *māyā* is the power of Īśvara, illusion which cannot be defined as either real or unreal. These verses do not supply the detail needed to affirm Brahman's causality in the way that Rāmānuja envisions it—in terms of an identity between the cause which is eternally differentiated and the effected state of Brahman. Moreover, the use of the term *māyā* in this upaniṣad to denote *prakṛti* requires additional clarification so as to reject rival interpretations such as that of Advaita. In fact, in both Chapters 3 and 4, these upaniṣad verses are interpreted using the VP. These passages suggest that Brahman is the cause, since it is matter (*prakṛti*) that is modified in its essential nature and not Brahman. In other words, these śṛuti passages cannot be adequately interpreted to claim Brahman as the cause as a whole and Brahman as the effect as a whole and that the manifest world, is real.

Bhagavadgītā support

Subsequent to quoting śruti and prior to turning to the VP, Rāmānuja also cites the BhG to support the view that matter (*prakṛti*) and individual selves (*puruṣa*) are both eternal and that they comprise Brahman who is the material cause as a whole. In order to ascertain the importance of the VP, it is necessary to evaluate the BhG's contribution in comparison to this purāṇa. As we have seen in the discussion of the Śvet Up passages, in the previous section, one of the initial moves in establishing Brahman as eternally differentiated is to establish these two entites as eternal and this is what the Śvet Up and BhG accomplish. Rāmānuja utilizes five BhG passages, but in fact the commentary on three of these verses in his *Bhagavadgīābhāṣya* relies on the VP. That is, these BhG passages themselves cannot be interpreted adequately as Viśiṣṭādvaitic without the aid of the VP:

> Be sure that matter (*prakṛti*) as well as individual self (*puruṣa*) are both without beginning
> and the transmutations and *guṇas* alike are the products of *prakṛti*.
>
> (BhG 13.19)

> Earth, water, fire, wind, ether, *manas*, *buddhi*, and *ahaṃkāra* are the eight components of my nature (*prakṛti*).
>
> (BhG 7.4)

> Know, however, that I have still another nature (*prakṛti*) which is of a higher order than the former,
> a nature (*prakṛti*) that is constituted by embodied souls, on which this material world is dependent O' Arjuna.[37]
>
> (BhG 7.5)

Rāmānuja in his commentary on BhG 13.19 states that only matter and the individual selves that are distinct entities associate with each other due to karma. Though he does not at this juncture state these two as the modes of Kṛṣṇa, he assumes that the reader is interpreting this BhG verse in light of this soul–body paradigm. This is due to the fact that in his commentary on 13.4 he utilizes VP (2.13.69–71, 2.13.89, 2.13.102–3) to establish that matter and individual selves comprise the body of Brahman who is their inner self. This is also the case with BhG 7.4–7.6, where VP 1.2.24 and VP 6.4.38–39 are utilized to the same effect. The significance of these VP passages for Rāmānuja's interpretation of BhG verses is discussed in Chapter 4 and is not addressed here in detail. However, we may note that it does support the theory that the VP provides certain details not to be found elsewhere and that to even read certain BhG passages requires the purāṇa, for Rāmānuja. In this particular context of the VS, these BhG passages (13.19, 7.4–5), reiterate the Śvet Up claim that matter, liberated selves, and embodied selves are eternal and constitute Kṛṣṇa's very nature (*prakṛti*). Rāmānuja concludes with two more passages from Chapter 9 of the BhG:

> taking my material from my own nature (*prakṛti*) I create again and again.
>
> (BhG 9.8cd)

> and under my guidance the matter (*prakṛti*) with its animate and inanimate beings is brought forth.[38]
>
> (BhG 9.10)

BhG 9.8cd and BhG 9.10 also support matter and individual selves as eternal in Brahman who has complete control over them. In summary, though Rāmānuja cites the BhG here, some of the passages themselves require the VP to be interpreted according to Viśiṣṭādvaita. In regard to BhG 9.8 cd and 9.10, these passages do contribute to the concept of Brahman's lordship over the eternal matter (*prakṛti*) and individual selves (*puruṣa*) but are still inadequate to support the concept of Brahman as the material cause as a whole. As we see in Chapter 4, thc VP is crucial in establishing Kṛṣṇa as the eternally qualified cause who transforms into the world.

Viṣṇu Purāṇa support

The VP cited here as corroboration along with the BhG, provides details on the relationship not found in the previous śruti and BhG passages. Rāmānuja states the following prior to citing from this purāṇa:

> Thus, matter (*prakṛti*) also constitutes the body of Īśvara (Viṣṇu). The term *prakṛti* denotes Īśvara, who is the inner self of *prakṛti* and has it as a mode. The term individual self (*puruṣa*) also denotes Īśvara, who is the self of *puruṣa* and has it as a mode. Therefore, Īśvara is the inner self of the modifications of *prakṛti* as well as *puruṣa*. Regarding this it is said—*Viṣṇu is the manifested and unmanifested creation, puruṣa, and time* (VP 1.2.18), *He the supreme lord is the agitator and that which is agitated* (VP 1.2.31).[39]

According to Rāmānuja, the VP supports matter and individual selves as eternal, but also that they are related to Brahman as His modes. Some of the details that were not supported by śruti passages but are evident in the VP verses are: a) Viṣṇu *is prakṛti, puruṣa*, and time, and thus all entities are eternal; b) matter is what modifies upon creation but since it is identified with Viṣṇu, its independent causality is refuted; c) although the VP passages that have been stated do not suggest a soul–body relationship, this is implied from the fact that Brahman is both *agitator and the agitated*. The complete context of the verses that Rāmānuja has only partially stated, support all these details and the soul–body relationship:

> Viṣṇu being the manifested and unmanifested creation, *puruṣa*, and time, sports like a playful boy, as you shall learn by listening to his frolics.
>
> (VP 1.2.18)

> Puruṣottama is both the agitator and the thing agitated;
> Being present in matter both when it is contracted and expanded.[40]
>
> (VP 1.2.31)

The fact that Viṣṇu is *present in matter both when it is contracted and expanded* suggests for Rāmānuja, that He is the inner self of matter that is eternal. Hence, Rāmānuja's previous comment about modes is justified. It also confirms the individual self as distinct from Brahman and disputes matter as an independent cause.

Rāmānuja concludes his discussion of Brahman's causality with a description of creation and dissolution for which he again turns to the VP:

> Thus Brahman, when his body (*śarīra*) is constituted by matter (*prakṛti*) and individual selves (*puruṣa*) in their subtle form, not distinguishable by differences of name and form, is the causal state (*kāraṇāvasthā*). The passing of the world to this phase of existence is termed 'dissolution'. Brahman having, as its body, the individual selves and nature, in their gross manifested condition distinguished by differentiation of name and form is in the state of effect (*kāryāvasthā*). Brahman's assuming this mode of manifestation and grossness is described as creation. As Bhagavān Parāśara says—*He is the cause of effects, the unborn prakṛti and puruṣa.*[41]
>
> (VP 1.9.37)

The context of VP 1.9 is the narrative of the churning of the ocean and this passage is taken from Brahmā's eulogy to Viṣṇu as the causeless cause. For Rāmānuja, this narrative presents creation not as a new entity coming into being, but as simply a different state of the causal Brahman. These two stages of creation/dissolution are the same since the changes taking place in the modes do not affect the complex as a whole (due to the soul–body relation). Rāmānuja sums up his argument by quoting from VP 1.9.37, which reiterates the eternal nature of a differentiated Brahman into matter, and individual selves. Whereas most śruti passages need to be read assuming a differentiation of the causal Brahman into individual selves and matter, that is not the case here, with the VP.

Causality as an aspect of the essential nature of Brahman (*brahmsvarūpaviśeṣa*)

In the previous section, the VP is crucial in establishing an eternally differentiated Brahman that remains the same as far as its essential nature is concerned even through the creative process. The causal state (*kāraṇāvasthā*) of Brahman, which is an eternally differentiated whole, undergoes a change in its modes into what is called the effected state (*kāryāvasthā*) of Brahman. In addition to Brahman as the material cause as a whole (*aviśeṣaṇakāraṇa*), another way in which Rāmānuja affirms the reality of the world is to define causality as a characteristic of Brahman's essential nature (*brahmasvarūpaviśeṣa*).[42]

Though other Vedāntins affirm the causality of Brahman, none characterize it as a quality of the essential nature of Brahman (*brahmasvarūpaviśeṣa*).[43]

Three constituents characterize Rāmānuja's definition of *brahmasvarūpaviśeṣa*: a) Brahman as the cause; b) Brahman as inseparable from the world; c) Brahman as the Lord over His creation from which he is completely distinct and transcendent. While śruti affirms Brahman as the cause, his creative activity is not discussed as a characteristic of his essential nature (*svarūpaviśeṣa*) in the three-fold sense stated above.

Prior to utilizing the VP, Rāmānuja also quotes MBh passages, 12.182.1, 12.182.12, 12.7074.[44] Here, Nārāyaṇa as the inner self of the world is declared as *jaganmūrti*, one who has the world as His body. While it does underscore the soul–body aspect of Brahman's causality, the MBh does not compare to the VP in terms of the detail it offers, and serves instead to foreshadow the content of the purāṇa. Moreover, the TD scarcely discusses these passages, noting only that the MBh is also a *sāttvic*[45] text and therefore authoritative.[46] This scant attention to MBh passages by the commentator, as compared to the VP passages, and also the sheer number of passages from the latter cited by Rāmānuja, suggests that the purāṇa is the main scripture for Rāmānuja on matters of causality.

What does Rāmānuja gain by positing such a nature for Brahman? The concept of causality as *brahmasvarūpaviśeṣa* allows him to affirm the positive nature of reality in contrast to the Advaitin, for whom empirical reality is an illusion. Furthermore, the causality of Brahman seen as an aspect of his essential nature (*brahmasvarūpaviśeṣa*) is much different from Bhāskara's Bhedābheda Vedānta of the created world as essentially limited or conditioned (*aupādhika*). Rāmānuja uses the VP, to delineate this three-fold character of the essential nature of Brahman: Brahman as the cause, Brahman as inseparable from the world, and Brahman's lordship over creation. Though śruti passages can be interpreted to yield all these three characteristics of Brahman separately, there are no śruti texts utilized by Rāmānuja that affirm the three-fold combination of characteristics, that is, causality as *brahmasvarūpaviśeṣa* as he understands it.

Throughout the discussion of the VP in this section, Rāmānuja uses the term *brahmasvarūpaviśeṣa* in his exegesis of the VP passages. To begin with, he states that passages such as VP 1.1.31, to be discussed subsequently, have the sole purpose of expounding an aspect of the essential nature of Brahman (*brahmasvarūpaviśeṣa*).[47] Several passages later, when he compares the VP to the *Nārāyaṇa Anuvāka* of the *Taittirīya Āraṇyaka,* he twice declares that the VP's sole aim is the determination of this specific nature of Brahman alone.[48] Having established the VP's authority as a valid means of knowledge of Brahman, Rāmānuja cites twenty-five VP passages to support his view of causality as *brahmasvarūpaviśeṣa.* I will not analyze all of these VP citations which address causality as a *svarūpaviśeṣa* of Brahman, but only highlight the content of some of the significant passages.

Rāmānuja's first citations from the VP establish the relevance and authority of the VP by noting that this purāṇa shares the same goals as the upaniṣads and the *Brahma Sūtras* in the kinds of questions it seeks to answer:

> Every wise man of the East, North, South, and West relies on the VP in the determination of each and every duty (*dharma*) and in each and every ultimate reality (*tattva*); for that reason I have embraced this very text without reservation. We learn from the sūtra: *from whom birth etc. of this proceed* (Br Sū 1.1.2) that the cause of the birth etc. of the world is Brahman. Now, the VP in answer to the question: *what has caused the world to be born etc.* (VP 1.1.4–5), says: *it has originated from Viṣṇu* (VP 1.1.31). Everyone agrees that this answer has only one purpose, namely, to establish an aspect of the essential nature of Brahman (*brahmasvarūpaviśeṣa*) … even as in all śrutis the *Nārāyaṇa* section serves only to set forth a certain aspect of the Supreme Brahman's essential nature (*brahmasvarūpaviśeṣa*), so does the VP.[49]

The fact that the discussion of Brahman's causality as his *svarūpaviśeṣa* begins with a eulogization of the authority of the VP suggests that the VP's contribution is significant and that Rāmānuja's use of this smṛti text might be objected to by other Vedāntins. Rāmānuja affirms the VP's authority in several ways: first, he invokes its pan-Hindu popularity as a scripture of importance regarding matters of duty (*dharma*) and ultimate reality (*tattva*). Second, in regard to the issue of Brahman's causality, he compares the authority of the VP to that of the *Brahma Sūtras*, the summary text of Vedānta philosophy, and to the *Nārāyaṇa Anuvāka*, a section of the *Taittirīya Āraṇyaka*. Having validated the VP as an authority on the issue of Brahman's causality as he defines it, Rāmānuja provides specific verses that qualify it as a source of Vedānta.

The first VP passage, *all this has originated from Viṣṇu* (VP 1.1.31), identifies Brahman as the supreme cause. He then quotes two passages to clarify the origin of the world from Viṣṇu. With these verses Rāmānuja and the commentator introduce the concept of an eternally differentiated Brahman:

> Both that which I (*Parāśara*) have called matter (*prakṛti*) with a manifest and unmanifest nature,
> and individual self (*puruṣa*) dissolve in the Supreme Self.
>
> (VP 6.4.39)

> The Supreme Self is the highest lord, the substratum of everything.
> He is praised in the Vedas and upaniṣads[50] as Viṣṇu.[51]
>
> (VP 6.4.40)

The context of VP 6.4 is the description of the different types of world dissolution. This chapter describes the regression of the material world into Viṣṇu and speaks of matter and the individual self as portions of Viṣṇu. To counter the view that Brahman or a part of Brahman is modified in this process, the TD interprets the term *substratum* in VP 6.4.40 as suggestive of the soul–body relationship, "*He is the substratum* indicates the soul–body relationship."[52] Note also that matter in its two forms as both manifest and unmanifest is congruent with the theory that it is matter alone that undergoes change. Additionally, the identity of the supreme self as the deity Viṣṇu is also established.

Subsequently, two VP passages from the beginning of the purāṇa are stated. In this section of VP 1.1., Maitreya requests Parāśara for instruction on the nature of the world. The specificity of Maitreya's questions in VP 1.1.4–5 is exactly what Rāmānuja needs as an entry point to the details of the cosmology needed to establish the concept of *brahmasvarūpaviśeṣa*:[53]

> I wish to hear from you, O' righteous one,
> the way the world was and how it will be again.
>
> (VP 1.1.4)

> O' Brahmin, what is the stuff the world is made of? Where do these animate and inanimate beings come from?
> How and into what is it brought to dissolution and into what does it dissolve?[54]
>
> (VP 1.1.5)

For Rāmānuja these are very specific questions about the causal state and the effected state of Brahman, particularly the relation of matter (*prakṛti*) and the individual self (*puruṣa*) to Brahman. Though the context is the dissolution of the world, this scenario holds equally true for world origination as well. The commentary indicates that the answer to these questions points to specific types of causal theories:

> Because people who have studied Vedānta ask the question how creation relates to Brahman, with the word 'how' the VP introduces a question in order to teach the ways of dissolution such as emptiness, illusion, modification, direct cause, or indirect cause etc.[55]

These passages (VP 1.1.4–5) do not simply qualify as questions on whether Brahman is the cause of the world; they question *how* Brahman is the cause of the world. The VP then is said to provide the answers to these important queries. As the commentary states Brahman can be the material cause in different ways. Creation can be a modification of Brahman, a direct cause of Brahman or an indirect cause of Brahman etc. Multiple Vedānta theories of causality are referenced here. Both Rāmānuja and the commentator utilize these VP passages for a specific purpose, namely, to express the exact nature of Brahman's involvement in the creative process and in effect distinguish Viśiṣṭādvaita from other types of Vedānta.

According to Rāmānuja, the next eleven VP passages he utilizes answer the question *what is Brahman*,[56] but the context is still causality as a unique aspect of the essential nature of Brahman. Earlier, Rāmānuja quotes only a part of VP 1.1.31 to validate the authority of the VP, whereas now he cites the complete verse:

> This world was produced from Viṣṇu Himself (*sakāśāt*) and it exists in Him.
> He is the cause of its preservation and dissolution.
> He is the world.[57]
>
> (VP 1.1.31)

This passage describes Viṣṇu's function as the material and efficient cause of the universe. The fact that Viṣṇu is the world could suggest identity in essential nature between the two. However, one of the interpretations that the TD offers for *sakāśāt* is that the world evolves out of a part of Brahman:

> *sakāśa* means *pārśva*, 'side', 'flank', 'ribs', so that *viṣṇoḥ sakāśāt* means 'from a part of the body of Viṣṇu'.[58]

Once again, the commentator tries to limit the effects of modification, a conseqeunce of being the material cause, to only a part or portion of Brahman, but this still subjects Brahman to change and impermanence. To define "part" within the soul–body paradigm, the commentator goes back to the context of this passage (1.1.31) in the VP. According to him, the word "Viṣṇu" in "*this world was produced from Viṣṇu himself*" (VP 1.1.31) denotes Viṣṇu with his constituent parts, matter (*prakṛti*) and individual selves (*puruṣa*), which are modes of Brahman. To establish the Lordship and transcendence of Brahman over his creation, the commentary claims that because of the soul–body paradigm, Brahman's engagement can be understood as indirect, yet inseparable:

> The question of the place of dissolution expressed by the phrase, *into what* in 1.1.5, is answered with *there.* The world exists *in Him alone* means in Viṣṇu alone. Here, too, it is understood that the place of dissolution is indirect (*sadvāraka*).[59]

Thus, Brahman as an eternally differentiated entity possesses matter and individual souls as his modes. Even in the state of dissolution, when the world is reabsorbed into Brahman, they abide in him and are distinct, yet inseparable, and so Brahman is the indirect (*sadvāraka*) cause. The three-fold definition of *brahmasvarūpaviśeṣa*—Brahman as the cause, Brahman as inseparable from the world, and Brahman as the transcendent Lord distinct from the world, is supported by the VP according to Rāmānuja and his commentator.

Having established Brahman who is eternally differentiated as the cause, the next VP passages are used to declare Brahman's transcendent nature and His absolute difference from all entities. This emphasizes the third component of the *brahmasvarūpaviśeṣa* paradigm. The transcendent nature of Brahman is two-fold—he is the cause of the world and yet he is completely different from everything and every being. This dual affirmation of the transcendent nature of Brahman is the main contribution of VP 1.2.10–14 discussed below:

> He is the highest of the high, he is the supreme almighty, he resides in the individual self
> and is without characteristics such as form and color etc.[60]
>
> (VP 1.2.10)

The context of VP 1.2 is world evolution. In this chapter, it is declared that matter in its manifest and unmanifest forms, individual selves, and time, denote the supreme condition of Viṣṇu. As the self of all, He enters into matter and spirit to promote creation. The fact that the supreme condition of Viṣṇu is comprised of the matter and individual selves is contrary to Bhāskara and Yādavaprakāśa's view. The VP also discusses the evolution of matter from Viṣṇu, while affirming his transcendence over it.

Utilizing the VP, Rāmānuja maintains the continuity of being, but at the same time rejects Brahman's conditioning by the changes in his modes. Here, I shall only list some of the VP passages cited that declare such a transcendent nature of Brahman and his Lordship over creation:

> He is free from decay, destruction, birth, change; He alone always exists.
>
> (VP 1.2.11)

> Since he resides everywhere the wise call him Vāsudeva.
>
> (VP 1.2.12)

> He is Brahman, supreme, eternal, unborn, without decay, imperishable, ever of the same essential nature, and because he has not faults, is stainless.
>
> (VP 1.2.13)

> All this is nothing but him. His own essential nature (*svarūpa*) encompasses what is manifest and what is unmanifest,
> and he exists in the form of (individual selves) *puruṣa* and in the form of time.[61]
>
> (VP 1.2.14)

The three-fold definition of causality as *brahmasvarūpaviśeṣa* is constantly affirmed in these VP passages. Brahman is transcendent, yet resides everywhere and since nothing exists apart from him, he is the cause of the world (1.2.11). VP 1.2.13 characterizes Brahman as entirely different, even as matter and individual selves constitute his essential nature (*svarūpa*) (VP 1.2.14).

The discussion of causality as an aspect of Brahman's essential nature continues with the next five VP passages (6.5.83–87). VP 6.5 begins with a discussion of the evils of the worldly existence and the different types of hells. The last section which utilizes VP 6.5.83–87 is a discussion of the meaning of the term *bhagavat* which is a synonym for Viṣṇu in Śrīvaiṣṇavism. This section of the VP effectively identifies *bhagavān* as Vāsudeva, who is the supreme Brahman. Once again, I shall only address some of these utilized passages:

> O' Lord, He is beyond matter (*prakṛti*) of all beings, beyond mutations, and beyond the faults of *guṇas* etc.
> He is beyond all concealment; He is the self of everything; everything between heaven and earth is encompassed by Him.[62]
>
> (VP 6.5.83)

> He consists of all auspicious qualities; with a tiny portion of his power (*śakti*) He holds up the world.[63]
> At his own discretion, if he so desires, he takes on a large body, accomplishing the welfare of the entire world.
>
> (VP 6.5.84)

Even as Brahman encompasses the world, he is unaffected due to the soul–body relationship, and so he is the essence of all auspicious qualities. This is the participative-partitive theology that is the hallmark of Rāmānuja's theological method (Lipner 1986: 83–86). The important concept of incarnation is also articulated in 6.5.84 suggesting that His interest in the welfare of a world that is illusory negates the importance of the concept of incarnation. Brahman's direct activity in his creation via his descents (*avatāra*) is said to be for the benefit of a world that is real. The bodies that Viṣṇu assumes during his incarnations are different from the *vigraha*, his divine form, which is discussed in the next section. The VP, then, allows for a reading that underscores salient Viśiṣṭādvaita principles more so than śruti.

The concept of the dual-character, *ubhayaliṅgatva*, which is characteristic of Rāmānuja's definition of Brahman in these passages, asserts his auspicious qualities and at the same time denies any faults due to *prakṛti*:

> He is Īśvara, encompassing individual and aggregate existence, encompassing manifest and unmanifest existence,
> lord (*Īśvara*) of all, all pervasive, all knowing, and he is called *paramātman*.[64]
>
> (VP 6.5.86)

> Through which this pure, stainless, transcendent, faultless, indivisible, sole reality
> is known that is true knowledge, all that is contrary to this is ignorance.
>
> (VP 6.5.87)[65]

> This is the explanation for the determination of the essential characteristics of the Supreme Brahman (*brahmasvarūpaviśeṣa*).[66]

These VP passages chosen by Rāmānuja, to confirm causality as an aspect of Brahman's essential nature are a strong refutation of the defnitions of causality held by other schools of Vedānta. He concludes with the following passages to sum up his argument that causality is indeed an aspect of Brahman's essential nature (*svarūpaviśeṣa*):

> Because the imperishable one is the immanent soul of all beings and is embodied by all, therefore creation etc localized in these beings are ultimately useful to Him alone.
>
> (VP 1.2.69)

> So Viṣṇu, most excellent, beneficient and benevolent, is embodied by all, in the various modes of Brahmā etc., in which he is creating and created, protecting, consuming, and protected.[67]
>
> (VP 1.2.70)

The mention of the world as an embodiment of Viṣṇu agrees with Rāmānuja's soul–body paradigm. As the imperishable one, He is also the *creator and created*, the *protector and protected*. In other words, the world *is* Brahman. Passages 1.2.68–70 affirm the three-fold definition of causality as an aspect of Brahman's essential nature. They offer support for Brahman as the cause of the world that is inseparable from Him, and yet his complete transcendence over it. Rāmānuja elaborates:

> *because the imperishable One is the immanent soul of all beings and embodied by all*, i.e. because the imperishable One is this by all embodied immanent soul of all beings. Later on the text will declare that *all this is in truth Hari's body* (VP 1.22.36). In other words, there is no contradiction in that Viṣṇu, the supreme Brahman is imperishable and yet ensouls the world in so far as all constitute his body: for this defines the respective natures of body and soul from each other.[68]

The VP is the formative text for Rāmānuja to organize and refine the details of his ontology. Brahman possesses an imperishable nature as he is the soul of all things and even in the causal state, Brahman is the soul of all things.

Rāmānuja's view of the causality of Brahman as an aspect of his essential nature (*brahmasvarūpaviśeṣa*), supported by the VP, illustrates creation as a positive cosmological development. The fact that both matter (*prakṛti*) and individual selves (*puruṣa*) are eternal in order for Brahman to be the cause, as Rāmānuja understands it, is discussed in the section on Brahman as the cause as a whole. If *prakṛti*, *puruṣa*, and Brahman are all eternal, and the former two constitute His body, then the world which is the effect is not something that originates anew, but is simply a change in condition (*avasthā*). Rāmānuja weaves together a list of VP passages that illustrate the cosmology that can support his ontology. The evidence on the details of the causal state of

Brahman (with all its components), and the details of the effected state, along with the unchanging substantive self of Brahman, are the VP's most significant contributions, according to Rāmānuja.

The divine body of Brahman

In the VS, following the refutation of the Prābhākara-view of scripture, is a detailed account of the transcendent form of Viṣṇu (*divyarūpa*) and his abode (*divyasthāna*). Rāmānuja's argument is in two parts, each of which begins with summary descriptions of Brahman followed by scriptural support, from both śruti and smṛti. Upaniṣads such as the *Subāla Upaniṣad* and the *Mahānārāyaṇa Upaniṣad* identify Brahman as Viṣṇu, but they do not support a transcendent divine form, as Rāmānuja envisions it here. While he may find upaniṣadic evidence to support Brahman's many metaphysical qualities such as knowledge, bliss, and so on, the definition of Brahman as the four- or eight-armed Viṣṇu, the form he affirms for Brahman in the VS, is not found in these śruti. The VP is the key text that supports Rāmānuja's conceptions of the divine form. Furthermore, though BhG 11 describes Viṣṇu/Kṛṣṇa's universal form (*viśvarūpa*), this fiercesome cosmic form is not the form Rāmānuja has in mind.

Among Rāmānuja's predecessors there were some Vedāntins who did not accept the doctrine of the transcendent form of Brahman (Carman 1974: 167). Thus Rāmānuja, in affirming a divine form for Brahman, challenges his rivals with this unique feature of his Vedānta. To facilitate the identification of Brahman's form as that of the deity Viṣṇu, Rāmānuja differentiates between two concepts, the essential nature (*svarūpa*) and the divine form (*divyarūpa*). Distinct from Brahman's essential nature, Rāmānuja affirms a divine form which is "unique to him, anthropomorphic and male in appearance, having physical properties, yet constituted of a special substance which is neither matter (*prakṛti*) nor the result of karma and the focus of the heavenly abode" (Lipner 1986: 94). Whereas the divine form is "a body of some sort, owning a physical disposition of parts, localisable and localized" the essential nature is defined "by the five characteristics [reality, knowledge, bliss, purity, and infinitude] … not localisable in the manner of the supernal form" (Lipner 1986: 95).

Although Rāmānuja's use of *svarūpa* is flexible enough to allow the description of Brahman from different perspectives, "there is a strict use of *svarūpa* … at least in the sense of Brahman's quiddity or essential nature, i.e. Brahman per se or in himself, in his innermost core" and this definition of Brahman's *svarūpa* is from *Taittirīya Upaniṣad* 2.1.1, *Brahman is reality, consciousness, and bliss* (Lipner 1986: 80). Though these three qualities form the "core" of Brahman's *svarūpa*, elsewhere, Rāmānuja expands these three characteristics to five defining attributes, reality (*satya*), consciousness (*jñāna*), bliss (*ānanda*), infinity (*anantatva*), and purity (*amalatva*), and this he believed to be the upaniṣadic definition of the supreme self (Carman 1974: 93). This understanding, however, is much different from what he calls the divine form characterized by ornaments, weapons, and so on. Thus for Rāmānuja, Brahman's *svarūpa* is defined in metaphysical terms such as brilliance, knowledge, bliss and so on, but the *divyarūpa* is akin to the images of Viṣṇu possessing a (somewhat) anthropomorphic form.

In the VS, VP 6.7 is the only text Rāmānuja depends on to articulate this specific form for Brahman. In his rather long discussion of Brahman's divine form, Rāmānuja attempts to reconcile this distinction between *svarūpa* and *divyarūpa*. After a brief overview of the structure of Rāmānuja's argument, the following sections address the exegetical use of the VP in establishing a divine form for Brahman.

Structure of Rāmānuja's argument

As mentioned earlier, Rāmānuja's argument is divided into two subsections, each of which begins with a summary description of Brahman followed by scriptural support from both śruti and smṛti. In the two descriptions of Brahman, Rāmānuja seamlessly alternates between defining Brahman in terms of essential nature (*svarūpa*) and divine form (*divyarūpa*). The purpose of the two sections to establish a divine form of Brahman is an exegetical manoeuver to reconcile the upaniṣadic descriptions of Brahman's *svarūpa* with the *divyarūpa* depictions from popular religion, prevalent in the texts such as the purāṇas. As a member of the Śrīvaiṣṇava religious community such purāṇic depictions of the deity were very important for devotion and worship. Though Rāmānuja views the *svarūpa* and *divyarūpa* of Brahman as "twin manifestations" of the divine being that are inseparable, the fact that a *divyarūpa* was not accorded to Brahman by previous Vedāntins makes a study of the distinction and relation between *svarūpa* and *divyarūpa* all the more important (Sydnor 2008: 19). The structure of Rāmānuja's two descriptions of Brahman's form, then, reflects his attempts to introduce a divine form for Brahman into the Vedānta tradition.

Whereas, the first description of Brahman is followed by scriptural support from both śruti and smṛti, the second description of Brahman is followed by support from śruti only. However, this second description itself is influenced by VP 6.7. Overall, though it seems that Rāmānuja adheres to the traditional exegetical method of citing śruti first and then using smṛti corroboratively, his dependence on the VP is considerable.

In regard to the two descriptions of Brahman, the second description is the 'locus classicus' of the experience (*anubhava*) of the divine form (Lipner 1986: 94). This characterization of the body of God is a limb-by-limb enjoyment of the deity, a head-to-toe description based on VP 6.7.79–83 (Hopkins 2002: 146–156).

The context of VP 6.7 is a discussion on yoga between the brothers Khāṇḍikhya and Keśidhvaja. In Chapter 7, beginning with verse 6.7.46 the conversation turns to the auspicious object (*śubhāśraya*) of meditation. According to Rāmānuja, this section espouses meditation on the divine form of Viṣṇu, different from the material world which is also theologically understood as a form of the deity. VP 6.7 provides the definitive description for Rāmānuja's second and final description of Brahman's transcendent divine form, the *divyarūpa*, which is suggestive of the iconic forms of Viṣṇu.[69]

The first description of Brahman's divine form[70]

Rāmānuja begins with a summary description, followed by scriptural support:

> this supreme Brahman, Nārāyaṇa's, essential nature (*svarūpa*) is one of consciousness, bliss, and purity that is indivisible he has countless auspicious qualities (*kalyāṇaguṇa*) that are unsurpassed and perfect; such as consciousness, power, strength, sovereignty, vigor, and radiance he produces by his own will, the aggregate of all things sentient and insentient, which are different from him; his uniform divine form (*ekarūpadivyarūpa*) is agreeable and appropriate to him; his endless variety of unsurpassed, auspicious ornaments are suited to him; his various types of marvelous, endless, immeasurable, weapons are suited to his power.[71]

Two points regarding this description are important. First, Rāmānuja begins by enumerating Brahman's essential nature (*svarūpa*) and ends with a description of Brahman's divine form (*divyarūpa*). Second, the śruti passages he cites as scriptural evidence support the former *svarūpa* description but not the *divyarūpa*.

The first compound in the above decription, enumerates three of the five metaphysical qualities, consciousness, bliss, and purity, which constitute the "core" of Brahman (Lipner 1986: 80). There is no mention of a divine form here. In the next compound, Rāmānuja states the six auspicious qualities (*kalyāṇaguṇa*) of Viṣṇu: consciousness, power, strength, sovereignty, vigor, and radiance. This order of listing the auspicious qualities is in fact, close to the enumeration that is found in VP 6.5.79. Another essential quality of Brahman is also stated, namely, his role as the creator and inner controller of all creation. This concept of creation by Brahman's own will or *satya-saṃkalpa* is mentioned in the upaniṣads, such as Ch Up 8.1.5 and Ch Up 3.14.2.[72] The next aspect of Brahman mentioned in this first description is his one divine form (*ekarūpadivyarūpa*), and that he is adorned with various ornaments and weapons suited to him. According to Rāmānuja this description is "supported by thousands of śruti".[73] However, we shall see that there is no description of Viṣṇu's ornaments and weapons, at least not in the upaniṣads that Rāmānuja has utilized.

In the above-mentioned first description of Brahman, the distinction between *svarūpa* and *divyarūpa* is supported by the commentator as well as Rāmānuja:

> The words essential nature (*svarūpa*) denote qualities that describe Brahman's essential nature (*svarūpanirūpakadharma*). Its essential nature is said to be indivisible. Knowledge, bliss, and purity etc. are Brahman's qualities. The term *he produces by his own will* indicates that it has a manifestation (*vibhūti*). The manifestation of qualities that comprise Brahman's essential nature is the divine form, established by examples from scripture; this establishes the divine form (*vigraha*) etc. Brahman's essential nature, qualities, and *vibhūti* are given as examples for the authoritativeness of *divyarūpa* etc. The divine *vigraha* etc. remains to be proved.[74]

According to Sudarśanasūri, qualities (*guṇa/dharma*) such as *jñāna*, *bala*, *aiśvarya*, and so forth are the defining attributes of Brahman's defining essential nature (*svarūpanirūpakadharma*) and so can be equated with the essential nature (*svarūpa*) itself and the world that he creates by his own will is a manifestation (*vibhūti*) of these essential defining qualities (*svarūpanirūpakadharma*) of Brahman.[75] The divine form is also a manifestation of the essential nature of Brahman, such as consciousness, bliss, purity, and so on; but as the commentator points out this "divine *vigraha* etc. remains to be proved". What is provided thus far is the authoritativeness or rationale to establish a divine form generally.

The commentary's identification of the words *vigraha* and *divyarūpa* suggests that a connection between these two is perfectly acceptable. The term *vigraha* utilized to denote the divine form of Brahman is a term commonly used to suggest both a concrete form/figure and the images of deities. As we shall see, śruti evidence for such a form is not adequate. Both Rāmānuja and his commentator agree on the distinction between essential nature and form, but each expresses this agreement in a slightly different manner: while the commentator explicitly describes the relationship between the essential nature and the divine form of Brahman, Rāmānuja infers it. This first summary description of Brahman, then, affirms a distinction between his essential nature and his divine form, and in order to establish a relation between these two, the commentator states that the divine form is a manifestation of the qualities that comprise Brahman's essential nature.

Following this first description of Brahman, Rāmānuja provides a series of śruti and smṛti passages as evidence for his conclusions. The upaniṣad definitions of Brahman, for the most part, support Rāmānuja's definition of the essential nature (*svarūpa*) of Brahman as knowledge, bliss, and so forth. However, even when the śruti passages affirm a Brahman with form it is quite general and the specifics of form such as a head-to-foot description that mention Viṣṇu's ornaments, his beauty, and his weaponry is supplied by smṛti. At most Rāmānuja is successful in using śruti to prove that Brahman has a form, which by Vedāntic standards was quite radical; however, for the four-armed form of Viṣṇu, he relies on smṛti.

Śruti support

To support this first description of Brahman, Rāmānuja follows the traditional method of citing the relevant śruti first, and then smṛti. The information declared in the śruti passages is meant to support a divine form for Brahman. Śruti passages, however, do not speak of a divine form, akin to Viṣṇu's divine form, with ornaments and other accoutrements:[76]

> I know that immense person, having the color of the sun (*ādityavarṇa*), and beyond darkness (*tamas*).[77]
>
> (Śve Up 3.8)

> the golden (*hiraṇmaya*) person we see within the sun ... his eyes are like deep blue lotuses.[78]
>
> (Ch Up 1.6.6–7)

> In the space here within the heart lies the immortal and golden person (*puruṣa*) consisting of the mind.[79]
>
> (Taitt Up 1.6.1)

> All flashes of lightning originate from this *puruṣa*.[80]
>
> (Mahā Nār Up 1.6)[81]

In these passages, Rāmānuja identifies *puruṣa* as Brahman, possessed of a form and a golden complexion, with eyes like a lotus. This interpretation is rather forced, as will be seen after the examination of the context of each passage. Note that the above-mentioned passages and their contexts have been analyzed only in so far as the concept of a divine form of Brahman, as defined by Rāmānuja, is concerned. Though Rāmānuja does not cite the whole verse of the *Śvetāśvatara Upaniṣad* 3.8, it is as follows:

> only when a man knows him does he pass beyond death; there is no other path for getting there.
>
> (Śve Up 3.8)

> This whole world is filled by that person, beyond whom there is nothing; beneath whom there is nothing; smaller than whom there is nothing; larger than whom there is nothing; and who stands like a tree firmly planted in heaven.[82]
>
> (Śve Up 3.9)

In the *Śvetāśvatara Upanisad*, *puruṣa* is spoken of in metaphysical terms and, though suggestive of a form, it is not exactly the form of Viṣṇu which Rāmānuja has in mind. The upaniṣad goes on to describe the form of Brahman as follows:

> The person has a thousand heads, a thousand eyes, and a thousand feet. Having encompassed the earth on all sides; he extended ten fingers' breadth beyond it.
>
> (Śve Up 3.14)

> With hands and feet everywhere, with eyes, heads, and faces everywhere, and with ears everywhere, that remains encompassing everything in the world.[83]
>
> (Śve Up 3.16)

Though these passages suggest a form for *purusa*, the context is completely cosmic, conveying an inexpressible dimension of this being. Thus although Rāmānuja has cited Śve Up 3.8 as proof for Viṣṇu's form, only a general form can be inferred from the scriptural support that is provided.

The *puruṣa* motif is also present in *Chāndogya Upaniṣad* 1.6.6–7. Here, too, some information regarding a general form is given:

> Now, the golden person we see within the sun—he has golden hair and a golden beard; he is completely golden, down to the very tips of his nails.
>
> (Ch Up 1.6.6)

> His eyes are replendent like the lotus. His name is 'Up' (*ud*), for he has risen up (*udita*) above all evils.[84]
>
> (Ch Up 1.6.7)

Again, though this passage supports a general form and several other features, such as golden hair, for Brahman, the context of speculation here remains one of cosmic correspondences. Likewise, *Taittirīya Upaniṣad* 1.6.1:

> In this space here within the heart lies the immortal and golden person consisting of the mind. And this thing that hangs like a nipple between the two palates; it is Indra's passage. Bursting through the two halves of the skull at the point where the hairs part, he establishes himself in the fire by making *bhūr*, in the wind by making the call *bhūvas.*[85]
>
> (Taitt Up 1.6.1)

The correspondences between the cosmos, the body, and sacrifice suggest that the context is rooted in Vedic ritual. There is nothing here that implies that the divine form of Brahman is Viṣṇu's form. So also is the case with the *Mahā-nārāyaṇa Upaniṣad* 1.6,[86] where *puruṣa*, i.e., Brahman, is described as the source of lightning, though Rāmānuja interprets this passage to be declaring Brahman's complexion.

He cites additional passages from the upaniṣads to support Brahman's possession of a divine form:

> Like a bright flash of lightning in the middle of a dark cloud.[87]
> (Mahā Nār Up 3.12)

> … it is made of mind; the vital functions are its physical form; luminous is its appearance; the real is its intention; space is its essence; it contains all actions, all desires, all scents, all tastes; it has captured this whole world; it neither speaks nor pays any heed.
> (Ch Up 3.14.2)

> … like a golden cloth.[88]
> (Bṛ Up 2.3.6)

At most, these passages can be understood to support a form for Brahman in a general way, but they still do not provide any specific support of Brahman as the deity Viṣṇu. Rāmānuja, interpreting *Mahānārāyaṇa Upaniṣad* 3.12 says:

> that bundle of flames that burns within the space in the middle of the heart of the lotus and within it the essential nature (*svarūpa*) of the supreme self shines bright like a blue cloud; he blazes like a flash of lightning that has a dark cloud within it.[89]

Although there is no reference to the divine form of Brahman, the TD interprets the word *svarūpa* as "referring to *vigraha*", which as we mentioned earlier he uses to designate the divine form.[90] The commentary tries to ascribe a divine form to Brahman by indicating that "complexion" implies a divine form. Moreover, the word *svarūpa* is not found in the upaniṣad passage itself.[91] We see here, both Rāmānuja and the commentator extending the meaning of the śruti passages to support a divine form for Brahman.

In *Chāndogya Upaniṣad* 3.14.2, Brahman is identified as one's self within the heart. Again, there does not seem to be specific information here regarding Brahman's divine form. Once again, the TD, as in its comment on *Mahānārāyaṇa Upaniṣad* passage 3.12, interprets this passage as a description of Brahman's form:

> Thus, by these two phrases, *he has all actions and has all desires*; the fact that Brahman has both manifestations (*ubhayavibhūti*) is stated. With the phrase *has all smells and all tastes*, the form (*vigraha*) of Brahman is established.[92]

Other than the fact that Brahman "possesses all tastes and all scents", which is, according to the TD, suggestive of a form (*vigraha*), the other descriptions do not establish anything in regard to Brahman's form. The commentator too, is unable to argue convincingly that the upaniṣad passages Rāmānuja has utilized do support the divine form of Viṣṇu. Even the introduction of the concept of *ubhayavibhūti*, which is the dual manifestation of the eternal realm (*nityavibhūti*) and the realm of sport or creation (*līlāvibhūti*), does not convey specifics on the divine form of Viṣṇu, except that he possesses a form of some sort.

The context of the last example from the *Bṛhadāraṇyaka Upaniṣad* 2.3.6 is a discussion of the two visible appearances of Brahman, one in reference to the divine sphere and the other in reference to a physical form. Here again, the text makes correspondences between the macrocosm and the microcosm. The complete passage, which is not cited by Rāmānuja, is as follows: "Now the visible appearance of this person is like (*yathā*) a golden cloth, or white wool, a red bug, or a flame, or a white lotus, or a sudden flash of lightning" (Bṛ Up 2.3.6). The TD interprets this to mean saffron-robed: "*Mahārajata* is a kind of dye or coloring substance; *mahārajata* is something dyed with it.[93] The commentator does not specify the color, but only interprets the term *mahārajata*, to denote the possession of color. Here *appearance of this person like a golden cloth* is interpreted as suggestive of divine form, since this "person" is depicted as robed in gold-colored cloth. This seems a contrived interpretation of the term "something dyed with it", and is not at all convincing.

In conclusion, it is difficult to envision Brahman, from these, śruti examples, as more than *puruṣa* with lotus eyes, golden complexion, golden hair, thousand-headed and in golden robes, that is, possessing a general form. Certain characteristics from Rāmānuja's first description have not even been touched upon by the scriptural evidence, such as possession of auspicious ornaments, weapons, attendants and retinue, and the divine abode. Neither Rāmānuja nor the commentator is able to support Brahman's divine form from the śruti passages.

Smṛti support

The smṛti support, which is discussed in this section, begins to establish the kind of divine form that Rāmānuja envisions for Brahman. However, prior to citing from smṛti texts, Rāmānuja thinks it necessary, yet again, to establish the authority of smṛti literature:

> The epics and purāṇas which augment the Vedas declare the same truth—
> seeing that both (Lava and Kuśa) were intelligent and well-established in the Vedas
> the Lord, took them on as his students in order to corroborate the Vedas.[94]
>
> (*Rāmāyaṇa* 1.4.6)

Just as in the discussion on Brahman's casuality (VS #110) where the importance of the VP is reiterated, so once again, he undertakes to defend the purāṇa's authority. A possible reason for this repetition is that the smṛti passages function as more than corroborative evidence. That is, they introduce something entirely new that is lacking in śruti. Having justified the use of smṛti, Rāmānuja cites evidence from the *Rāmāyaṇa*, and the VP:

> The divine form as stated in the *Rāmāyaṇa* verses is considered first:
> that great yogin, the supreme self, the primeval one,
> is without a beginning, middle, or end, he is great beyond the great.[95]
> (*Rāmāyana* 6.1.4.14)

This passage is reminiscent of the many śruti passages that affirm Brahman in abstract metaphysical terms. Indeed, this passage speaks more to the universe as a form of Brahman than it does to the divine transcendent form which is actually the topic of the discussion. According to the commentary, *without beginning, middle, or end,* declares "the essential nature or *svarūpa* of Brahman as eternal",[96] but there is little to be gleaned here regarding the *divyarūpa*. The first indication of Viṣṇu's divine form is provided by the next verse:

> He is beyond matter, he is the creator who bears the conch, discus, and mace
> He has the *Śrīvatsa* mark on his chest; He has Śrī eternally for his consort,
> he is invincible, eternal, and immutable.[97]
> (*Rāmāyaṇa* 6.1.4.15)

The ornaments and weapons specific to Viṣṇu are iconographic details and such specificity is not seen in the śruti passages. The *Rāmāyaṇa* is then the first text, śruti or smṛti, which addresses Viṣṇu's divine form that is consonant with Rāmānuja's description of Brahman's divine form. The other *Rāmāyaṇa* passages utilized are:

> the various types of arrows and the drawn-bow assumed personal forms
> and accompanied the descendent of Kākutstha, all follow him.
> (7.109.7)

> with body and with his entourage he enters the realm of Viṣṇu.[98]
> (7.110.13ab)

These verses are not explained by the commentator. However, they deal primarily with the incarnated form and its relation to the supernal form of Viṣṇu rather than the latter, which is the topic of discussion here. The description of Viṣṇu adorned with his various ornaments and weapons is evidence for the kind of divine form that Rāmānuja intends and additionally, these epic passages provide scriptural support for the connection between Viṣṇu's transcendent form (described in *Rāmāyaṇa* 6.1.1.14) and his incarnations. For Rāmānuja, the incarnation "is a particular manifestation of the supernal form itself." However, the "supernal form [divine form], though closely related to the Lord's avatāric forms … is logically closer to the divine quidditative center than the [supernal form]"(Lipner 1986: 96). Moreover, the incarnation derives from the supernal form and is conditioned by factors such as the particular world epoch, which does not apply to the divine form.

The *Rāmāyaṇa* verses establish the incarnations themselves, as forms not only worthy on their own merits, but all the more so because of their accessability to the worshipper. The fact that Rāma and his followers passed into the realm of Viṣṇu with their bodies, indicates that they are not comprised of matter (*prakṛti*). Even the incarnations, though of human or animal form, are not material. The contribution of the *Rāmāyaṇa* passages is that for the first time a scripture is cited from which Viṣṇu's form does not need to be *inferred*, but its main function is to establish the concept of Viṣṇu's incarnations.

To support his interpretation that Brahman has a divine supernal form, Rāmānunja utlilizes additional passages from the VP followed by some passages from the MBh:

> Wherever, all these powers are established, O' King,
> there is another grand form that is different from Hari's universal form (*viśvarūpa*).[99]
>
> (VP 6.7.70)[100]

What are the two forms that are mentioned here? Sudarśanasuri does not comment on this passage in the TD, but does so in his commentary, the *Śrutaprakāśikā*, on the *Mahāsiddhānta* section of the ŚBh 1.1.1. He notes that the form of Brahman in which all the powers are established is the divine form of Brahman:

> Now, in this very purāṇa, even though at the conclusion he (Rāmānuja) quotes texts in detail, he demonstrates that Brahman has a divine form, a *vigraha* as in VP 6.7.70 … That is different from the universal form (VP 6.7.70) means that the two forms do not coincide.[101]

The VP indicates two distinctly different forms of Viṣṇu. One, the form of Hari with the universe in the effected state, the other is his divine form. In other words, different from the world that comprises the body of Brahman, there is another divine form. The powers that are mentioned in VP 6.7.70 are the three powers (*śakti*) that are said to abide in this particular form of Hari known theologically as the body of Brahman. The primary power is the energy which resides in the supreme nature of Viṣṇu; a secondary power results when that energy is embodied, while the third power is ignorance (VP 6.7.69–71). By using this VP passage Rāmānuja intends to differentiate between the divine transcendent body, which is the current topic of discussion and the material world envisioned as a divine form as well.

The term *viśvarūpa* that occurs in VP 6.7.70 stated above has a different connotation in the BhG, where it refers to the terrible form of Viṣṇu in both his creative and destructive capacities; even in the BhG, there is a distinction made between the *viśvarūpa* and the more benign four-armed form. Kṛṣṇa claims that the *viśvarūpa* is only accessible by divine vision. Terrified of this *viśvarūpa*, Arjuna implores Kṛṣṇa to once again assume his benign four-armed form. It is important to note here that Rāmānuja does not cite any passages from Chapter 11 of the BhG, which elaborates on the divine form, because the form depicted therein is frightening and is unlike the divine form Rāmānuja depicts here. In the VP context, the term *viśvarūpa* designates the transcendent divine body of Brahman akin to icons.

The next set of scriptural passages is from VP 1.22, which also differentiates two forms of Brahman:

> Viṣṇu as comprising all powers is the highest essential nature of Brahman
> This form is reflected on first by yogins at the beginning of their yogic practices.
>
> (VP 1.22.59)

> Hari is the highest and closest of all the powers of Brahman
> O' Great Sage, Hari is a form (*mūrta*) of Brahman, he comprises the entire Brahman.[102]
>
> (VP 1.22.61)

Rāmānuja only cites the first half of 1.22.61ab, but this section of the VP identifies Hari as a form of Brahman. Moreover, the form of Hari presented here is the one endowed with weapons and ornaments. The different weapons and ornaments in this section are identified with different aspects of the universe (VP 1.22.65ff). For example, *pradhāna* or matter is identified with the *Śrīvatsa* mark (VP 1.22.67), and his necklace, *Vaijayanti*, composed of five precious stones, is said to be the aggregate of the five elements, and so on. The importance of the VP passages cited here is that the embodied form of Viṣṇu, with ornamentation and weaponry, is declared to be real and different from the *svarūpa.*[103] Whereas, the *Rāmāyaṇa* passages establish the connection between the divine form and the incarnations, the VP passages establish that the world as Brahman's body is quite different from his divine form.

In the first section, then, the śruti examples cited to support Rāmānuja's definition of the divine form are inadequate. The divine form as suggested by Rāmānuja's first summary are developed mainly with the use of the VP, and to a certain degree, the *Rāmāyaṇa*. The descriptive summary in the second section, though it does not utilize the VP directly, is influenced by the VP (van Buitenen 1956: 290).

It is interesting that Rāmānuja only cites śruti passages as support for this second section on the divine form. It would seem that if the whole discussion on the divine form of Brahman is taken into account, Rāmānuja does not want to draw attention to the definitive description of Brahman in the second part. The interpretive strategy of Rāmānuja in this section is worth noting. He begins, as tradition requires, with support from śruti, but these passages only portray the essential nature of Brahman in metaphysical terms. Both Rāmānuja and the commentator create, through exegesis, the possibility to associate the two separate concepts (*svarūpa* and *divyarūpa*) to combine in such a way that the VP definitions of the iconic form of Viṣṇu can be incorporated into Vedānta.

The second description articulates the divine form of Viṣṇu, not His essential nature (*svarūpa*) and it is the former not the latter that commands worship and devotion from devotees. One of the main differences between these two descriptions is that the former affirms the divine form of Brahman in a general way. That is, Brahman is declared to possess auspicious qualities, weapons, ornaments, consorts, and a divine abode, but no specifics are provided to identify His unique form of divinity. Such a description could be used to describe many divinities in the Hindu pantheon. However, Rāmānuja's goal is to identify Brahman as the deity Viṣṇu, his task is not yet complete. He begins with a second description of Brahman and provides a new set of śruti passages as support.

The second description of Brahman's divine form

In support of the second description only śruti passages are cited. However, this description of Brahman itself is taken from the VP and so in a sense Rāmānuja is citing the VP first and then interpreting śruti through the information gained from the purāṇa. In this description, as in the first, Rāmānuja begins with an upaniṣadic depiction of *puruṣa*, but the rest of the imagery is not found in śruti. It begins with a description of the metaphysical qualities of Brahman:

> He dwells inside the circular orb of the sun; he has the splendor of a colossal mountain of molten gold, whose brilliance is like that of the rays of hundreds of thousands of suns; his long eyes, spotless like the petals of a lotus that sprouting from deep waters on a stalk, blooms in the rays of the sun.[104]

This description of Brahman is reminiscent of śruti passages, which have been already cited in support of the first description. Here, I only evaluate the new citations. Included among these are the views of the Bhāṣyakāra (Dramiḍa), and the Vākyakāra[105] (Ṭaṅka), on the *Brahmasūtras.*[106] All these passages reiterate the lordship of Viṣṇu over creation, but do not provide details on the divine form (*divyarūpa*).[107] Even the comments of the Bhāṣyakāra and the Vākyakāra do not supply the needed specifics for Rāmānuja's definition of the divine form (*divyarūpa*), although they do affirm that Brahman possesses *a* form.

Proof of Rāmānuja's attempt to connect these śruti passages to the smṛti passages declaring the divine form of Viṣṇu is evident from the examples we have already evaluated. Furthermore, the TD's view that the smṛti examples are for the explication of *Chāndogya Upaniṣad* 1.6.6, which itself does not provide support in regard to the specifics of the divine form, is further evidence of this insufficiency. Additional evidence is provided by Rāmānuja's concluding remarks. Here he attempts to relate the divine form to the *svarūpa* of Brahman:

> Because in the text *being alone this was in the beginning my dear son, one only without a second* (Ch Up 1.6.6), his attendants, his abode etc. are included in the essential nature (*svarūpa*) of the supreme Brahman, which possesses a host of auspicious qualities such as knowledge, strength, sovereignty.[108]

The word *svarūpa* is here used to denote essential attributes such as knowledge, bliss, and so on, but it now also includes attendants and the divine abode. This meaning of "essential nature" does not correlate with the commentator's definition of essential nature as distinct from the the divine form, mentioned in the discussion of the first description of Brahman. The commentator himself seems aware of this discrepancy, since he once again re-defines divine form:

> Just as the qualities of knowledge and so on are included in the cause, those qualities such as the abode etc., cannot be explained as non-existent in it. Therefore, because the eternal realm (*nityavibhūti*) is included in the cause as known from scripture such as *being only*, by the words *being only, one alone, without a second*, the inner nature of Brahman is understood.[109]

This is a circuitous way to argue for a divine form and abode for Brahman. The causal state of Brahman, which includes everything, according to Ch Up 1.6.6, is taken to include divine form and divine abode. This is a re-interpretation of Ch Up based on the fact that smṛti affirms a divine form.

Continuing with Rāmānuja's second description of Brahman's form, we see a head-to-foot description of Viṣṇu similar to the one found in the VP passages. The juxtaposition of his second description of Brahman with the VP passages underscores the vocabulary common in both. Beginning with Viṣṇu's forehead, the description does not match any śruti passages that Rāmānuja has thus far cited. The vocabulary that is common to both the VP and Rāmānuja's second description of Brahman are highlighted:

> he has a **forehead** with beautiful eyebrows and a handsome nose; his coral-like lips are **smiling pleasantly**; his **cheeks** are tender and radiant;

> his **conch-like neck** is raised uplifted and pendulous; his divine **ears**, tender as buds hang touching his divine shoulders.[110]

Some of the VP passages that correspond to the description of Viṣṇu's forehead, his pleasant smile, his cheeks, forehead, conch-like neck, broad chest, and so on, are:

> Let him meditate on the one who is Brahman: a **pleasantly smiling** face,
> eyes resembling lotus leaves,
> lovely **cheeks**, beautiful wide **forehead**, shining and flat.
>
> (VP 6.7.80)

> ornamented with beautiful **earrings** placed close to the **ears**
> a **conch-like neck**, a **broad chest** adorned by the Śrīvatsa.[111]
>
> (VP 6.7.81)

Though such details are not unique to the VP and can be found in many other smṛti texts as well, the fact that Rāmānuja in his first description employs numerous passages from the VP, especially VP 6.6, makes it likely that he was again inspired by VP 6.7.80–84. In this section of the VP, the divine form of Viṣṇu as the auspicious object (*śubhāśraya*) of worship is established and is an important section of the purāṇa for Rāmānuja.[112] Moreover, earlier in the VS, Rāmānuja himself states that the sixth book of the VP is the source text for information on Brahman's body, the divine body and its incarnations.[113]

The rest of the second description of Brahman's form according to Rāmānuja is as follows:

> his **arms** are round, well-developed, and long; his beautiful palms are reddish adorned with fingers that are the same color; his body, slender waist, and **broad chest** are well-proportioned in all places; his shape is of an inexpressibly divine form; his color is pleasing; his **feet** are as beautiful as budding lotuses; he wears a **yellow robe** that suits him; he is adorned with immeasurable, divine, endlessly marvelous ornaments like a spotless **crown** (*kirīṭa*), **earrings** (*kuṇḍala*), necklaces (*hāra*), the kaustubha gem, **bracelets** (*keyūra*), **armlets** (*kaṭaka*), anklets (*nūpura*), belt (*udarabandhana*) and so on, a **conch** (*śaṅkha*), **discus** (*cakra*), **mace** (*gadā*), **bow** (*śārṅga*), the *śrīvatsa* curl, and the garland (*vanamāla*).[114]

The following passages are suggestive of the description stated above and provide information on Viṣṇu's arms, ornaments, weapons, and his robe:

> the navel caving into the three folds of the belly and by the belly
> eight long **arms**, hanging, or even four-armed Viṣṇu.
>
> (VP 6.7.82)

firm thighs and calves, well-formed **feet** and toes
[…] he who is in a pure **yellow robe**.

(VP 6.7.83)

wearing a beautiful **crown** (*kirīṭa*), **bracelets** (*keyūra*), and **armlets** (*kaṭaka*) holding in his hands the **bow** (*śārṅga*),
conch (*śaṅkha*), **mace** (*gadā*), sword (*khaḍga*), and the mighty **discus** (*cakra*).[115]

(VP 6.7.84)

This description of Viṣṇu's divine form, either four-armed or eight-armed, does not correlate exactly to any of the iconographic specifications of images found in texts such as the *Vaikhānsāgamas* (Champakalaksmi 1981). Nevertheless, it is evocative of Viṣṇu images and is in stark contrast to the descriptions of Brahman from the upaniṣads.

Following the head-to-foot description of Viṣṇu, Rāmānuja ends with a reiteration of qualities of the divine form that evokes devotion from the worshipper:

> By his surpassingly sublime beauty he captivates the eyes and hearts of all; the nectar of his pervasive loveliness fills and overflows the entire existence, sentient and non-sentient; his eternal and inconceivable youthfulness is infinitely marvelous; he is delicately tender as blossoming flowers; he perfumes the endless expanse of the universe with his divine fragrance; he shines in his supreme majesty as he enevelops the three worlds; he looks at his devotees with a look of compassion and affection.[116]

Carman (1974: 79) in his discussion of Viṣṇu's auspicious qualities (*kalyāṇaguṇa*) notes that *saundarya* or beauty of bodily form was important for Rāmānuja as "this characterized the Lord both in his transcendent realm and his incarnations." Descriptions of divine beauty however are rare in śruti passages. To comment on these last descriptive statements, the TD cites mostly from the *Rāmāyaṇa*. It reiterates that all the descriptions of Viṣṇu thus far (taken from smṛti) are meant to explain divine descriptions in passages such as Ch Up 1.1.6–7. However, the addition of information from the VP has made it possible to broaden the context for understanding the nature of the divine form.[117] Rāmānuja concludes his description of the divine form by citing a series of śruti passages to substantiate this second description of Brahman's divine form. These examples all refer to Brahman's metaphysical qualities and not to a specific form of Brahman. Furthermore some of these passages were already cited as evidence in the discussion on the first description of Brahman.[118]

This rather long two-part discussion of the divine form illustrates that Brahman as Viṣṇu is possessed of a divine form, and to substantiate this

Rāmānuja depends on the VP. For Rāmānuja, then, Brahman or Viṣṇu possesses an essential nature (*svarūpa*) comprised of metaphysical attributes such as knowledge, brilliance, bliss, splendor, support for which is readily available in Vedānta. Additionally, Brahman possesses a divine transcendent form (*divyarūpa*) comprised of a non-material substance, which is four armed with ornamentation and weaponry. It is an embodied form that is exclusively proper to Brahman and for this Rāmānuja turns to the VP.

Conclusion

In the course of this chapter we have examined Rāmānuja's exegetical use of the VP in the *Vedārthasaṃgraha* to support the concepts fundamental to his theology namely, the essential nature of the individual self, Brahman's causality, and His divine form. In the discussion on the individual self, Rāmānuja follows the principle of corroboration (*upabṛṃhaṇa*) and cites the upaniṣads and then the VP as scriptural evidence for his view of the nature of the individual self. In the śruti examples that he utilizes, he finds support for Brahman's relationship to the individual self as one of soul to body. The śruti examples offer little on the individual self as a distinct entity *sans* its relation to Brahman. Since for Rāmānuja, although the liberated individual self shares certain qualities with Brahman such as knowledge and bliss, it has a real and distinct existence, though always in relation to Brahman. The terminology to describe the essential nature of the individual self as one of knowledge (*jñānasvarūpa*), as one of knowledge and bliss (*jñānandaikaguṇa*), and as indescribable (*vācām agocara*) is provided by the VP. Furthermore, the purāṇa also provides evidence to argue the metaphysical reality of the embodied individual self. First, the individual self is said to be a power (*śakti*) of Viṣṇu and then the concealment of its attributive nature by another power of Viṣṇu, namely karma is stated. Associating with karma the individual self is said to exist in all beings with its attributive nature concealed to different degrees (*tāratamya*).

In contrast to Advaita, Brahman's causality is an important aspect of Rāmānuja's Vedānta. For him any discussion of the world as empirically real is related to the issue of Brahman's causality. Utilizing the VP, Rāmānuja argues for the concept of Brahman as eternally differentiated into matter and individual selves and thus the material cause as a whole (*aviśeṣaṇakāraṇa*). Included in this discussion is creation as simply a transformation in the causal condition (*kāraṇāvasthā*) of Brahman to its effected condition (*kāryāvasthā*). For the cosmological details such as Brahman as eternally differentiated into matter and individual selves and his lordship over the two entities that comprise his body, Rāmānuja finds in the VP passages such as *Viṣṇu is manifest and unmanifest creation, He is the Lord and the agitator and that which is agitated, He is present in matter both when it is contracted and expanded, He is the cause of effect, the unborn matter (prakṛti) and individual selves (puruṣa)*. While śruti, BhG, and MBh passages precede the VP citations, they do not compare to the specifics on creation that are found in the purāṇa. The *Śvetāśvatara Upaniṣad* does speak of matter (*prakṛti*) as eternal and as manifesting from Brahman, but it also goes on to describe it as illusory (*māyā*) and Brahman as the illusionist (*māyāvin*) which then would require clarification of the term *māyā* in a positive light. The five BhG passages cited prior to the VP verses provide more detail than śruti, but considerably less than the VP. Moreover, the fact that Rāmānuja turns to the VP to interpret most of the BhG passages in his commentary on that text suggests that the purāṇa is vital to the "correct" reading of the BhG as well.

To support causality as a unique attribute of Brahman's essential nature (*brahmasvarūpaviśeṣa*) also, Rāmānuja relies on the VP. The three-fold definition of causality as a unique quality of Brahman's essential nature requires the simultaneous affirmation of Brahman as the cause, Brahman as inseparable from the world, and Brahman as the lord over his creation. Rāmānuja does not even cite śruti in this context, but spends considerable time legitimizing the authority of the VP as equal to that of the certain upaniṣads and the *Brahma Sūtras*. Brahman's causality as envisioned in the VP fulfills the criteria that comprise the concept of *brahmasvarūpaviśeṣa* such as: *the world produced from Viṣṇu exists in him … he is the world, He resides in the individual self, His own essential nature (svarūpa) encompasses what is manifest and unmanifest, he exists in the form of puruṣa and in the form of time, he holds up the world with a tiny portion of his power and takes on form … for the welfare of the world, encompassing manifest and unmanifest, he is the Lord of all.* For Rāmānuja's purposes śruti passages are too general and only the VP provides concrete details needed to affirm the causality of Brahman and the reality of the the world.

Lastly, in addition to the conception of the world as the body of Brahman, Rāmānuja affirms a divine body (*divyarūpa*) that is akin to the iconic forms of Viṣṇu, and support for this is lacking in śruti. The divine body of Brahman is a specific form of Viṣṇu and the discussion of the auspicious object (*śubhāśraya*) of meditation in VP 6.7 is the sole scriptural source. While the śruti evidence is adequate to establish the essential nature of Brahman (*svarūpa*), it is ill-suited as support for the divine form. That is, descriptions of Brahman such as *like a bright flash of lightning, luminous in appearance, whose visible appearance is like a golden cloth* are starkly different from purāṇic portrayals such as *a pleasantly smiling face, eyes resembling lotus leaves, lovely cheeks, beautiful wide forehead, shining and flat, ornamented with beautiful earrings placed close to the ears, a conch-like neck, and a broad chest adorned by the Śrīvatsa.*

Notes

1 Whereas, Śaṅkara accepts the reality of creation only provisionally, Bhāskara (tenth century CE), the proponent of Aupādhika Bhedābheda (identity and

difference due to adjuncts) Vedānta advocates the influence of adjuncts such as karma on Brahman as the cause of creation (Dasgupta 1991: Vol. III, 6–11). According to him, though Brahman possesses auspicious qualities and is free from sin, due to limiting adjuncts it transmigrates in *saṃsāra*. Yādavaprakāśa (eleventh century CE), who championed Svābhāvika Bhedābheda (identity and difference due to Brahman's way of being), declares that Brahman itself, through its potential power (*śakti*), differentiates into God (*Īśvara*), matter (*acit*), and individual selves (*cit*). God, according to Yādavaprakāśa, is not the same as Brahman but is possessed of only a part of Brahman's perfections (Oberhammer 1997: 10–11).

2 For more on *svarūpa* and *svabhāva*, see Carman 1974: 88–97 and Lipner 1986: 158 fn 6.

3 VS #4.

4 VS #4. Bṛ Up 3.7.22 and Sub Up 2 are van Buitenen's translations. Here and elsewhere, all the upaniṣad translations are from Olivelle 1998, unless otherwise indicated.

5 ṣaḍvidhatātparyaliṇgopetatvāt tatprathamam uktam (TD 9).

6 TD 9.

7 dehātiriktātmasvarūpatatsvabhāva iti. svarūpaṃ jñānānadaikalakṣaṇam. svabhāvo bhagavaccheṣatvam (TD 8).

8 eṣu vākyeṣu jīvaparayoḥ svarūpaṃ kathaṃ pratipannam ity ākāṅkṣāyām upabṛṃhaṇānugṛhītaśrutipratipannam tayos svarūpaṃ vivakṣan (TD 10).

9 VS #5, 43, 78–79, 143–44.

10 jīvātmanaḥ svarūpam devamanuṣyādiprakṛtipariṇāmaviśeṣarūpanānāvidhabhedarahitam. jñānānandaikaguṇam. tasyaitasya karmakṛtadevādibhede' padhvaste svarūpabhedo vācāmagocaraḥ svasaṃvedyaḥ jnanasvarūpam ityetāvadeva nirdeśyam. tacca sarveṣām ātmanāṃ samānam (VS #5).

11 jñānasvarūpam akhilam jagad etad abuddhayaḥ
arthasvarūpaṃ paśyanto bhrāṃyante mohasaṃplave.
(VP 1.4.40) (TD 11)

12 Indicated by TD and van Buitenen 1956: 186; fn 34.

13 tathātmā prakṛteḥ saṅgādahammānādidūṣitaḥ
bhajate prākṛtāndharmān anyastebhyo' pi so' vyayaḥ.
(VP 6.7.24)
pumān na devo na naro na paśur na ca pādpaḥ
śarīrākṛtibhedās tu bhūpaite karmayonayaḥ.
(VP 2.13.94) (TD 10)

14 jñānadaikaguṇam ity anena
nirvāṇmaya evāyamātā jñānamaya' malaḥ
duḥkhājñānamalā dharmāḥ prakṛtes te na cātmanaḥ.
(VP 6.7.22)
ity asyārtho' bhipretaḥ. (TD 10)

15 karmakṛtadevādibhede' padhvaste ity anena
ekasvarūpabhedo hi bāhyakarmāvṛtiprajaḥ
devādibhede' padhvaste nāstyevāvaraṇo hi saḥ.
(VP 2.14.33)
ityasyārtho vivṛto bhavati. (TD 10–11)

16 VP 2.14.33 ab is slightly different in the critical edition of the VP. It reads: ekatvaṃ rūpabhedaśca bāhyakarmāvṛtiprajaḥ.

17 svarūpabhedo vācāmagocaraḥ svasamvedyam ity anena pratyastamitabhedam (VP 6.7.53). ityādivacanaṃ vyākhyātaṃ bhavati. The compelete VP verse is
pratyastamitabhedam yat sattāmātram agocaram
vacasām ātmasamvedyaṃ tajjñānaṃ brahmasaṃjñitam.
(VP 6.7.53) (TD 11)

18 A reference to Buddhism.
19 tucchutvavyāvṛtyarthamāha ātmasamvedyam' iti. tac ca svarūpato dharmataś ca jñānam (TD 11).
20 VS #74.
21 nirvāṇmaya evāyamātmā jñānamayo' malaḥ
duḥkhājñānamalā dharmāḥ prakṛteste na cātmanaḥ.
(VP 6.7.22) (VS #79)
22 nanu ca bhavato' pi vijñānasvarūpa ātmābhyupagantavyaḥ. sa ca svayamprakāśaḥ. tasya ca devādisvarūpātmābhimāne svarūpaprakāśatirodhānam avaśyāśrayaṇīyam. svarūpaprakāśe sati svātmany ākārāntarādhyāsāyogāt. ato bhavataścāyam samāno doṣaḥ. (VS #41)
23 evamabhyupagacchatām asmākam ātmadharmabhūtasya caitanyasya svabhāvikasyāpi karmaṇā pārmārthikaṃ saṅkocaṃ vikāsaṃ ca bruvatāṃ sarvamidaṃ parihṛtam. bhavatastu prakāśa eva svarūpamiti prakāśo na dharmabhūtas tasya saṅkocavikāsau vā nābhyupagamyate. prakāśaprasārānutpattim eva tirodhānabhūtāḥ karmādayaḥ kurvanti. (VS #43)
24 avidyā cet tirodhānaṃ tirodhānabhūtayā' vidyā svarūpabhūtaprakāśanāśeti pūrvamevoktaḥ. asmākaṃ tv avidyārūpeṇa karmaṇā savrūpanityadharmabhūtajñānaprakāśaḥ saṅkucitas. tena devādirūpātmābhimāno bhavatīti viśeṣaḥ. (VS #43)
25 Rāmānuja only cites VP 6.7.61cd.
26 yathā uktam—
viṣṇuśaktiḥ parā proktā kṣetrajñākhyā tathāparā
avidyā karmasamjñānyā tṛtīyā śaktir iṣyate.
(VP 6.7.61) (VS #43)
27 yayā kṣetrajñaśaktiḥ sā veṣṭitā nṛpa sarvagā
samsāratāpān akhilān avāpnoti atisantatān.
(VP 6.7.62)
tayā tirohitatvāc ca śaktiḥ kśetrajñasamjñitā
sarvabhūteṣu bhūpāla tāratamyena vartate.
(VP 6.7.63) (VS #43)
28 The VP also identifies karma as matter (*prakṛti*).
29 The atomic nature (*aṇutva*) of the individual self is discussed in Lipner 1986: 63–68.
30 tāratamyena vartate ityanena jñānasya saṅkocavikāsau siddhau. na hy aṇumātrasya svarūpasya tāratamyam. tasmād dharmabhūtajñānadvārakameva ātmanas tāratamyamiti. jñānadvārakatvaṃ ca tatraivoparitanaiḥ ślokair vivṛtam aprāṇavatsu svalpālpā sthāvareṣu tato' dhikā. (VP 6.7.64 ab)
ityādibhiḥ. (TD 95)
31 Prior to this discussion, Rāmānuja begins his *siddhānta* by citing scriptural evidence from both, śruti and smṛti. The śruti passages utilized are Bṛ Up 3.7.3; Bṛ Up 3.7.22 (Mādhyandina); Sub Up 7. Muṇḍ Up 3.1.1; Taitt Āra 3.11; Taitt Up 2.6; Ch Up 6.3.2; Śvet Up 1.6; Śvet Up 1.12; Śvet Up 6.13. The smṛti examples are from the *Rāmāyaṇa* 6.120.26; VP 1.22.36; BhG 10.20; BhG 15.15. According to Rāmānuja, these scriptures prove that Brahman is the self of all, that matter and individual selves comprise Brahman's body, and therefore the whole world can be said to be Brahman's body. Additionally, because of the soul–body relationship between the world and Brahman, world and Brahman can be identified with each other through *sāmānādhikaraṇya*. That is, the term "world" denotes not just creation, but Brahman who is the inner self of this creation (VS #65). Though these examples suggest the distinction between Brahman, individual selves, and matter, and the soul–body relation shared by these three, it is difficult to use them as proof when describing the transformation of the causal state of Brahman into the effected state. Only the BhG and VP passages contribute to the concept of Brahman as the material cause as a whole.

32 etaduktaṃ bhavati brahmaivam avasthitam ityatraivam śabdārthabhūtaprakāratayaiva vicitracetanācetanātmakaprapañcasya sthūlasya sūkṣmasya ca sadbhāvaḥ. (VS #66)

33 VS #69.

34 ataḥ prakṛtipuruṣamahadahamkāratanmātrabhūtendriyatadārabhdhacaturdaśabhuvanātmakabrahmāṇḍatadantarvartidevatiryaṅmanuṣyasthāvarādisarvaprakārasamsthānasamsthitaṃ kāryamapi sarvaṃ brahmaiveti, kāraṇabhūtabrahmavijñānādeva sarvaṃ vijñātaṃ bhavatītiyekavijñānena sarvavijñānam upapannataram. tadevaṃ kāryakāraṇabhāvādimukhena kṛtsnasya cidacidvastunaḥ parabrahmaprakāratayā tadātmakatvam uktam. (van Buitenen translation) (VS #69)

35 ajām ekāṃ lohitaśuklakṛṣṇāṃ bahvīṃ prajāṃ janayantīṃ sarūpām
ajo hyeko juṣamāṇo'nuśete jahāty enāṃ bhaktabhogām ajo'nyaḥ.
(Śvet Up 4.5)
iti prakṛtipuruṣayor ajatvaṃ darśayati. (VS #72) my own translation.

36 asmān māyī sṛjate viśvam etat tasmiṃś cānyo māyayā sanniruddha; māyām tu prakṛtiṃ vidyān māyinaṃ tu maheśvaram. (Śve Up 4.9–10) (VS #72)

37 prakṛtiṃ puruṣaṃ caiva viddhyanādī ubhāvapi
vikārāṃśca guṇāṃścaiva viddhi prakṛtisaṃbhavān.
(BhG 13.19)
bhūmirāpo'nalo vāyuḥ khaṃ mano buddhireva ca
ahamkāra itīyaṃ me bhinnā prakṛtiraṣṭadhā.
apareyamitastvanyāṃ prakṛtiṃ viddhi me parām
jīvabhūtāṃ mahābāho yayedaṃ dhāryate jagat.
(BhG 7.4–5) (van Buitenen translation) (VS #72)

38 prakṛtiṃ svāmavaṣṭabhya visṛjāmi punaḥ punaḥ. (BhG 9.8)
mayādhyakṣeṇa prakṛtiḥ sūyate sacarācaram. (BhG 9.10) (van Buitenen translation) (VS #72)

39 evaṃ ca prakṛiterapīśvaraśarīratvāt prakṛtiśabdo'pi tadātmabhūtasyeśvarasya tatprakārasamsthitasya vācakaḥ. puruṣaśabdo'pi tadātmabhūtasyeśvarasya puruṣaprakārasaṃsthitasya vācakaḥ. atas tadvikārāṇāmapi tathaiśvara evātmā. tadāha vyaktaṃ viṣṇustathāvyaktaṃ puruṣaḥ kāla eva ca (VP 1.2.18), sa eva kṣobhako brahman kṣobhayaśca parameśvaraḥ (VP 1.2.31) iti (VS #73).

40 vyaktaṃ viṣṇustathāvyaktaṃ puruṣaḥ kāla eva ca
krīḍato bālakasyeva ceṣṭāṃ tasya niśānaya.
(VP 1.2.18)
sa eva kṣobhako brahman kṣobhaśca puruṣottamaḥ
sa sankocavikāśābhyāṃ pradhānatve' pi ca sthitaḥ.
(VP 1.2.31)

41 tad evaṃ nāmarūpavibhāgānarhasūkśmadaśāpannaprakṛtipuruṣaśarīraṃ brahma kāraṇāvastam. jagatas tadāpattireva ca pralayaḥ. nāmarūpavibhāgavibhaktasthūlacidacidvastuśarīraṃ brahma kāryāvastham. brahmaṇas tathāvidhasthūlabhāva eva jagataḥ sṛṣṭir ityucyate. yathoktaṃ bhagavatā parāśareṇa *pradhānapuṃsorajayoḥ kāraṇaṃ kāryabhūtayor* iti. (VP 1.9.37) (VS #74)

42 Van Buitenen titles this VS section as "Miscellaneous Discussions", suggesting that this section is simply an addendum to the previous more important sections that discuss the identity of Brahman as Viṣṇu. However, in light of the connection between this section and the beginning of the *siddhānta* on Brahman's causality (the *aviśeṣaṇakāraṇa* section), this VS section is in fact the conclusion of Rāmānuja's argument begun earlier. Making use of the VP in this section, Rāmānuja establishes the supreme cause as the unique quality of the essential nature of Nārāyaṇa—*brahmasvarūpaviśeṣa*. Thus these two sections, in terms of content, which is Brahman's causality, comprise a complete unit.

43 For a succinct exposition on Brahman's causality in Vedānta, see Lipner 1978: 60–64.

44 Only MBh 12.7074 is included in the MBh critical edition.
45 For Rāmānuja's classification of smṛti as sāttvic (most authoritative), rājasic, and tāmasic, see Adluri 2006.
46 TD 247.
47 ... ityādinā brahmasvarūpaviśeṣapratipādanaikaparatayā pravṛttam (VS #110).
48 ... kevalaparabrahmasvarūpaviśeṣapratipādanāyaiva pravṛtto nārāryaṇānuvākas tathedam vaiṣṇavam ca purāṇam (VS #110) and ... ityparabrahmasvaūpaviśeṣanirṇayāyaiva pravṛttam. (VS #110)
49 prācyodīcyadākṣiṇātyapāścātyasarvaśiṣṭaiḥ sarvadharmasarvatattvavyavasthāyām idameva paryāptam ity avigānaparigṛhītaṃ vaiṣṇavaṃ ca purāṇaṃ. janmād yasya yata (Br Sū 1.1.2) iti jagajjanmādikāraṇaṃ brahmetyavagamyate. tajjanmādikāraṇaṃ kimiti praśnapūrvakaṃ viṣṇoḥ sakāśād udbhūtam. (VP 1.1.31) ityādinā brahmasvarūpaviśeṣapratipādanaikaparatayā pravṛttam iti sarvasaṃmatam ... yathā sarvāsu śrutiṣu kevalaparabrahmasvarūpaviśeṣapratipādanāyaiva pravṛtto nārāyaṇānuvākas tathedaṃ vaiṣṇavaṃ ca purāṇaṃ. (VS #110)
50 Since Vedānta is in the plural, I have translated it as the "upaniṣads".
51 prakṛtir yā mayākhyātā vyaktāvyaktasvarūpiṇī
puruṣaś cāpy ubhāv etau līyete paramātmani.
(VP 6.4.39)
paramātmā ca sarveṣām ādhāraḥ parameśvaraḥ
viṣṇunāmā sa vedeṣu vedānteṣu ca gīyate.
(VP 6.4.40) (VS #110)
52 ādhāra iti śarīrātmabhāvaḥ (TD 249)
53 Also see Lacombe 1966: 108.
54 so'ham icchāmi dharmajña śrotuṃ tvat tu yathā jagat
babhūva bhūyaś ca yathā mahābhāga bhaviṣyati.
(VP 1.1.4)
yanmayaṃ ca jagadbrahman yataścaitaccarācaram
līnam āsīd yathā yatra layameṣyati yatra ca.
(VP 1.1.5) (VS #110)
55 śrutavedāntasya praśnatvāt tucchatvavivartatvapariṇāmatvasadvārakatvādvārakatvādiprakārajñāpanārthaṃ 'yathā' iti praśnaḥ. (TD 250)
56 paraṃ brahma kimiti prakramya. (VS #110)
57 viṣṇoḥ sakāśād udbhūtaṃ jagattatra evaca sthitam
sthithisaṃyamakartāsau jagato'sya jagacca sa.
(VP 1.1.31) (VS #110)
58 sakāśaḥ pārśvaḥ, śarīraikadeśād ity arthaḥ. (TD 251)
59 'yatra' iti layasthānapraśnasyottaram āha tatra iti. tatraiva. viṣṇāveva. atrāpi viṣṇuśabdena layasthānatvaṃ sadvārakam iti siddham. (TD 251–52)
60 paraḥ parāṇāṃ paramaḥ paramātmātmasaṃsthitaḥ
rūpavarṇādinirdeśaviśeṣaṇavivarjitaḥ.
(VP 1.2.10) (VS #110)
61 apakśayavināśābhyāṃ pariṇāmardhijanmabhiḥ
varjitaḥ śakyate vaktuṃ yaḥ sadāstīti kevalam.
(VP 1.2.11)
sarvatrāsau samastaṃ ca vasaty atreti vai yataḥ
tataḥ sa vāsudeveti vidvadbhiḥ paripaṭhyate.
(VP 1.2.12)
tad brahma paramaṃ nityam ajam akśayam avyayam
ekasvarupaṃ ca sadā heyābhāvāc ca nirmalam.
(VP 1.2.13)
tad eva sarvamevaitad vyaktāvyaktasvarupavat
tathā puruṣarūpeṇa kālarūpeṇa ca sthitam.
(VP 1.2.14) (VS #110)

62 sa sarvabhūtaprakṛtiṃ vikārān guṇādidoṣāṃśca mune vyatītaḥ
atītasarvāvaraṇo'khilātmā tenāstṛtaṃ yad bhuvanāntarāle.
(VP 6.5.83) (VS #110)

63 VP 6.5.84 ab is slightly different in the critical edition: samastakalyāṇaguṇātmako hi svaśaktileśāvṛtabhūtasargaḥ.

64 sa īśvaro vyaṣṭisamaṣṭirūpo'vyaktasvarūpaḥ prakaṭasvarūpaḥ
sarveśraḥ sarvadṛk sarvavettā samastaśaktiḥ parameśvarākhyaḥ.
(VP 6.5.86) (VS #110)

65 In the critical edition, VP 6.5.87 cd states *avagamyate* instead of *adhigamyate*.

66 samjñāyate yena tadastadoṣaṃ śuddhaṃ paraṃ nirmalam ekarūpam
samdṛśyate vāpy adhigamyate vā tajjñānamajñāmato' nyad uktam.
(VP 6.5.87)
iti parabrahmasvarūpaviśeṣanirṇayāyaiva pravṛttam. (VS #110)

67 sa eva sarvabhutatma viśvarupo yato' vyayaḥ
sargādikaṃ tato'syaiva bhūtastham upakārakam.
(VP 1.2.69)
sa eva sṛjyaḥ sa ca sargakartā sa eva pātyatti ca pālyate ca
brahmādiavasthābhir śeṣamūrtir viṣṇur variṣṭho varado vareṇyaḥ.
(VP 1.2.70) (VS #112)

68 sa eva sarveśvaraḥ parabrahmabhūto viṣṇureva sarvaṃ jagaditi pratijñāya sarvabhūtātmā viśvarupo yato' vyaya iti heturuktaḥ. sarvabhūtānām ayamātmā viśvaśarīro yato' vyaya ityarthaḥ. vakṣyati ca—tat sarvaṃ hares tanur iti (VP 1.22.36). etad uktaṃ bhavati. asyāvyayasyāpi parasya brahmaṇo viṣṇor viśvaśarī ratayā tādātmyam aviruddham ityātmaśarīrayośca svabhāvā vyavasthitā eva (van Buitenen translation) (VS #113).

69 For more on icons and images in Śrīvaiṣṇavism see Nayar 1992.

70 In this first section, a description of Brahman's divine form also includes discussion of Brahman's divine abode and his consort (s). I address only the discussion of the divine form and the scriptural examples utilized to support the existence of a divine form. Additionally, I exclude discussions on the nature of the divine abode and the meaning of the important yet ambiguous term *paramaṃ padam* (VS #128–31).

71 tasyetasya parasya brahmaṇo nārāyaṇasyāparicchedyajñānānandāmalatvasvarūpavajjñānaśakti balaiśvaryavīryatejaḥprabhṛtynavadhikātiśayāsaṃkhyeyakalyāṇaguṇavatsvasaṃkalpapravartyasvetarasamastacidacidvastujātavatsvabhābhimata svānurūpaikarūpadivyarūpataducitaniratiśayakalyāṇavividhān antabhūṣaṇasvaśaktisadṛśāparimitānantāścaryanānāvidhāyudha … (VS #127).

72 Also Ch Up 8.1.5, 8.7.1, 8.7.3, and Maitri Up 7.7 (Jacob 1891: 961).

73 … sahasraśaḥ śrutayaḥ santi (VS #127).

74 svarūpaśabdaḥ svarūpanirūpakadharmavācī. aparicchedyeti svarūpam uktam. jñāneti guṇā uktāḥ. svasaṃkalpeti vibhūtimattvam uktam. svarūpatadguṇavibhūtayo divyarūpādīnāṃ prāmāṇikatve dṛṣṭāntatayā uktāḥ. divyavigrahādayaḥ sādhyāḥ (TD 306).

75 For more on the concept of *vibhūti*, see Oberhammer 2000.

76 I do not discuss all the śruti passages because their contribution is identical to that of the other examples discussed here. These passages are: Muṇḍ Up 3.1.8, Sub Up 6, Taitt Saṃhitā 2.2.12.5, Mahā Nār Up 1.5, Taitt Up 2.1, RV 10.129, RV 10.90. Additionally, I do not discuss śruti passages that mention the divine abode and Viṣṇu's consorts (Taitt Saṃhitā 4.4.12.5; Taitt Ār 3.13.1) as these passages refer to "Viṣṇu's abode" and "Śrī and Hrī as his consorts" and do not mention his divine form (VS #127).

77 Van Buitenen 1956 and Olivelle 1998 translate *tamasaḥ* as darkness, but it can also denote one of the three qualities (*guṇa*) of matter (*prakṛti*), which is how

Rāmānuja interprets this term in VS #131. In the same way *rajas*, is also rendered as "matter" by Rāmānuja.

78 Van Buitenen 1956, VS #127, translates *kapyāsaṃ puṇḍarīkam evam akṣiṇīsam* as "many-colored lotus." He summarizes the discussion regarding the meaning of *kapyāsaṃ puṇḍarīkam evam akṣiṇī*, as found in the TD (TD 323ff). The three acceptable meanings van Buitenen lists are: *ādityakṣitaṃ śrīmattvāt* (splendor) emitted by the sun, for (the lotus) is resplendent, *nālāsanam, jalabhuvam*. The reasoning for a translation of "many-colored" is not clear. There are variant readings for *kapyāsam*. See Olivelle 1998: 536.

79 Rāmānuja explains the word comprised of the mind as follows: the *mayaṭ* affix denotes a relation of abundance; here the relation is different, and it is one of grasping and being grasped. The meaning is as stated in śruti: *however, by the pure mind [it is known]*.

80 vedāhametaṃ puruṣaṃ mahāntam ādityavarṇaṃ tamasaḥ parastāt (Śve Up 3.8).
ya eṣo'ntarāditye hiraṇmayaḥ puruṣaḥ ... tasya yathā kapyāsaṃ puṇḍarīkam evam akṣiṇī (Ch Up 1.6.6–7).
sa ya eṣo'ntarhṛdaya ākāśaḥ. tasminn ayaṃ puruṣo manomayo'mṛto hiraṇmayaḥ manomaya (Taitt Up 1.6.1).
sarve nimeṣā jajñire vidyutaḥ puruṣād adhi (Mahā Nār Up 1.6) (VS #127).

81 Mahā Nar Up 1.6 translation is my own.

82 tameva viditvāti mṛtyumeti na anyaḥ panthā vidyate'yanāya (Śve Up 3.8).
yasmāt paraṃ nāparamasti kiṃcidyasmānnāṇīyo na jyāyo'sti kiṃcit
vṛkṣeva stabdho divi tiṣṭhaty ekastenedaṃ pūrṇaṃ puruṣeṇa sarvam.
(Śve Up 3.9)

83 sahasraśīrṣā puruṣaḥ sahasrākṣaḥ sahasrapāt
sa bhūmiṃ viśvato vṛtvā atyatiṣṭhaddaśāṅgulim.
(Śve Up 3.14)
sarvataḥ pāṇipādaṃ tatsarvato'kṣiśiromukham
sarvataḥ śrutimalloke sarvamāvṛtya tiṣṭhati.
(Śve Up 3.16)

84 atha ya eṣontarāditye hiraṇmayaḥ puruṣo dṛśyate hiraṇyaśmaśrurhiraṇyakeśa ā praṇakhātsarva eva suvarṇaḥ.
(Ch Up 1.6.6)
tasya yathā kapyāsaṃ puṇḍarīkamevamakṣiṇī. tasyoditi nāma. sa eṣa sarvebhyaḥ pāpmabhya uditaḥ. udeti ha vai sarvebhyaḥ pāpmabhyo ya evaṃ veda.
(Ch Up 1.6.7)
Olivelle 1998 translation.

85 sa ya eṣo'ntarhṛdaya ākāśaḥ. tasminn ayaṃ puruṣo manomayaḥ. amṛto hiraṇmayaḥ. antareṇa tāluke. ya eṣa stana ivālambate. sendrayoniḥ. yatrāsau keśānto vivartate. vyapohya śīrṣakapāle. bhūrityagnau pratitiṣṭhati. bhuva iti vāyau.
(Taitt Up 1.6.1)
Olivelle 1998 translation.

86 For more on this upaniṣad, see Varenne 1960.

87 In Mahā Nār Up 3.12, *nīlatoyadamadhyasthā vidyullekheva bhāsvarā* is translated as, the middle of the blue cloud is radiant like a streak of lightning. However Rāmānuja takes *nīlatoyadamadhyasthā* to be a *bahuvrihi* compound rather than a *ṣaṣṭhi tatpuruṣa, madhyastanīlatoyadāvidyullekheva*. The TD provides the rationale for this—the compound "within the blue-cloud" is a *bahuvrīhi*; the irregular position of the first member is accepted as a Vedic exception (TD 308).

88 nīlatoyadamadhyasthā vidyullekheva bhāsvarā (Mahā Nār Up 3.12).
manomayaḥ prāṇaśarīro bhārūpaḥ satyakāmaḥ satyasaṃkalpaḥ. ākāśātmā sarvakarmā sarvakāmaḥ sarvagandhaḥ sarvarasaḥ sarvamidam abhyātto' vākyānādaraḥ.
(Ch Up 3.14.2)

mahārajanaṃ vāsa (Bṛ Up 2.3.6) (VS #127).
Olivelle 1998 translation.

89 madhyasthanīlatoyadā vidduyullekheva seyaṃ daharapuṇḍarīkamadhyasthākāśavartinī vahniśikhā svāntarnihitanīlatoyadābhaparamātmasvarūpā svāntarnihitanīlatoyadā vidyudivābhāti ityarthaḥ (VS #127). *madhyastanilatoyada* here, is a forced interpretation (van Buitenen 1956: 283).

90 svarūpaśabdo vigrahaparaḥ (TD 308).

91 The term *svarūpa* is found in a handful of upaniṣads such as Maitri Upaniṣad 7.11, Sarva Upaniṣatsāra 3–5, Gopichandana 5, Muktika Upaniṣad 1.3, and 2.60 (Jacob 1891: 1063).

92 evaṃ padadvayena ubhayavibhūtimattvam uktaṃ bhavati. sarvagandhaḥ sarvarasaḥ ityanena ca vigrahasiddhiḥ (TD 308–9).

93 mahārajataṃ rāgadravyaviśeṣaḥ; tena rañjitaṃ mahārajatam (TD 309).

94 itihāsapurāṇayor vedopabṛmhaṇayoś cayam artha ucyate
tau te medhāvinau dṛṣṭvā vedeṣu pariniṣṭhitau
vedopabṛmhaṇārthāya tāvagrāhayata prabhuḥ.
Rāmāyaṇa 1.4.6 (VS #133)

95 vyaktam eṣa mahāyogī paramātmā sanātanaḥ
anādimadhyanidhano mahataḥ paramo mahān.
(*Rāmāyaṇa* 6.1.4.14) (VS #133)

96 anādimadhyanidhana iti svarūpanityatvam (TD 321).

97 tamasaḥ paramo dhātā śaṅkhacakragadādharaḥ
śrīvatsavakṣā nityaśrīr ajayyaḥ śāśvato dhruvaḥ.
(*Rāmāyaṇa* 6.1.4.15) (VS #133)

98 śarā nānāvidhāś cāpi dhanurāyatavigraham
anvagacchanta kākutsthaṃ sarve puruṣavigrahāḥ.
(*Rāmāyaṇa* 7.109.7)
viveśa vaiṣṇavam tejaḥ saśarīraḥ sahānugaḥ (*Rāmāyaṇa* 7.110.13ab) (VS #133) (not found in the critical edition of the epic).

99 samastāḥ śaktyaścaitā nṛpa yatra pratiṣṭhitāḥ
tadviśvarūpavairūpyaṃ rūpam anyad hareḥ mahat.
(VP 6.7.70)

100 Alternate readings for VP 6.7.70 cd are *tadviśvavairūpyaṃ rūpam anyad hareḥ mahat* in VS #164 and in the critical edition of the VP it is *tadviśvarūparūpaṃ vai rūpam anyad hareḥ mahat.*

101 atha tasminneva yogaprakareṇa upasaṃhāre'pi saviśeṣaparavākyāni darśayan divyavigrahavatvaṃ cāha samasteti … tad viśvarūpavairūpyamiti sanniveśavailakṣaṇyam uktam. (ŚP. Vol I.215)

102 sarvaśaktimayo viṣṇuḥ svarūpaṃ brahmaṇo' param
mūrtaṃ yad yogibhiḥ pūrvaṃ yogārambheṣu cintyate.
(VP 1.22.59)
sa paraḥ sarvaśaktīnāṃ brahmaṇaḥ samanantaraḥ
mūrtaṃ brahma mahābhāga sarvabrahmamayo hariḥ.
(VP 1.22.61) (VS #133)

103 I do not address additional smṛti examples as they do not add anything to the argument at hand. These passages are VP 1.8.39, VP 4.1.84ab, MBh 12.5.27, and MBh 12.191.9ab (VS #133). In closing the discussion of this first description of Brahman, Rāmānuja ends by citing Br Sū 1.1.21, which he claims suggests that Brahman has a transcendent form. But, this sūtra only mentions the term "attributes".

104 yo'sāvādityamaṇḍalāntarvartī taptakārtasvaragirivaraprabhaḥ sahasrāṃśuśatasahasrakiraṇo gambhīrāmbhaḥ samudrabhūtasumṛṣṭanālaravikaravikasitapuṇḍarī kadalāmalāyatekṣṇaḥ … (VS #134)

105 Rāmānuja refers to the Vedānta of predecessors such as Bodhāyana, Taṇka, and Dramiḍa whose works are not extant, as support for his view.
106 Van Buitenen 1956: 24–29.
107 VS #135.
108 eteṣāṃ parijanasthānādīnāṃ *sad eva somyedam agra āsīd* ity atrajñānabalaiśvaryādikalyāṇaguṇagaṇavatparabrahmasvarūpāntarbhūtatvāt (VS #132).
109 yathā kāraṇavastvantarbhūtatvāj jñānādiguṇānāṃ *sad eva* ityādivākye teṣām abhāvo na pratipādyate; evaṃ nityavibhūter api kāraṇavastvantarbhūtatvāt *sad eva* ityādivākyagataiḥ *sad eva, ekam eva, advitīyam* iti śabdair brahmāntarbhāvo' vagamyate. nityavibhūtiviśiṣṭaṃ brahmaiva avagamyatetyarthaḥ (TD 319).
110 subhrūlalāṭaḥ sunāsaḥ susmitādharavidrumaḥ surucirakomalagaṇḍaḥ kambugrīvaḥ samunnatāṃsavilambicārurūpadivyakarṇakisalayaḥ ... (VS #134).
111 prasannacāruvadanaṃ padmapatropamejñaṇam
sukapolam suvistīrṇalalāṭaphalakojjvalam.
(VP 6.7.80)
samakarṇāntavinyastacārukarṇavibhūṣaṇam
kambugrīvaṃ suvistīrṇaśrīvatsāṅkitavakṣasam.
(VP 6.7.81)
112 ŚBh 1.1.1.
113 VS #133.
114 ... pīnavṛttāyatabhujaścārutarātāmrakaratalānuraktāṅgulībhiṛ alaṃkṛtas tanumadhyo viśālavilakṣḥasthalaḥ samavibhaktasarvāṅgo'nirdeśyadivyarūpasaṃhananaḥ snigdhavarṇaḥ prabuddhapuṇḍarīkacārucaraṇayugalaḥ svānurūpapītāmbaradharo'malakirīṭakuṇḍalahārakaustubhakeyūrakaṭakanūpurodarabandhanādyaparimitāś caryānantadivyabhūṣaṇaḥ śaṅkhacakragadāsiśārṅgaśrīvatsavanamālālaṃkṛtaḥ (VS #134).
115 valītribhaṅginā magnanābhinā codareṇa vai
pralambāṣṭabhujaṃ viṣṇum athavāpi caturbhujam.
(VP 6.7.82)
samsthitorujaṅghaṃ ca susthitāṅghrikarāmbhujam
cintayed brahmabhūtaṃ taṃ pītanirmalavāsasam.
(VP 6.7.83)
kirīṭacārukeyūrakaṭakādivibhūṣitam
śārṅgaśaṅkhagadākhaḍgacakrākṣavalayānvitam.
(VP 6.7.84)
116 anavadikātiśayasaundaryāhṛtāśeṣamanodṛṣṭivṛttir lāvaṇyāmṛtapūritāśeṣacarācarabhūtajāto'tyad bhutācintyanityayauvanaḥ puṣpahārasasukumāraḥ puṇyagandhavāsitānantadigantarālas trailokyākramaṇapravṛttagambhīrabhāvaḥ karuṇānurāgamadhuralocanāvalokitāśritavargaḥ puruṣavaro darīdṛśyate (VS #134).
117 evaṃ ya eṣo' ntarāditye (Ch Up 1.6.6) ityādi vākyasyārtha uktaḥ (TD 329).
118 Ch Up 1.6.7, Bṛ Up 4.4.22, Ch Up 8.1.5, Mahā Nar Up 11.2–3, Muṇḍ Up 3.1.8, Bṛ Up 2.3.6, Śvet Up 3.7, Taitt Sam 4.4.12.5, Taitt Ār 3.13.1, Taitt Up 2.1, Muṇḍ Up 2.3.10 (VS #135–37). There is also one passage whose source is unknown (VS #135).

3 Brahman, the individual self, and ignorance in the *Śrībhāṣya*

In the last chapter on the *Vedārthasaṃgraha* (VS), we examined Rāmānuja's use of the *Viṣṇu Purāṇa* (VP) as valid means of knowledge (*śabdapramāṇa*) in consolidating his views on the individual self, the causal nature of Brahman and the divine form. This chapter examines the importance of the VP as valid means of knowledge (*śabdapramāṇa*) in Rāmānuja's commentary on the *Brahma Sūtras* (Br Sū), the *Śrībhāṣya* (ŚBh). In the ŚBh, Rāmānuja cites 161 passages from the VP considerably exceeding the 133 from the *Bṛhadāraṇyaka Upaniṣad* and 132 from the *Bhagavadgītā* (Hohenberger 1960: 20–21). An interesting characteristic of the ŚBh is its lengthy commentary on Br Sū 1.1.1. It is in the commentary on this *sūtra* in particular, that we find sustained use of the VP. For this reason, this chapter addresses the significance of the VP in the commentary on Br Sū 1.1.1 only. Furthermore, ŚBh 1.1.1, is comprised of two sections addressing the *prima facie* view—a Minor Objection (*Laghupūrvapakṣa*) and a Major Objection (*Mahāpūrvapakṣa*), and two corresponding conclusions (*siddhānta*)—a Minor Conclusion (*Laghusiddhānta*) and a Major Conclusion (*Mahāsiddhānta*).[1] Of these it is only the Major Objection, which presents the Advaita perspective, and the Major Conclusion, that are relevant to our evaluation of the exegetical function of the VP.

The VP is crucial in Rāmānuja's arguments in ŚBh 1.1.1 in three ways. First, it helps define and provides support for Brahman's nature. Second, it conclusively differentiates the individual self (both in its liberated and embodied states) from Brahman. Third, it explains the relationship between Brahman and ignorance (*avidyā*). In contrast to the VS, the ŚBh as a commentary on the *Brahmasūtras* constrains Rāmānuja's exegetical freedom in some ways; however, an interesting strategy of symmetry is evident in regard to his use of the VP. The very same scriptural passages cited as support of the *prima facie* view in the Major Objection are then reinterpreted in the Major Conclusion. Some possible reasons for such a hermeneutic strategy, I address below; however, the fact that the sections on scriptural support in the Major Objection more or less mirror those in the Major Conclusion seems to be a unique feature of the ŚBh. This is not something that we witness in the VS, perhaps due to the fact that it is not a commentary on a primary text. Since in the course of my analysis of ŚBh 1.1.1 I frequently refer to the structure of the sections of the Major Objection and the Major Conclusion that address scripture as a valid means of knowledge, I summarize the data in Table 3.1.

Though there are similarities in terms of the specific scriptural passages that are discussed in the Major Objection and the Major Conclusion, there are also important variations as concern the VP. In the Major Objection, Rāmānuja has the Advaitin cite śruti, *Brahma Sūtras*, *Viṣṇu Purāṇa*, and the *Bhagavadgītā* to argue that Brahman alone is the only reality lacking any differentiations or qualities whatsoever. In the Major Conclusion, he first refutes the interpretation of these śruti and Br Sū passages and then cites an additional thirty-three VP passages to establish the Viśiṣṭādvaita perspective on the nature of Brahman (noted in italics in Table 3.1). Though it may seem that Rāmānuja turns to śruti first and then smṛti, namely the VP, we shall see that it is the passages from the purāṇa that directly address his concerns; in fact, he interprets śruti based on his reading of the VP. Thus, in this section it is the content of this purāṇa that supports his vision of the nature of Brahman.

After refuting the Advaita interpretation of śruti, Rāmānuja then turns to the VP passages and BhG passages cited in the Major Objection. He refutes these passages by a detailed examination of the context of these verses and cites additional śruti and smṛti to argue that the VP passages do not, as the Advaitin claims, support attribute-less Brahman, but in fact address the individual self. Thus, the role of the VP in this second section of this chapter is to support the metaphysical reality of the individual self and to define its essential nature, something that is not of concern to the objector. Having established that the VP passages cited in the Major Objection in fact address the individual self rather than Brahman, Rāmānuja goes on to cite additional VP and śruti to establish the distinction between the individual self (in both its embodied and liberated states) and Brahman. These topics are examined in the third section of this chapter.

Lastly, in the Major Objection, śruti and VP passages are utilized as support for ignorance as indescribable as either an entity or a non-entity and as the cause of the superimposition of the empirical world on Brahman. Subsequently, in the Major Conclusion, after a refutation of the Advaita understanding of ignorance as indefensible by means of logic, Rāmānuja argues that scripture also does not support such a notion of ignorance. He does this by re-interpreting certain terms such as *anṛta*, *satya*, *sat*, *asat*, and so on, which denote ignorance (*avidyā*) for the Advaitin. Additionally, Rāmānuja also undertakes a systematic re-interpretation of sections of the VP that were used in the Major Objection to support the *prima facie* view and uses these in turn to interpret śruti. This discussion on the nature of ignorance is covered in the last section of the chapter.

Why does Rāmānuja have the objector utilize the VP passages to support the Advaita worldview? There are three possible reasons for such use of the VP. First, Rāmānuja, intending to use the VP later in his Major Conclusion, gives the Advaitin the opportunity to utilize the same scripture. Second, the VP may have been an important text within the Advaita tradition and a

Table 3.1 Scriptural Use in the Major Objection and Major Conclusion of Śrībhāṣya 1.1.1

Major Objection (Mahāpūrvapakṣa)	*Major Conclusion* (Mahāsiddhānta)
Scripture supports attributeless Brahman	Scripture does not teach a Brahman devoid of all difference
	Nature of Brahman
• Ch Up 6.2.1, Muṇḍ Up 1.1.6, Taitt Up 2.1.1, Śvet Up 6.19, Kena Up 2.3, Bṛ Up 3.4.2, Taitt Up 3.6.1, Bṛ Up 4.5.7[2], Bṛ Up 4.4.19,[3] Bṛ Up 2.4.14,[4] Ch Up 6.1.4,[5] Taitt Up 2.7.1, Br Su 3.2.11, Br Su 3.2.3	• Ch Up 6.2.1, *Br Su 2.1.5*,[6] Muṇḍ Up 1.1.6, Taitt Up 2.1.1, *Ch Up 6.2.3*, 6.2.1, *Adhy Up 68*, Śvet Up 6.19, Muṇḍ Up 1.1.9, *Ch Up 6.2.3*, *Ch Up 6.2.1*, *Ait Up 1.1*, *Kaṭh Up 5.13*, *Śvet Up 6.13*, *Śvet Up 1.9*, *Śvet Up 6.7–8*, *Ch Up 8.1.5*, *8.7.1*, *8.7.3*, *Taitt Up 2.8*, *Taitt Up 2.1.1*, *Ch Up 8.1.1*, *Ch Up 3.14.1*, Kena Up 2.3, *Taitt Up 2.1.1*, *Muṇḍ Up 3.2.9*, Taitt Up 2.6.1, *Bṛ Up 2.4.14*, Bṛ Up 3.4.2, *Taitt Up 3.6.1*, *Bṛ Up 3.9.28*, *Taitt Up 2.8.1*, *Taitt Up 2.9.1*, Bṛ Up 4.4.19, Bṛ Up 2.4.14, *Taitt Up 2.6.1*,[7] *Taitt Up 2.7.1*, Br Su 3.2.11, Br Su 3.2.3 • *BhG 10.3, 9.4–5, 7.6–7, 10.42, 15.17–18* • *VP 6.5.82–87, 6.5.72–77, 6.7.70–72, 1.22.53, 1.2.10–14, 6.4.39–40, 1.22.53–54, 6.7.61–63, 2.7.29–31, 1.22.60*
	Nature of the Individual Self
• VP 6.7.53, 1.2.6, 1.4.38–41, 2.14.31, 2.13.86, 2.14.32, 2.16.23–24, 6.7.96	• VP 6.7.53, *Śvet Up 3.8*, *BhG 8.9*, *VP 6.7.55*, *6.7.69–70*, *Viṣṇu Dharm 114.23–26*, VP 1.2.6, *Taitt Up 3.1.1*, *MBh 1.1.264*, *VP 1.1.4–5*, *VP 1.1.31*, *VP 1.2.10*, *VP 1.1.2*, *VP 1.3.1–3*, VP 1.4.38–41
	Plurality of Individual Selves
	• VP 2.14.31, *BhG 5.18–19*, VP 2.13.86, 2.14.32, 2.16.23–24, *VP 6.7.96*, *Muṇḍ Up 3.1.1*, *Kaṭh Up 3.1*, *Taitt Āraṇ 3.21*, *VP 6.5.83.85*, *6.7.61–62*, *Br Su 1.2.21*, *1.1.22*, *2.1.22*, *Bṛ Up (Mādhy) 3.7.22*, *Bṛ Up 4.3.21*, *4.3.35*
	Liberated Self is also distinct from Brahman
	• *VP 2.14.27*, *BhG 14.2*, *VP 6.7.30*, *Br Su 4.4.17*, *4.4.21*, *1.3.2*, *Ch Up 8.1.6*, *Taitt Up 2.1.1*, *Taitt Up 3.10.5*, *Ch Up 8.12.3*, *Taitt Up 2.7.1*, *Muṇḍ Up 3.2.8*, *Muṇḍ Up 3.1.3*, *Br Su 3.3.11*, *3.3.57*, *Muṇḍ Up 3.2.9*, *Muṇḍ Up 3.2.8*, *Ch Up 8.3.4*, *VP 6.7.93–95*, *2.14.33*, *6.7.96*, *Viṣṇu Dharm 120*, *VP 6.7.61*, *BhG 13.2*, *15.16–17*, *18.61*, *15.15*
• BhG 10.20, 13.2, 10.39	• BhG 10.20, 13.2, 10.39 • *BhG 10.41–42*

Table 3.1 (continued)

Major Objection (Mahāpūrvapakṣa)	*Major Conclusion* (Mahāsiddhānta)
Scripture supports ignorance (*avidyā*) • Ch Up 8.3.2, 8.3.1, RV 10.129.1–3, Śvet Up 4.10, Br Up 2.5.19, BhG 7.14, Muṇḍ Up 2.21 • VP 2.12.39–40, VP 2.12.43–45	Scripture does not teach ignorance (*avidyā*) • Ch Up 8.3.2, 8.3.1, RV 10.129.1–3, *Sub Up 2*, Śvet Up 4.10, VP 1.19–20, Śvet Up 4.9, *Māṇḍ Up 2.21*, *Br Up 2.5.19*, *BhG 7.14* • VP 2.12.39–40, VP 2.12.43–45 • *VP 2.12.36, 2.12.38, 1.22.86, 1.22.38, 1.2.69, 2.12.39,* 2.12.40, 2.12.41–45, *2,12,38, 2.12.45–47, 2.13.100, 2.14.24, VP 2.13.2, VP 2.12.38*

detailed analysis of this purāṇa was a means of appropriating it as a Viśiṣṭādvaita text. To my knowledge, there is no evidence of the use of the VP in the Vedānta treatises of Śaṅkara's immediate disciples. This does not rule out, however, the possibility that the VP was popular within Advaita Vedānta interpretive communities as mentioned in Chapter 1.[8] A third reason might be that Rāmānuja was better able to counter the Advaita claim of attributeless Brahman with the VP. In the analysis that follows, reasons two and three seem the most plausible.

The nature of Brahman

In the Major Objection, Rāmānuja has the Advaitin claim the following about Brahman:

> Brahman alone, who is only consciousness and contrary to all characterizing attributes, is real; all entities other than it, such as the distinctions of knowledge due to various types of knower and the known are thought to exist in him and are unreal.[9]

As pure consciousness, Brahman is perceived with attributes due to adjuncts (*upādhi*), when in fact it is identical with supreme knowledge and is the absolute reality (*vastusat*) (De Smet 1953: 64, 83–84). To fully comprehend the significance of the VP, in this discussion of the nature of Brahman we begin by juxtaposing Rāmānuja's summary statement on the nature of Brahman with that of the Advaitin:

> The Highest Brahman, by his very nature, is declared to be devoid of association with all faults, has the nature of all auspicious qualities, and

> for purposes of sport (*līlā*), creates the world, preserves it, destroys it, enters into it, and controls it; all sentient and insentient beings under all kinds of conditions are undoubtedly real and are said to be the bodily form of the Highest Brahman; the world has been stated to be so by words such as body (*śarīra*), form (*rūpa*), body (*tanu*),[10] part (*aṃśa*), power (*śakti*), and glorious manifestation (*vibhūti*) and so on; and by *sāmānādhikaraṇya*[11] these are equated with the word 'that' (as in *you are that* Ch Up 6.8.7); the sentient being, which forms the *vibhūti* of Brahman, exists in its own essential nature, and in the form of the embodied soul due to its association with insentient matter, because the condition of the embodied self, which is veiled by ignorance (*avidyā*) in the form of meritorious and sinful acts, does not recognize its essential nature as comprised of sentience, but as having the nature of matter. Therefore, the Highest Brahman who is possessed of attributes and the world, which is his manifestation (*vibhūti*), is known to be undoubtedly real as well.[12]

This description of Brahman utilizes terminology from the VP. Rāmānuja finds several concepts in the purāṇa that are important in establishing the soul–body paradigm he uses so often to interpret śruti such as: the world as Brahman's glorious manifestation[13] (*vibhūti*), the world as His body (*śarīra/tanu*), the concept of *ubhayaliṅgatva* (fact of possessing dual characteristics—infinite auspicious qualities and no faults whatsoever), Brahman's creative activity as divine sport (*līlā*), and the nature of the individual self and its association with ignorance (*avidyā*). These concepts for which he finds support in the VP to counter the Advaita view of the world as only provisionally real are fundamental to his articulation of Vedānta. In contrast to his refutation of such a non-dual interpretation of śruti which focuses mainly on proving that the upaniṣads teach a Brahman possessed of various attributes, the information provided by the VP is vastly different not only in terms of the detail they provide, but also support for the soul–body framework so central to Viśiṣṭādvaita Vedānta.

Thus, as far as the nature of Brahman is concerned, in the Major Conclusion, both śruti and VP passages have been utilized, even though the purāṇic passages are mentioned only by Rāmānuja. Though, it may seem that he has utilized śruti and then smṛti maintaining the traditional view of the corroborative function of smṛti, his re-interpretation of śruti mentioned in the Major Objection is only to establish that a Brahman devoid of attributes is not what the upaniṣads teach. That is, he engages with śruti cited in support of the *prima facie* view only to argue that Brahman is not quality-less (*nirguṇa*). For the additional information which characterizes his view of Brahman, as stated in the summary statement above, he resorts to the VP. I first evaluate Rāmānuja's refutation of the śruti that is mentioned in the Major Objection and then address the BhG and VP passages, which are introduced by Rāmānuja in his Major Conclusion.

Śruti support

In the Major Objection the following śruti passages are utilized to support the Advaita view of Brahman as devoid of all attributes: Ch Up 6.2.1, Muṇḍ Up 1.1.6, Taitt Up 2.1.1, Śvet Up 6.19, Kena Up 2.3, Bṛ Up 3.4.2, Taitt Up 3.6.1, Bṛ Up 4.5.7,[14] Bṛ Up 4.4.19,[15] Bṛ Up 2.4.14,[16] Ch Up 6.1.4,[17] Br Sū 3.2.11, Br Sū 3.2.3. In the Major Conclusion, Rāmānuja takes up these passages to refute the Advaita characterization of Brahman. We will not discuss all of these passages, but rather look at the exegetical strategies he employs to counter the *prima facie* claims.[18] To establish that the śruti in question in fact support the Viśiṣṭādvaita point of view he utilizes the soul–body paradigm, the concept of Brahman's dual nature (*ubhayaliṅgatva*), and the postulate of scriptural harmony (*samanvaya*). For re-interpreting the Br Sū passages 3.2.11 and 3.2.3 he depends indirectly on the VP.

Ch Up 6.2.1, *in the beginning, son, this world was simply what is existent, one only, without a second* is the first scripture that is provided as support by the objector. Chapter 6 of the *Chāndogya Upaniṣad* is the source text for the *satkāryavāda* doctrine, that the cause and effect are non-different. For Śaṅkara, however, these "creation texts are no more than a device for suggesting the idea that the individual self and the highest self are (in their true nature) identical" and are only a means to point beyond empirical reality (Alston 1980, Vol. II: 191). For Rāmānuja, on the other hand, Brahman's originative causality is an important aspect of "God's relatedness to finite being" and this passage is indeed one of Rāmānuja's *mahāvākyas*, "great utterances" that embody core Vedāntic truths (Lipner 1986: 82). Refuting the Advaitic interpretation of this śruti as supporting a Brahman devoid of all attributes, he argues instead that this scripture affirms the highest Brahman denoted by *sat* as the material and efficient cause of the world, who is omniscient, omnipotent, wills the truth, pervades all, supports all, controls all, and is characterized by innumerable auspicious qualities and is the inner self or soul to the world that comprises his body. Thus, unless the soul–body paradigm is invoked to read Ch Up 6.2.1, it will not yield an interpretation conducive to Viśiṣṭādvaita, in this particular instance. Indeed, "Rāmānuja's belief that finite selves [and matter] constitute the body of the Supreme Self is for him, not the conclusion of a rational argument, but a fundamental fact vouched for by scripture" (Carman 1974: 127).[19]

The soul–body paradigm is also closely associated with Rāmānuja's concept of Brahman's causality and the rejection of the world's status as provisionally real, and it is crucial in his redefinition of the concepts of diversity and manifoldness. Bṛ Up 4.4.19/Bṛ Up 4.5.15 is cited in the Major Objection as evidence that there is no other reality than the attribute-less Brahman:

> there is here nothing diverse at all. From death to death he goes, who sees here any kind of diversity[20]

> when however, the whole has become one's very self, then who is there for one to see and by what means?[21]

Once Again, Rāmānuja notes that the Advaitic view is to be dispensed with:

> this whole world being an effect of Brahman and having Brahman as its inner ruler is one with Brahman, because Brahman is its self. Manifoldness contrary to this (understating of diversity) is rejected by these texts.[22]

Additionally, he employs the principle of scriptural harmony (*samanvaya*) to claim that unless these passages are interpreted in this way they would contradict other śruti such as *may I become many, may I be born* (Ch Up 6.2.3). Rāmānuja redefines what "diversity" means in this upaniṣad as something that issues forth from the unitary complex of Brahman, matter, and individual selves, and as such is not contrary to the "one-ness" that this scripture teaches.

The second mode of interpretation that Rāmānuja employs is the concept of *ubhayaliṅgatva*, the fact that Brahman possesses all auspicious perfections and is devoid of any imperfections whatsoever (Carman 1974: 88). Muṇḍ Up 1.1.5–6 states:

> whereas the higher (knowledge) is that by which one grasps the imperishable. What cannot be seen, what cannot be grasped, without color, without sight or hearing, without hands and feet; what is eternal and all-pervading, extremely minute, present everywhere ... that is immutable, which the wise fully perceive.[23]

Applying the concept of dual characteristics of Brahman to the passage, the conclusion he reaches is that this passage only denies Brahman's possession of defects pertaining to matter (*prakṛti*), but that it does not in fact support a Brahman that is attribute-less. That is, Rāmānuja takes all the qualities denied of Brahman by scripture and the Advaitin as only those that concern material nature. He elaborates that "[i]n Muṇḍ Up 1.1.5–6, the highest Brahman is said to possess innumerable auspicious qualities, is all-knowing, is the root of all beings, immutable, omnipresent, subtle, manifest, eternal and free from qualities of matter (*prakṛti*)".[24] Whereas, for the Advaitin Brahman qualified with attributes, even auspicious perfections results from the very same adjuncts that produce ignorance (De Smet 1953: 47). Similarly, Rāmānuja interprets śruti such as ... *without parts, inactive, tranquil, unblemished, spotless* (Śvet Up 6.19) as affirming the perfections of Brahman and the negation of all faults. In fact, for Rāmānuja this dual nature of Brahman in regard to the qualities He possesses is one of the unique and defining features of Brahman and which distinguishes Him from all other entities (Carman 1974: 103–4).

As a third exegetical strategy, Rāmānuja resorts to the concept of scriptural harmony (*samanvaya*) to re-interpret passages such as *Kena Upaniṣad* 2.3, which states:

> it is envisioned by one who envisions it not; but one who envisions it knows it not. And those who perceive it perceive it not; but it is perceived by those who perceive it not.
>
> (Kena Up 2.3)

According to Śaṅkara, in this upaniṣad:

> it is first said that the projection of the world procccds from the Absolute. And in the end it is declared that one finds perfect stability bringing freedom from all fear, in identifying oneself with the absolute bereft of all relation with the perceptible and imperceptible aspects of the world.
>
> (Sarasvati 1989: 75)

So, while one's inner Self, Brahman as pure consciousness, is beyond the distinctions of subject, object, and the act of knowing, the realization of this Self is initialized through the study of scripture (Hirst 2005: 39ff; Rambachan 1991: 113–16).

Rāmānuja replies that if indeed Brahman is not an object of knowledge as the objector claims, then other scriptural passages such as *he who knows Brahman attains the highest* (Taitt Up 2.1.1), *he who knows Brahman becomes Brahman himself* (Muṇḍ Up 3.2.9) that speak of the effect of the knowledge of Brahman would contradict the Advaita reading of *Kena Upaniṣad*. Note here, that the Muṇḍ Up passage is more conducive as support for the Advaita perspective. However, Rāmānuja counters that this cannot be the meaning of Muṇḍ Up 3.2.9, otherwise passages which affirm the identity of Brahman with the world such as, *Brahman, you see, is this whole world. With inner tranquility, one should venerate it as jalān*[25] (Ch Up 3.14.1) would be meaningless. Rāmānuja as we mentioned earlier takes Brahman's originative causality as one of the defining features of the divine essential nature, and so this passage which identifies Brahman with the world can only make sense if Brahman is understood as a differentiated whole and the knowledge of *such a* Brahman is stated in scripture to be of the form of worship and meditation.

Lastly, the Major Objection also cites *Brahma Sūtras* (Br Sū) as support for an attribute-less Brahman.[26] Though the Br Sū is a smṛti text, since it is a summary text of the meaning of śruti, it is deemed as a relevant source after the śruti citations. For instance Br Sū 3.2.11 is utilized which states, *not even according to place, two fold characteristics belong to the highest for everywhere (it is taught)*. This *sūtra* is meant to reconcile two types of śruti, the ones that affirm that Brahman possesses attributes and those that claim that it is devoid of any qualities. Śaṅkara argues in his commentary on this *sūtra* that it is not logical to uphold both these assertions in regard to Brahman and concludes that those texts that speak of Brahman endowed with qualities are simply due to limiting adjuncts which result from ignorance. Rāmānuja on the other hand, utilizing VP 6.5.84–85 and VP 1.22.53, argues essentially what he has done in his exegesis of Muṇḍ Upa 1.1.5–6 which we mentioned earlier. This strongly suggests that Rāmānuja needs VP particulars to interpret śruti passages according to Viśiṣṭādvaita. This is a rather ingenious exegetical move and we have come across this even in the VS where he cites BhG passages as support for his point of view, but his reading of those very verses (in the *Bhagavadgītābhāṣya*) utilize the VP. Thus this purāṇa is, in a sense, the thread (*sūtra*) on which hangs Rāmānuja's interpretations of scripture through his various texts and commentaries.

In summary, some of the exegetical strategies Rāmānuja employs to interpret śruti to refute the Advaita interpretation of śruti are: to utilize the soul–body paradigm coupled with his view of Brahman's originative causality to re-interpret concepts of diversity and manifoldness; the concept of Brahman's dual characteristics (*ubhayaliṅga*) and also the use of the concept of scriptural harmony (*samanvaya*) to reconcile contradictions within texts on the nature of Brahman. Moreover, in some of the *Brahma Sūtras* that are cited, Rāmānuja utilizes the VP to interpret the *sūtra* according to Viśiṣṭādvaita. What is striking in this polemic on the interpretation of śruti is that he engages with the Advaitin only in so far as to argue against a quality-less Brahman, whereas in his engagement with smṛti, which immediately follows and which he himself introduces, he broadens the scope of this rather limited definition of Brahman.

In the next two sections we discuss Rāmānuja's citations from the BhG and VP as support for his views on the nature of Brahman. Again, these passages are not cited in the Major Objection. The insertion of such smṛti support in the Major Conclusion is significant, particularly the VP, because the vocabulary Rāmānuja utilizes to define Brahman in his summary statement is taken entirely from this purāṇa, details essential to support the very paradigms (soul–body and so on) he has utilized to read śruti.

Bhagavadgītā support

Prior to citing passages from the VP, Rāmānuja also quotes eight verses from the BhG that he has not had the Advaitin utilize in the Major Objection. The main function of the BhG passages is to foreshadow the content of the VP. In a sense they give more information than the śruti, but considerably less than the subsequent VP verses. The first BhG passage is taken from Chapter 10 traditionally referred to as *vibhūtiyoga* that emphasizes Kṛṣṇa's lordship over creation. As we saw earlier in this chapter, in Rāmānuja's summary statement, the concept of the world as a manifestation (*vibhūti*) of Brahman is one of the ways in which the Advaita view of Brahman is countered. According to

Rāmānuja, BhG 10.3 ab, *he who knows me as unborn, beginning-less and the great Lord of the universe*[27] conveys the knowledge of Kṛṣṇa's true nature (*yāthātmyaviṣayajñāna*), specifically as the supreme creator and controller over his created manifestation which he pervades (Carman 1974: 140). This BhG passage is also indirectly related to the VP.

In his *Bhagavadgītābhāṣya*, commenting on BhG 10.3, Rāmānuja references VP 6.7.46ff on the three innate tendencies (*bhāvana*) that characterize all embodied beings.[28] *Karmabhāvana* is the suitability to work, *brahmabhāvana* translates as fitness for meditation and yoga, and *ubhayabhāvana* is the capability to engage in both actions and meditation. All beings operate within these three propensities and the point of the VP is that Brahman is unique in that he is beyond such tendencies, which fall under the purview of matter and *saṃsāra*. The importance of this section of the VP, called the *Śubhāśrayaprakaraṇa* (*Treatise on the Auspicious Object*) is solely devoted to the description of Viṣṇu as the most auspicious and worthy object of meditation, who as the supreme reality, is indeed a unique being, both creator and the created and stands as the controller of his manifest creation. The fact that the commentary on BhG 10.3ab itself which is cited here as evidence depends on the VP, highlights Rāmānuja's dependence on the VP as a text that is crucial even for reading the BhG in a "correct" way.

While BhG 10ab is meant to support Rāmānuja's view of Brahman as the supporter and controller of a world that is his glorious manifestation, the next two BhG passages highlight another aspect of Viṣṇu's lordship:

> All beings abide in me, however I do not abide in them.
>
> (BhG 9.4cd)

> And yet beings do not abide in me. Behold my divine yoga
> I am the upholder of all beings and yet I do not abide in them
> My will keeps them in existence.[29]
>
> (BhG 9.5)

According to Rāmānuja's commentary on these passages the idea of Brahman as the abider or pervader of all creation (9.4cd) intimates that he is the inner controller and the master (*śeṣin*) who rules and controls the world that he pervades. So too 9.5, where he interprets *upholder of beings* as the supporter who sustains all simply with his will. These two BhG passages along with 10.3 highlight the important aspects of the soul–body paradigm of the support/supported (*ādhāra*/*ādheya*), controller/controlled (*niyanta*/*niyamana*), and master/servant (*śeṣin*/*śeṣa*) (Carman 1974: 127ff). Though these BhG passages as Rāmānuja interprets them seem more comprehensive in refuting the Advaita view of an attribute-less Brahman than śruti, the specific details that provide evidence for this soul–body relationship itself is mentioned only in the VP.

Rāmānuja also cites BhG 10.42cd, 7.6cd, 7.7, 15.17, and 15.18 in his Major Conclusion. In his commentary on all these BhG passages he utilizes the VP. I discuss the importance of this purāṇa in countering an Advaita interpretation of these BhG verses in Chapter 4.[30] The use of the BhG prior to the VP signals its importance within Vedāntic circles. After all, it was one of the three foundational texts of Vedānta philosophy in addition to the *Brahma Sūtras* and the upaniṣads. More importantly, Rāmānuja takes Kṛṣṇa's instructions as a "theological directive" seriously as he understands the BhG as Brahman's self-revelation (Ram-Prasad 2013: 112). So, how can we evaluate the contribution of the BhG passages on the nature of Brahman? The fact that the VP is utilized to interpret a majority of these BhG passages illustrates the importance of this purāṇa and that Rāmānuja has it in mind regardless of whether he's commenting on the upaniṣads, the *Brahma Sūtras* or the *Bhagavadgītā*. As we shall see in Chapter 4 on the *Bhagavadgītābhāṣya*, though the BhG itself may provide Rāmānuja with the general Viśiṣṭādvaita framework, much more so than some śruti, the VP is essential for particulars that serve as evidence for important doctrines such as the soul–body paradigm and to his overall project of establishing certain scripture as expositions of Viśiṣṭādvaita Vedānta.

Viṣṇu Purāṇa support

Thus far, to support the nature of Brahman as envisioned in Viśiṣṭādvaita, Rāmānuja has countered the Advaita interpretation of śruti cited in the Major Objection and has then gone on to provide evidence from the BhG. Subsequently, he cites an additional thirty VP passages as support. Though at first, it may seem that he has primarily relied on śruti and then cited smṛti as support, it is the VP that provides concepts salient to his philosophy that are lacking in śruti, at least the ones that he has utilized. In the previous section we saw that even smṛti passages such as the BhG need the VP to interpret Kṛṣṇa as the supreme Brahman eternally differentiated and as the ensouler of creation. While Rāmānuja imposes the soul–body paradigm to read śruti, the VP is the source, where he finds direct evidence of such a relationship to begin with, at least in this particular section of his Br Sū commentary.

The rest of this section evaluates the significance of some of the VP passages, which provide details on the nature of Brahman not found in śruti. The first set of passages (VP 6.5.83–87) is taken from Chapter 6.5 of the purāṇa describes the various types of dissolutions, hells, and heavens, and ends with a syllabic exegesis of the term "Lord" (*bhagavān*), which is said to primarily denote Vāsudeva, the Supreme Brahman (VP 6.5.5.69–79):

> O' sage, He is beyond matter that comprises all beings, its modifications[31] and faults such as those arising due to the qualities of matter. Beyond all

> concealment, He is the self of all, and in this way[32] invincible, He pervades whatever is in the intermediate region.[33]
>
> (VP 6.5.83)

> His nature is constituted of all auspicious qualities, he supports the whole of creation with a small part of his power; assuming at will any desired form, He accomplishes the good of the world.[34]
>
> (VP 6.5.84)

> He is a collection of qualities such as splendor, strength, sovereignty, knowledge, renown, and power. He is the highest of the high, who is the lord of the high and low devoid of faults and so on.[35]
>
> (VP 6.5.85)

> He is the lord, has the form of separate and aggregate matter, He has the essential nature of the unmanifest and manifest; He is the lord of everything, seeing everything, omniscient, having power over everything, and called the highest lord.[36]
>
> (VP 6.5.86)

> That by which it (Brahman) is understood as devoid of faults, pure, highly stainless, of one form,
> that is knowledge; all else is called ignorance.[37]
>
> (VP 6.5.87)

In his re-interpretation of Muṇḍ Up 1.1.5–6 earlier, Rāmānuja depends on the concept of *ubhayaliṅgatva*, the fact that Brahman possesses auspicious qualities and is, in addition, devoid of any fault or imperfections associated with matter. This is in contrast to the Advaitin, for whom this upaniṣad conveys a Brahman who is devoid of any qualities. Since the upaniṣad itself does not mention particulars to support either view, the VP, which is much more direct on this issue serves a significant purpose. VP 6.5.83 rejects Brahman's association with matter and the faults thereof and read together with 6.5.84–85 which states Brahman as *beyond all concealment*, *invincible* and as the repository of auspicious qualities, offers direct evidence of the dual nature of Brahman. As far as the nature of the world and its relationship to Brahman go, these passages in no uncertain terms assert creation as a positive manifestation of Brahman. Even while rejecting Brahman's association with matter, these verses speak of the world of *separate and aggregate matter* as His form (*rūpa*) and the *unmanifest and manifest* as comprising his essential nature (*svarūpa*).

Additionally, support for the reality of the world and its connection to Brahman is found in VP 6.5.84. That Brahman incarnates and is concerned with world welfare contradicts the Advaita perspective. The concept of Viṣṇu's incarnation has no reference in śruti that Rāmānuja has utilized. Moreover, the commentator on the ŚBh, Sudarśanasūri, connects the incarnation of Viṣṇu to a worshipable form of the deity, he states that when the VP claims that "He accomplishes the good of the world by means of this very descent", the use of this (form) as a *vigraha* (worshipable form) is established.[38] The term *vigraha* suggests a concrete image, perceptible to the human eye. Both Rāmānuja and the commentator contextualize the world, incarnations, devotion and worship as relevant and real contra-Advaita. For Śaṅkara, Brahman as the Lord over his creation who incarnates periodically is a possibility only in the realm of ignorance.

The VP passages that follow, 6.5.86–87, affirm the identity between Brahman and the world and, at the same time, underscore His difference from them precisely because he is bereft of the faults of matter *(prakṛti)*. The fact that 6.5.86 states that matter and spirit are the very form (*rūpa*) of Brahman over which he exercises power, also contradicts the Advaita view of an attribute-less Brahman alone as real. The commentator notes that:

> the expression *separate and aggregate matter*, stands for the whole of intelligent beings, in their condition (*avasthā*) of cause and effect … That Brahman has these as his form means that they constitute His body. That Brahman has this manifestation as His essential nature (*svarūpa*) means that it is a body unique to Him alone.[39]

As Brahman's body, creation in its manifest and unmanifest forms is real. And as His body, it does not affect the essential purity of Brahman. VP 6.7.87 then goes on to define knowledge of Brahman as the possessor of a body over which he is sovereign.

We mentioned earlier that though these VP passages are clear on the nature of Brahman as Rāmānuja envisions it, there are some phrases that are problematic and can be taken as supportive of the Advaita perspective. Two phrases in VP 6.5.83 might be seen as problematic, that Brahman *is the self of all* and that *he pervades* certain cosmic regions, which are Advaitic in tenor. However, as we have already seen in the discussion of BhG 9.4cd and 9.5, Rāmānuja interprets pervasion in the context of the soul–body relationship. To refute the Advaita interpretation of the world as unreal, the commentator of the ŚBh interprets pervasion (*āstṛta*), in VP 6.5.83, as follows: "in the intermediate region (6.5.83) means within the two-fold manifestation (*vibhūti*)".[40] This is a reference to the world of sport/creation (*līlāvibhūti*) and the eternal manifestation (*nityavibhūti*) which comprises the supreme glorious manifestation (*anantamahāvibhūti*) of Viṣṇu in later Śrīvaiṣṇavism. The introduction of the concept of *vibhūti* is meant to refute the Advaita concept of the empirical reality as an illusion.[41] Even in the VS, using the concept of *vibhūti*, Rāmānuja prevails over the Advaita idea of the world as illusion. Thus the VP is not entirely amenable to a Viśiṣṭādvaitic reading and after all Rāmānuja has the Advaitin cite this very purāṇa as support in the Major Objection; however, he weaves together passages from various sections of the purāṇa to accentuate details such as world as the form (*rūpa*) of Brahman and creation as an essential nature (*svarūpa*) of Brahman that assist him greatly.

The next four VP passages (6.7.70–72; 1.22.51) introduce the reason for creation as well as present more information on the different forms of Brahman. I will only discuss VP passages 6.7.70–71 here, as VP 6.7.72 and 1.22.51 assert the transcendence of Brahman from the world, which is a concept also mentioned in śruti:

> O' King, where all these powers are established, that is another
> great form of Hari, that is a different form[42] from the universal form.[43]
>
> (VP 6.7.70)

> Out of His own playfulness, He causes that form, endowed with all powers to manifest as gods, animals, men, and so on.[44]
>
> (VP 6.7.71)

The first passage affirms two forms of Brahman: the *universal form* of Hari *wherein the three powers of Viṣṇu are established* and the *great form of Hari*. The former is the very form that manifests itself as created beings and is mentioned in earlier passages of the same VP chapter (6.7.60–61) and also in VP 6.7.71 here. The second form, the great form of Hari, is the divine form or *divyarūpa* discussed in the VS from which result the various incarnations of Viṣṇu. The concept of divine sport (*līlā*) and the fact that the world is simply a transformation of one of the forms of Viṣṇu also affirms creation and its positive relationship to Brahman. This association between Brahman and the world as a vital part of the nature of the supreme reality is a strong critique of Advaita.

Brahman as the inner self of both individual selves and matter is addressed in VP 1.2.10–14[45] and VP 6.4.39–40, and forms the basis for the soul–body paradigm that Rāmānuja takes for granted in his earlier re-interpretation of śruti such as Ch Up 6.2.3:

> The supreme self is the highest of the high, the highest self; He abides in the self
> and is devoid of distinguishing attributes such as form, color, and so on.[46]
>
> (VP 1.2.10)

> He is everywhere, and all things abide in him,
> therefore He is called Vāsudeva by the learned.[47]
>
> (VP 1.2.12)

> That Brahman is the highest, eternal, unborn, imperishable, and indivisible
> of one essential nature and is pure, always devoid of faults.[48]
>
> (VP 1.2.13)

> That alone is all this, possessing the essential nature of manifest and unmanifest;
> and also existing in the form of the individual self (*puruṣa*) and time.[49]
>
> (VP 1.2.14)

In 1.2.10, Brahman as *the highest self* is said to *abide in the self*, thereby distinguishing the individual self from Brahman, for Rāmānuja. This verse clarifies the ambiguity we saw with VP 6.5.83, where Brahman is declared as the *self of all*, which had an Advaitic tenor. The commentator also notes that with this phrase, Brahman's continuity with things (*vastvapariccheda*) is established.[50] That is, as the inner self of individual selves and matter, the originative causal link with Brahman is ever present. Whereas in VP 6.5.86 all things as forms of Brahman is mentioned, here, Brahman as the inner self of the (individual) self, highlights the soul–body paradigm.[51] Two other concepts from this previous verse (6.5.86) are also echoed in VP 1.12.13–14. First, to illustrate the positive relation of Brahman to the world, these two passages speak of the world as an essential nature (*svarūpa*) of Brahman which we find in VP 6.5.86 as well.

Second, while describing Brahman as completely transcendent, entirely different from any other entity, and of one essential nature (*ekasvarūpa*), the VP also describes him as possessing the essential nature of the manifest and the unmanifest (*vyaktāvyaktasvarūpa*). To define creation as an aspect of Brahman's essential nature in this way conclusively denies the status of the world as only provisionally real. Having stressed the innate difference between creation and Brahman, Rāmānuja affirms Brahman as the source from which everything manifests and is reabsorbed.[52] The fact that 1.2.10–14 articulate different aspects that comprise the soul–body relationship makes the discussion of emanation and reabsorption of the world from and into Brahman distinct from that of Śaṅkara who also asserts the same, though not in an ultimate sense.

VP 1.2.14 mentions individual self (*puruṣa*) and matter (*prakṛti*) as powers or forms of Brahman and these next two passages from VP 1.22 are an elaboration of this concept. The fact that Rāmānuja cites passages from the beginning of Book One, Chapter 1.2 and then the last chapter of the same book 1.22, suggests that for him, this purāṇa as a coherent whole supports his Vedānta:

> Brahman has two forms,[53] embodied and unembodied; these two forms, perishable and imperishable, exist in all beings.
>
> (VP 1.22.53)

> The imperishable is the highest Brahman, the perishable is this entire world. Just as fire situated in one place spreads all around, so is this whole world the manifestation of Brahman's power.[54]
>
> (VP 1.22.54)

There may also be another reason that Rāmānuja mentions passages from VP 1.2 and VP 1.22 in conjunction. There is some ambiguity here as to what the *imperishable* in 1.22.53 denotes. Having stated that two forms of Brahman, the perishable and imperishable exist in all things, it is identified as the world, that is, the world of matter, whereas the imperishable is said to be the highest Brahman Himself. It is difficult to identify the imperishable here with the individual self which is mentioned in 1.2.14. Rāmānuja, however, reads this in the context of the soul–body paradigm. According to him, the statement *the imperishable is the highest Brahman* can refer to the individual self through *sāmānādhikaraṇya*. That is, the individual self can be referred to as Brahman, since Brahman has already been stated to be the inner self of the individual self in VP 1.2.10. Subsequent to this, Rāmānuja discusses the essential nature of the individual self and the concealment of the attributive nature of the individual self by karma (VP 6.7.61–63). I shall not discuss these here, as these passages are addressed in the section on the individual self in Chapter 2. However, they illustrate that we cannot speak of Brahman's nature without taking individual selves and matter into account.

Rāmānuja concludes the section on the nature of Brahman by citing two more passages from the VP:

> O' wise one, matter (*pradhāna*) and individual self (*puruṣa*) are enveloped by the power of Viṣṇu, which is the self residing in all beings.
>
> (VP 2.7.29)

> That same power is the cause of their separation and conjunction.[55]
>
> (VP 2.7.30ab)

Viṣṇu as the inner self residing in all beings wills (*saṃkalpa*) the association and dissociation of matter and individual selves. These passages again, could be read in an Advaita context; however, when read together with the previous VP passages they yield a different interpretation. Note that even in the state of dissolution, matter (*prakṛti*) and the individual selves (*puruṣa*) dissociate due to Brahman's will, but continue to exist as attributes of Brahman. Elaborating on the lordship of Brahman over his attributes, the individual self and matter, he quotes two more passages to decisively refute Brahman's direct association with them:

> Just as the wind when it touches water carries hundreds of drops so does the power of Viṣṇu carry the world consisting of *pradhāna* and *puruṣa*.[56]
>
> (VP 2.7.31)

> O' best among sages, this world, which undergoes modifications due to expansion, contraction, birth, and decay is imperishable and eternal.[57]
>
> (VP 1.22.58)

The claim in VP 1.22.58 that the world is eternal and imperishable coincides with Rāmānuja's thesis that Brahman is an eternally differentiated being and so matter (*prakṛti*) and individual self (*puruṣa*) are eternal. Thus change or transformation does not render *prakṛti* non-eternal, since as an eternal component of Brahman's body it merely undergoes change in its condition. The commentator expands on the metaphor of wind and rain used to convey this transcendent, yet immanent nature of Brahman:

> The example illustrates the distinction of the cause from the effect. The wind carries the drops of water away from it separately. Or else the example is illustrative of conjunction and separation: the wind carries the drops mutually connected or separated. Or else, the example illustrates that Viṣṇu is free from any traces of defects due to his association with matter and individual selves. Indeed the wind carries hundreds of drops of water without being affected in its nature.[58]

From these passages Rāmānuja finds support for what he has claimed is the nature of Brahman in his summary statement mentioned earlier: that the highest Brahman is declared by nature to be free from even the slightest of faults, is comprised of all auspicious qualities, and engages out of sport in the creation, preservation, destruction of the world, which is not an illusion but the divine body (*śarīra,rūpa*, *śakti*, *vibhūti*) itself. Ignorance itself is karma that conceals and is also real. The inner differentiation of Brahman comprised of matter and individual selves is a concept that is most clearly articulated in the thirty passages he introduces in the Major Conclusion to counter the *prima facie* view of attribute-less Brahman in the Major Objection.

In conclusion, based on the specifics from the VP, Rāmānuja states that the concepts of manifestation (*vibhūti*) and so on can be equated to the term "that" (Ch Up 6.8.7) by *sāmāṇādhikaraṇya* or co-ordinate predication. He understands this śruti to equate two different states (*avasthā*) of Brahman: the term *you* which refers to Brahman as the inner self of the individual self, and the term *that* denotes Brahman as the creator. Both these conditions of Brahman are non-different but not due to the fact that one's inner most self is ultimately Brahman itself.

As we mentioned at the beginning of this chapter, Rāmānuja has the Advaitin, in the Major Objection, also cite VP and BhG passages along with śruti discussed in this section. Rāmānuja has not addressed the smṛti support, BhG and VP from the Major Objection, yet. He proceeds to do this after his introduction of these VP passages. While certain VP passages are mentioned in the Major Objection as support of a non-dual Brahman, as the Advaitin envisions it, Rāmānuja claims that the context of these passages is in fact the individual self and not Brahman. Thus, utilizing the same VP evidence that supports the *prima facie* view of the attribute-less Brahman, Rāmānuja re-interprets these in his Major Conclusion. The next section examines his re-interpretation of the VP passages cited in the Major Objection as support.

The nature of the individual self

In reclaiming the VP as a Viśiṣṭādvaitic text, Rāmānuja undertakes a detailed analysis of the context of the VP passages cited in the Major Objection. He argues that the VP does not support a quality-less (*nirguṇa*) Brahman as the Advaitin claims, rather these passages refer to the individual self in its essential nature. For the Advaitin, the metaphysical reality of the individual self is not an issue of much importance, as it is for Rāmānuja. In ŚBrSuBh 1.2.6, Śaṅkara comments that "the supreme self is loosely spoken of by the immature souls as the embodied individual soul, taken to be limited by its apparent conditioning adjuncts, the body, sense-organs, mind and intellect ... this remains true as long as the teaching of the existence and the sole reality of the self in the text 'that thou art' has not been properly assimilated" (Sarasvati 1989: 59). Rāmānuja's counter-claim that the eleven VP passages cited in the Major Objection address the individual self rather than Brahman undercuts the *prima facie* view significantly. To establish the metaphysical reality of the individual self, three[59] important concepts are addressed: the essential nature of the self, the metaphysical reality of a plurality of individual selves, and Brahman as distinct even from the individual self that is liberated.

The essential nature of the individual self

The first VP passage utilized by the Advaitin to support a quality-less Brahman is VP 6.7.53:

> That in which distinctions have disappeared, which is only pure existence, inexpressible by words, self-knowing, knowing that is called knowing Brahman.[60]

It is easy to see why the Advaitin claims that the topic of discussion here is Brahman. Rāmānuja, however, launches into an exegesis of VP 6.7 to establish the individual self as the topic of discussion. VP 6.7.53 is part of the *Śubhāśrayaprakaraṇa* (*Treatise on the Auspicious Object*),[61] which is an important section for Rāmānuja. Indeed we have come across his use of this section of the VP in both the VS and the ŚBh (section on the nature of Brahman). To reiterate briefly, in VP 6.7, yoga is declared as the only means for the cessation of *saṃsāra* and then a detailed explanation of the various steps of this yogic path are stated. The discussion then turns to a worthy and appropriate object of meditation. The purāṇa posits as possibilities two forms (*rūpa*) of Viṣṇu, denoted as his two powers (*śakti*)—the unembodied power and the embodied power, that is the individual self in its essential nature and the embodied individual self associated with matter called ignorance (*avidyā*) or karma. Karma also is a power of Viṣṇu. After denying that these forms of Brahman, the embodied individual self and the unembodied individual self, are worthy as objects of meditation, the VP claims that only the universal form of Brahman that is the source of these three powers qualifies as the auspicious object of meditation.

Based on this interpretation of the context of VP 6.7, Rāmānuja elaborates:

> VP 6.7.53, declares that the essential nature of the self, even when associated with particular modifications of matter (*prakṛti*) such as gods, men and so on, is inexpressible by words which denote such distinctions, because it is devoid of distinctions existing in them; that it is defined solely as consisting of knowledge and existence; and that it is self-knowing, i.e., it is not known to the mind of one who is not competent in yoga. Therefore, from this passage the negation of the world does not follow.[62]

It is only when the individual self associates with matter that distinctions arise. That which is denoted as "Brahman" in VP 6.7.53 is, according to Rāmānuja, a form of Brahman, i.e., the individual self in its essential nature, which is eventually rejected for the divine form of Viṣṇu as an object worthy of meditation.[63] The VP passage cannot be used as support of a quality-less Brahman as has the Advaitin since the topic of discussion here is the individual self. The knowledge of the essential nature of the individual self is *knowing Brahman*. Thus *knowing Brahman* mentioned in the purāṇa is according to Rāmānuja knowing the essential nature of the individual self as the "body" of Brahman.

The second passage in the Major Objection that is provided as support for an attribute-less Brahman is VP 1.2.6:

> Him alone, who in reality is of the nature of knowledge and is infinitely pure,
> and who nevertheless exists in the form of material entities due to illusion.[64]
>
> (VP 1.2.6)

For the Advaitin, Brahman, which is of the nature of knowledge, is masked by adjuncts that arise due to ignorance. This one Brahman then, is said to exist in myriad forms such that it *seems* to be embodied. This continues until ignorance is sublated by true realization. Rāmānuja replies that:

> because it is said in the *śāstra* (VP) that Viṣṇu who is the highest Brahman is devoid even of any taint due to faults such as ignorance and so on, who is comprised of all auspicious qualities and who possesses the glorious manifestation (*mahāvibhūti*), it is not possible to have an illusory vision in regard to him. Moreover, it will be established immediately hereafter, saying that the world and Brahman are one due to their *sāmānādhikaraṇya*; it does not allow either one to be sublated, and is incontrovertible.[65]

Since the world and Brahman are equated by *sāmānādhikaraṇya*, due to the soul–body relationship, the world as the manifestation of Viṣṇu cannot be sublated as the Advaitin claims.

The context of VP 1.2 itself does not support the unreality of the world and the necessity of its sublation prior to liberation. VP 1.2 begins with Parāśara paying homage to the eternal, unchangeable Viṣṇu (1.2.1) and this is followed by a eulogy first to his three forms—the trinity of Brahmā, Hari, and Śaṅkara (1.2.2) and then his other forms such as embodied and unembodied selves (*sthūlasūkṣmātman*), and single and aggregate entities (*avyaktavyaktabhūta*) (1.2.3–4). Based on this, Rāmānuja argues that from the commencement of this purāṇa itself the reality of the world as a form of Brahman is affirmed and cannot thus support creation as illusory. However, Rāmānuja's perspective is not entirely unproblematic. The purāṇa still discussing the nature of Viṣṇu refers to Him as *of the nature of knowledge* and as existing in material form due to illusion (1.2.6). Clearly, it is Viṣṇu that VP 1.2.6 is addressing, but Rāmānuja interprets this verse as a reference to a form of Brahman, the individual self (*kṣetrajña*) that is embodied in *saṃsāra*. This interpretation of 1.2.6 is rather forced and there is no rationale in the content of the VP itself to conclude that this passage addresses the individual self. To counter this, Rāmānuja spends considerable effort and invokes the principle of scriptural harmony (*samanvaya*) to support his interpretation.

According to him one of the reasons as to why VP 1.2.6 does not articulate the Advaita view of Brahman is because it conflicts with śruti such as *Taittirīya Upaniṣad* 3.1.1: *that from which these beings are born; which once born, they live and into whom they pass upon death—seek to perceive that! That is Brahman!*[66] According to Rāmānuja, this upaniṣad passage teaches that Brahman is the cause of the world and as such the effect cannot be unreal and mirrors the commencement of VP 1.2. However, Rāmānuja is aware that alternate interpretations are also possible for this śruti, so he launches immediately into a passionate argument on the importance of smṛti (VP) and the principle of corroboration. He begins with a *Mahābhārata* (MBh) verse and then elaborates:

> The Veda should be amplified by the itihāsas and purāṇas.
> The Veda fears that he of little learning will do me wrong.
>
> (MBh 1.1.264)

> This is what is taught by scripture 'the act of amplifying' the meaning of epics (*itihāsa*) and *purāṇa*. To amplify means to gain a clear perception of the meaning of Vedic passages known to oneself, by means of the statements of those who know the entire Veda and its meaning and those who have directly perceived the essential nature of the Veda and its meaning, by means of the great power of their yoga. Indeed, amplification of Veda ought to be done, because without it one cannot reach a settled conclusion, since the knowledge of all the branches (of the Veda) is not comprehensible from listening to a small portion.[67]

In no uncertain terms Rāmānuja asserts that Taitt Up 3.1.1 cannot be read without the help of *the aid of those who know the entire Veda and its meaning,* such as the sage Parāśara of the VP who possessed the true knowledge of Brahman. And it is with this intention of amplifying his own knowledge of the Veda that Maitreya himself appeals to Parāśara for instruction (VP 1.1.6–7). Because Maitreya is well-versed in the Veda, his queries in the VP could not possibly contradict an important śruti text such as the Taitt Up 3.1.1. Moreover, the content of the upaniṣad itself is understood as an ideal response to questions posed in the VP such as:

> I wish to hear from you, O' knower of dharma, how this world came into existence, what it will become again, O' reverend one.
>
> (VP 1.1.4)

> What does the world consist of, wherefrom all the movable and immovable entities have arisen?
> Where was it resting? And into what will it be absorbed?[68]
>
> (VP 1.1.5)

In response to 1.1.4–5, the VP, in agreement with Taitt Up 3.1.1, according to Rāmānuja goes on to state that Brahman is the material and efficient cause of the world. The reply to Maitreya's question, *What does the world consist of?* which enquires about the nature of the creation, is given at the end of VP 1.1 in passage 31 as *this world is Brahman.*[69] That is Brahman as the cause of the world *is* this very world.

Rāmānuja is quick to point out that Brahman as the inner ruler or self of the world is the reason for this identity and it is not due to substantial oneness (*vastvaikya*). The concept of soul–body relationship is used to interpret the concept of pervasion in the VP passages themselves.[70] He reasons that the Advaita understanding of VP 1.2.6 as instruction on attribute-less Brahman cannot be justified as all the questions and answers in the VP, prior to this verse, would be inappropriate if the purāṇa was in fact a text devoted to the elucidation of the illusory nature of the world.

Thus not only is VP 1.2.6 to be understood in accordance with the broader scriptural tradition of the upaniṣads (Taitt Up 3.1.1) but also with the commencement and subsequent sections of the purāṇa as well. If in fact, the VP is understood to affirm Brahman whose nature is consciousness devoid of attributes, then the subject matter in the chapters that follow, that is 1.3, would not be understandable. Rāmānuja elaborates:

> If the VP is meant to establish that illusion based on Brahman, who is solely comprised of knowledge and without attributes, then there would be no place for the question:
> How is it possible for Brahman who is without qualities, unknowable, pure, and free from faults

to be the agent of creation, and the like.

(VP 1.3.1)

nor for the answer to it:

> O' best of ascetics, there are in all things powers which cannot be brought within the realm of the knowable
> and for that very reason those creative acts constitute the inherent powers of Brahman like heat constitutes the inherent power of fire.[71]
>
> (VP 1.3.2–2ab)

For Rāmānuja the VP itself by its context illustrates that creative agency is a peculiar power of Brahman alone, just as heat is the peculiar nature of fire and not of, for instance, water. However, if the world is thought to be an illusion, then all these passages of this purāṇa would be contradicted. Appealing to the harmony across different scriptures and harmony within a particular scripture (VP) seems to be Rāmānuja's main exegetical strategy in this rather lengthy reinterpretion of VP 1.2.6.

Plurality of individual selves

Having established the essential nature of the individual self, Rāmānuja reinterprets the next set of VP passages cited in the Major Objection. These are said to affirm Brahman as the sole reality, but in the Major Conclusion, he argues instead that they support the plurality of individual selves:

> Although he is to be found in one's own body and in that of others knowledge which is one, is, indeed the reality; dualists see things wrongly.[72]
>
> (VP 2.14.31)

While the Advaitin understands this passage as reference to Brahman, Rāmānuja does not agree. For him, the topic of discussion is the individual self and the purāṇa affirms the similar essential nature of individual selves though present in various bodies. Due to the associations with various physical forms the individual selves are seen as of different types. Note that Rāmānuja affirms the plurality of individual selves, but rejects their multiplicity based on difference in their essential nature, which is consciousness/knowledge. He elaborates:

> What is stated in this passage (VP 2.14.31), is that since all individual selves are similar because they are solely comprised of knowledge, the view of duality in the individual selves as though their association with specific modifications of matter, known as gods etc. denotes that they possess such a nature, is wrong.[73]

> The duality that exists in relation to masses of matter and in relation to different individual selves is not denied. It means that, the entity called the self, which associates with masses of varied, wonderful matter such as gods, men, etc., is all alike.[74]

Individual selves are countless but since all are similar in their essential natures they are all understood to be alike. The duality that exists between the individual self and the body/matter is not denied because 2.14.31 claims that something that is other than the body is found in one's own body and in those of others. Whereas, for the Advaitin the distinction spoken of here is a distinction between Brahman the sole reality and everything else, for Rāmānuja it is the distinction between the individual self and matter that is elucidated here.

As support for this interpertation of VP 2.14.31, Rāmānuja turns to what he claims has been stated by the Lord himself (*yathoktam bhagavatā*) in BhG 5.18 cd-19. These verses refer to the equanimity with which the advanced sages look upon a dog and an outcaste and view Brahman, devoid of all defects, as the same in all beings. Once again, the Advaitic sensibility of these BhG passages is evident as the subject of discussion is Brahman. Rāmānuja, however, reads the term "Brahman" as the individual self (*ātman*). Why? Commenting on BhG 5.16, in his *Bhagavadgītābhāṣya*, he explains that the plurality of individual selves is not due to adjuncts super-imposed on Brahman, but rather is the result of the contraction of the attributive consciousness of the individual self due to embodiment. We have already discussed this topic in Chapter 2. Rāmānuja seems to be making a subtle exegetical move here. What he is really concerned with is the rationale for the acceptance a plurality of selves. While the Advaitin claims that the plurality of individual selves is due to the effect of adjuncts, Rāmānuja does not deny the metaphysical reality of a plurality of selves or their embodiment, but simply rejects the Advaita reasoning. Though the use of BhG passages may not seem convincing, the point of citing them at this point is to convey that the term "Brahman" need not in fact refer to the supreme reality but rather can denote the individual self. Also, the authority of the BhG as Kṛṣṇa's self-revelation and the interpretation of BhG 5.18–19 as Viśiṣṭādvaitic perhaps validate their authority as well. Similarly, Rāmānuja interprets the next VP passage cited in the Major Objection as affirming the non-difference between individual selves based on their essential nature, which is all the same, but as rather due to physical embodiment:

> If there were anything else (*anya*) like me, or anything else (*para*) different from me,
> only then would it be proper to say that such a thing is me and such a thing is not me.[75]
>
> (VP 2.13.86)

Rāmānuja understands this passage to mean:

> if any individual self other than my own self is different in nature from consciousness which is my nature, then it is possible to say "I am of this nature," "he is of a different nature." However, this is not so, because all individual selves are equal as comprised of the same knowledge.[76]

The Advaitin reads VP 2.13.86 as evidence of Brahman, the sole reality:

> If there were any other thing than me then alone would it be possible to say that such a thing is me and such a thing is not me.
>
> (VP 2.13.86)

But Rāmānuja appeals to grammatical reasoning to refute the Advaita interpretation:

> In this passage the identity among individual selves is not taught, because it is not possible to use the word *para* and the word *anya* in one and the same sense as "if there were any one other than me." [See objector's translation above.] Indeed, the word *para* denotes another self which is distinct from one's own self, and, inasmuch as that self is also altogether of the nature of intelligence, the word *anya* denies that its nature is different from mine.[77]

He concludes in regard to VP 2.13.86 that since liberated selves are all comprised of knowledge, it is not possible to say one is different from the other as they are all, in this sense, of the same kind.

The difference denied is the one that exists between the true nature of the individual self, which is knowledge, and the perceived nature of the self as possessing material qualities. This is exemplified in the next VP passage, according to Rāmānuja:

> It is in consequence of the different holes in a flute that the distinctions of the air which pervades all without distinction is named *sadja* etc.;
> so also is the case with the distinction of the supreme self.[78]
>
> (VP 2.14.32)

He comments:

> there is no substantial sameness between particles of air, which are associated with several different holes of the flute, but there is only similarity of essential nature between them. Indeed all the particles of air have the same nature, because they possess the same nature of air. So also is the case with individual selves, the differences that result are due to names such as gods, men etc.[79]

He reiterates that "the difference in form of the individual selves is not due to their essential nature, but, due to their having entered various masses of matter known as gods, men, etc.; it is not declared in this example (VP 2.12.32) that all individual selves are one."[80] What this VP passage allows Rāmānuja to argue is the similarity of essential nature between individual selves without erasing the distinctions between them and all the while affirming their distinction from matter.[81]

The discussion on the plurality of individual selves concludes with VP 2.16.23cd–24ab and VP 6.7.96:

> He is me and he is you, and all this is the same as that,
> the essential nature of the self; give up the illusion of distinctions.
> Thus taught by Bharata that great king saw the highest reality and gave up distinction.[82]
>
> (VP 2.16.23cd–24ab)

These verses are taken from the narrative of Bharata, an important section of the VP for Rāmānuja. Contrary to the Advaitin, for whom these passages affirm ultimate reality as beyond all plurality and the destruction of multiplicity as the goal of right knowledge, for Rāmānuja, again, the distinction denied here is the one between individual selves in their essential nature. To further support this reading of the purāṇa passages, he resorts to the principle of intra-textual harmony. According to him "this teaching (of Bharata to the king), in fact begins with VP 2.13.89 that states *because the body which is characterized by head, hand etc., is different from the individual self (puruṣa)*."[83] Thus, the distinction between the body and the self mentioned here needs to be considered in the interpretation of later verses such as VP 2.16.23ce–24ab. Though these later passages when read independently of the former seem Advaitic, if the broader VP context is taken into account, the *prima facie* view that these passages refer to Brahman cannot be maintained. For similar reasons also the last passage utilized in the Major Objection, Rāmānuja argues, does not teach the identity of the individual self and Brahman:

> When the knowledge which produces distinctions has undergone complete destruction,
> then who will create the unreal difference between the self (ātma) and Brahman.[84]
>
> (VP 6.7.96)

So, for the Advaitin, *the knowledge which produces distinctions* is the perception of multiple individual selves, for Rāmānuja this plurality is based on their association with matter and not due to any difference in their essential natures.

With these last set of VP passages, Rāmānuja redirects the discussion from the Advaita concern of the non-difference of the Self and Brahman to the

Viśiṣṭādvaita issue of the non-difference between individual selves in their essential nature. In the Major Objection, scriptural support concludes after the VP verses, with BhG 10.20, 13.2, and 10.39. Though Rāmānuja has addressed all the VP passages from the Major Objection, he does not engage the BhG evidence (BhG 10.20, 13.2, 10.39) yet. He defers discussion of these passages and instead inserts an additional section at this juncture in his Major Conclusion on the distinction between the liberated self as distinct from Brahman. As this is not a concern for the Advaitin there is no scriptural support to argue this perspective. The next section evaluates the use of the VP in supporting this last claim of Rāmānuja on the topic of the individual self.[85]

The liberated self is distinct from Brahman

We have already encountered Rāmānuja's assertion that the liberated self is not identical to with Brahman. He now reiterates this claim and provides scriptural evidence:

> Even when one is released from ignorance (*avidyā*) by adopting the necessary means, essential identity with Brahman does not result, because that which is fit to be the seat of ignorance, can never become an entity that is unfit to be the seat of ignorance.[86]

Rāmānuja only cites from smṛti, specifically the VP and the BhG:

> The union of the self with the supreme self is said to be the greatest goal of all. But this is false, because one substance cannot acquire the nature of another substance.
>
> (VP 2.14.27)

> Relying on this knowledge, acquiring qualities equal to mine,
> they are neither born at the time of creation, nor suffer at the time of dissolution.
>
> (BhG 14.2)

> Brahman, by his own power makes his worshiper, who is deserving of change, acquire his own nature, even as a magnet attracts metal.[87]
>
> (VP 6.7.30)

First, these passages affirm that an essential identity between the liberated individual self and Brahman is impossible (VP 2.14.27). Second, once liberated, the individual self is said to acquire only certain qualities of Brahman and quits the cycle of birth and rebirth (BhG 14.2). Third, Brahman is said to be the goal to be attained by the individual self (worshiper) and absolute identity between the liberated self and Brahman is denied utilizing the illustration of magnet and pieces of metal. Just as a piece of metal can become magnetized by contact with a magnet, but does not become a magnet in nature, so also is the case with the liberated self and Brahman. The commentator points out that it is with such passages in mind that śruti which affirm the non-difference between the self and Brahman are to be interpreted.[88] Passages such as *one who knows Brahman, becomes Brahman*, one of the great statements (*mahāvākya*) for the Advaitin, are to be interpreted relying on the evidence from smṛti.[89]

A detailed explanation for why that which is fit to be the seat of ignorance (*avidyā*) never becomes Brahman is given in VP 6.7. Here, Brahman, the highest self, is affirmed as unique and different from individual selves because he is eternally free from the three dispositions (*bhāvana*) that characterize embodied selves[90]—*karmabhāvana*, *brahmabhāvana*, and *ubhayabhāvana*. This section of the VP was referenced earlier in this chapter in the discussion on the essential nature of Brahman. *Bhāvanas* are tendencies, capacities, or conceptions that envelop all embodied beings from Brahmā down to the lowest form of life. *Karmabhāvana* comprehends only actions, *brahmabhāvana* is the ability to achieve Brahman, and *ubhayabhāvana* is the capacity to engage in both actions and the capability of achieving Brahman. It is because of these tendencies that there is a difference in essential nature between Brahman and the individual selves and why even the liberated self cannot share all qualities of Brahman, such as His creative abilities. According to the VP, the embodied self that is worthy of liberation, has exhausted all these three *bhāvanas* and is hence worthy of liberation:

> O' King that which leads to the object of attainment is knowledge. Similarly, what has to be led is the individual self in whom all *bhāvanas* are extinguished.[91]
>
> (VP 6.7.92)

> the individual self is the user of the means (to liberation) and
> knowledge is the means to obtain what is to be obtained.
> Having gained liberation, and attained the object, that knowledge will cease to function.[92]
>
> (VP 6.7.93)

Once all the *bhāvanas* are extinguished, the practices such as acquisition of right knowledge and meditation cease to function as they lose their relevance. The description of liberation in the VP passages is, however, problematic as the passages are more conducive to an Advaita interpretation of the ultimate non-difference of the individual self and Brahman:

> When one attains the state (*tadbhāva*) that corresponds to that (Brahman),[93] then he is non-different (*abhāva*) from the highest self and differences are products of his ignorance (*ajñāna*).[94]
>
> (VP 6.7.94)

In contrast, for Rāmānuja, this passage does not assert non-difference of self and Brahman; rather it is:

> the essential nature of the liberated self [that] is stated in VP 6.7.94. The phrase *tadbhāva* means attributive qualities of Brahman, his attributive nature, not identity between the individual self and Brahman in essential nature; because if it did the second *bhāva* in *tadbhāvabhāva* would be useless. Also, this would be contrary to what has been taught previously in the VP.[95]

If this passage is interpreted from the Advaita point of view, Rāmānuja cautions that there would be a redundancy of the term *bhāva* as the second of the two *bhāva*-s in *tadbhāvabhāva* would be out of place. Moreover, he invokes intra-textual harmony to garner support for his interpretation—the teaching of the other VP passages stated such as VP 2.14.27 and VP 6.7.30 as contrary to VP 6.7.94.

Non-difference of the individual self and Brahman mentioned in 6.7.94 is also re-interpreted by Rāmānuja to mean only the sharing of some qualities:

> Because it possesses the same nature of consciousness, the individual self is of the same nature as the supreme self. The difference of the individual self from Brahman consists in its acquiring forms such as gods etc. These differences are a result of *ajñāna* in the form of karma. However, the distinctions such as god etc. is not due to the individual self's essential nature. When the karma, which has the nature of ignorance and forms the root of all distinctions, is destroyed by means of meditation on the supreme Brahman, then those distinctions cease due to the cessation of their cause. Therefore, the individual self does not differ from Brahman.[96]

To further disqualify an Advaita reading of VP 6.7.94, the commentator states that "the word ignorance (*ajñāna*) in VP 6.7.94 refers not to something that cannot be explained; [but] it derives from popular use, not from the *śāstra*. Its interpretation as denoting karma has been demonstrated in this very book (VP)."[97] Whereas the liberated individual self at one time in its embodied condition associates with karma and the three dispositions, Brahman never does. Non-difference means between Brahman and the individual self simply the sharing of the quality of consicousness.

Moreover, the scriptural statements that do affirm the non-difference of individual selves and Brahman can also be interpreted in another sense: the non-difference is said to be due to the fact that both the liberated self and Brahman are free from association with matter:

> However, the distinction of the one individual self from other[98] individual selves, which are of the same essential nature, is the result of the outer activity of karma.

When the distinctions such as gods etc. cease to exist, the activity ceases to exist and indeed he alone remains.

(VP 2.14.33)

When the knowledge which produces distinctions has undergone complete destruction
then who will create the unreal difference between the self and Brahman?[99]

(VP 6.7.95)

The context of VP 2.14.33 is the soul–body relationship and refers to ignorance or karma that renders one unable to discern the essential nature of the individual self from the body. VP 6.7.95 on the other hand, is concerned with the distinction between the individual self and Brahman. The contexts of 2.14.33 and 6.7.95 are different. Rāmānuja reconciles this by interpreting the word difference (*vibheda*) in VP 6.7.95 as denotative of distinctions that arise due to association with matter only, rather than difference between self and Brahman.[100] That is, when the individual self is liberated and free from association with karma, then distinctions of physical form and so on, which are thought to belong to the individual self cease to exist. Therefore, what is meant when Brahman and the liberated self are stated as non-different has to do with their freedom from material association and it is only in this sense that they do not differ.

An extension of the exegetical strategy of intra-textual coherence is to take passages such as *the power of Viṣṇu is said to be higher, the lower one is called the kṣetrajña, avidyā called karma is the third power* (VP 6.7.61) and *know the field-knower in all bodies as Myself* (BhG 13.2) into consideration. Using such passages scriptural statements that affirm the one-ness of the individual self and the supreme self are to be re-intepreted to mean that there is non-difference only due to the fact that Brahman constitutes the inner self, the internal ruler of all. Thus the identity between self and Brahman that is mentioned in scripture is to be read either utilizing the soul–body paradigm or in the sense that the non-difference is due to non-association of both entities with matter. That non-difference between Brahman and the liberated self is to be understood in this way is supported by the VP, according to Rāmānuja.

In concluding his discussion on the nature of the individual self, Rāmānuja once again invokes the principle of scriptural harmony (*samanvaya*) to argue that unless the identity of the liberated self and Brahman is understood in the above-mentioned way, there would be serious contradictions with certain BhG passages such as BhG 10.20, 13.2, and 10.39. These BhG passages were cited in the Major Objection to support an attribute-less Brahman, but here they are called on to support the Viśiṣṭādvaita perspective of the liberated self as distinct from Brahman. BhG 13.2 (also mentioned above), where Kṛṣṇa's claim that he is the field-knower in all fields is discussed in detail in Chapter 4 and so is not considered here. In the next chapter, the importance of the VP in interpreting this passage is discussed in the section on the field and the field-knower.[101]

In the Major Objection, Rāmānuja has the Advaitin cite from the upaniṣads, the VP, and the BhG. We have seen that he first counters the *prima facie* view of the quoted upaniṣads in his Major Conclusion in section on the nature of Brahman, but also includes a number of VP passages as support. He then refutes the Advaita interpretation of the VP passages to establish the distinction between Brahman and the individual self, once again inserting both śruti and VP to support his claims. He finally cites the BhG passages from the Major Objection at the end of this rather long section on the individual self and refutes the Advaita interpretation of them using the rationale of scriptural harmony between the BhG and the VP.

Defining ignorance

In the Major Conclusion, independently from the section on the nature of Brahman and the individual self discussed in the previous sections of this chapter, Rāmānuja undertakes a sustained refutation of the Advaita understanding of ignorance (*avidyā*). Titled, *the Seven Untenables* (*Saptvidhānānupapatti*), this section aims to disprove *avidyā* as posited by the Advaitin through valid means of knowledge (*pramāṇa*) such as perception, inference, and scripture.[102] We are only concerned here, with the last of the three valid means of knowledge. As mentioned at the beginning of this chapter, the section on ignorance in the Major Objection mirrors the one in the Major Conclusion in terms of scriptural citations (Table 3.1). That is, the very scripture utilized to support the *prima facie* view is now taken up by Rāmānuja for reinterpretation and to support the Viśiṣṭādvaita concept of ignorance as karma. The Major Objection cites both śruti and the VP to argue that ignorance is indescribable as neither existence nor non-existence and that it obscures the true nature of Brahman until it is sublated by the realization of true knowledge. We first examine Rāmānuja's refutation of the Advaitic interpretation of śruti as it concerns the topic of ignorance and then VP 2.12.39–40, 43–45. If his exegetical strategy in refuting the Advaitic interpretation of śruti is to resort to scriptural harmony across different upaniṣad texts, his approach in the discussion of VP is to rely on intra-textual coherence, that is reading a particular text, in this case the VP in a way that harmonizes passages from its various books and chapters.

Śruti support

In the Major Objection, the Advaitin describes unreality (*mithyā*) as the fault that misguides us and is beginning-less ignorance (*avidyā*) which cannot be described as either existence or non-existence and causes varied and manifold superimpositions on the essential nature of Brahman. Two śruti that purportedly support this definition of ignorance (*avidyā*) are:

> Indeed, being drawn away by the unreal (*anṛta*), they do not obtain this world of Brahman (*brahmaloka*).
>
> (Ch Up 8.3.2)

> Although they (desires) are real (*satya*), they have the unreal (*anṛta*) for a mask.[103]
>
> (Ch up 8.3.1)

The context of these passages is the investigation as to whether the space within the heart (*daharākāśa*) can be indentified as elemental space (*ākāśa*), the individual self, or Brahman. A full exposition of these passages in the context of Advaita and Viśiṣṭādvaita would lead our discussion far-a-field. I only discuss the terms that are of importance in the argument on ignorance.[104] For the Advaitin, the unreal (*anṛta*) denotes ignorance which masks the true nature of Brahman whereby the world of Brahman, is not obtained.[105]

Contrary to this interpretation, Rāmānuja understands *anṛta* as denoting actions that are performed without attachment to the results. The evidence for this he finds in Kaṭh Up 3.1 (*the two enjoying ṛta*) where *ṛta* is defined as karma free from attachment to the results of actions, and consists in the worship of the highest person (*paramapuruṣārādhana*). The goal (*pratiphala*) of such action is the attainment of Brahman. *Anṛta,* then, is not *avidyā* that superimposes the world on the true nature of Brahman, but it simply denotes karmic actions not performed as worship of Viṣṇu, without attachment to the results. In this instance, Rāmānuja relies on the context of other śruti to interpret the Ch Up 8.3.2 and 8.3.1 cited in the Major Objection. This seems to be his main strategy in the refutation of the Advaita interpretation of other śruti passages as well.

Ignorance (*avidyā*) is also referred to in scripture by the term *tamas*, according to the Advaitin, as in the following passage:

> Then, there was neither non-existence (*asat*) nor existence (*sat*) ... there was darkness (*tamas*). In the beginning knowledge was concealed by darkness (*tamas*).[106]
>
> (RV 10.129.1–3)

Śaṅkara in his commentary on Br Sū 2.1.8, claims that the subject of this passage is Brahman, and *tamas* as *avidyā* is neither existence (*sat*) nor non-existence (*asat*), which conceals Brahman. Rāmānuja counters this interpretation with *Subāla Upaniṣad* 2 that provides a different context for the term *tamas*: *unmanifest (avyakta) is absorbed into the imperishable (akṣara), the imperishable (akṣara) into darkness (tamas)*. The context of this upaniṣad is world dissolution and its reabsorption into Viṣṇu. In this sequential process of reabsorption darkness or *tamas* is unmanifest matter (*prakṛti*), which even in this primordial state exists as the body of Brahman.[107] So resorting to the doctrine of Brahman's causality, he attempts to reinterpret the meaning of *tamas* as something definable and that exists in a positive relation to Brahman. The *Subāla Upaniṣad*, though, does not clarify the relationship between Brahman and *tamas*. But since even Śaṅkara affirms the creation and dissolution of the world from Brahman, this passage as evidence is rather weak. Though, it is important in relocating the cognitive context of Advaita to the ontological one in Viśiṣṭādvaita—*tamas* as concealment of knowledge to *tamas* as the material substance (though unmanifest) of the universe. Rāmānuja's view on causality of Brahman discussed in the VS, requires more detail as he understands Brahman's causality in a much different sense than the Advaitin.

The Advaitin also interprets the term *māyā* as denotative of *avidyā* utilizing Śve Up 4.10: *know that māyā is prakṛti, and the Lord is the possessor of māyā.*[108] In his commentary on Br Sū 1.4.3, Śaṅkara notes that in this passage, *māyā* is the unmanifest (*avyakta*), which cannot be determined to be real or as unreal and is the limiting adjunct (*upādhi*) that brings about the state of personhood. Consequently, *prakṛti* as *māyā* is something unreal. Rāmānuja first counters this claim by turning to VP 1.19.20, *shielding the body of the boy, moving quickly it (Viṣṇu's discus) destroyed those thousand weapons (māyā) of Śaṃbara one after the other.* For now, we note that Rāmānuja defines *māyā* based on the VP context as a wonderful power of creation. Through *māyā* the demon Śaṃbara manifests real weapons, from which the boy Prahlāda requires protection. The reasoning here is that if the weapons were simply illusory, Viṣṇu's intercession would be meaningless. This passage is discussed in more detail in the section on *māyā* (BhG 7.14) in the next chapter as Rāmānuja's reading of this BhG passage itself requires the VP and so I do not address it here. It is significant that having cited VP 1.19. 19–20 Rāmānuja also turns to Śvet Up 4.9: *from that (prakṛti) the illusionist creates this whole world, and in it the other remains confined by the illusory power*[109] to support matter (*prakṛti/māyā*) as a source of wonderful manifestations. This means that he turns to VP in order to interpret the upaniṣad, which would otherwise risk rival Vedānta interpretation(s) as illustrated already by Śaṅkara's interpretation of Śvet Up 4.10.

Contrary to the Advaita claim that Brahman's nature is occluded by *māyā* and to support his view that it is a power that is wielded by Brahman (*māyāvin*) but who is very much in control of it, Rāmānuja cites passages such as:

> When the individual soul (*jīva*), that has been asleep under the influence of the beginning-less *māyā* wakes up.
>
> (Māṇḍ Up 2.21)

> Indra (Brahman) by his *māyā* moves about in many forms.[110]
>
> (Bṛ Up 2.5.19)

> He shines very much like Tvaṣṭṛ.
>
> (R.V 6.47.19)[111]

My *māyā* is difficult to overcome.[112]

(BhG 7.14)

For Rāmānuja in all these examples *māyā* is spoken of as the wonderful powers of Brahman (Bṛ Up 2.5.19), who since He shines forth like the god Tvaṣṭṛ cannot be concealed by something that is unreal (R.V. 6.7.19). Māṇḍ Up 2.21, identifies *māyā* as matter which conceals the individual self, the use of the tem *jīva* instead of *ātman* or Brahman allows for a less ambiguous interpetation. If this passage implies that matter is *māyā* that conceals the individual self, BhG 7.14ab, not cited here, affirms *māyā* as comprised of qualities (*guṇa*) and as matter quite clearly. The use of BhG 7.14 is also significant for one other reason. In his *Bhagavadgītābhāṣya* on this verse, Rāmānuja utilizes the VP to read this passage "correctly". Thus far Rāmānuja has refuted the śruti interpretations of the Advaitin utilizing other śruti, but also relyies on the VP. He cites VP 1.19.20 to clarify his definition of *māyā* and to use it as a guide to read Śvet Up. He also cites BhG 7.14 that identifies *avidyā* as *prakṛti* with the three qualities (*guṇa*) which is the nature (*prakṛti*) of Kṛṣṇa, but as mentioned, the connection to the VP is quite significant as we explore in Chapter 4.

In each of the śruti examples discussed above, the Advaitin interprets the terms *anṛta*, *tamas* and *māyā* in the context of sublation. That is, *anṛta* masks what is real, *tamas* conceals Brahman, and *māyā* is the limiting adjunct that brings about the illusion of personhood. It is only when ignorance is sublated by true knowledge that Brahman is realized. What Rāmānuja needs to counter ignorance defined in terms of concealment and sublation is to find scriptural evidence that transposes the focus from the cognitive context to an ontological one. Utilizing other śruti he argues that *anṛta* denotes actions (*karma*) that are not dedicated to Viṣṇu, *tamas* signifies unmanifest matter (*prakṛti*), and *māyā* as wonderful creations or manifestations that are real. He only accomplishes this much in his refutation of śruti but his ultimate goal as we see in the next section is to define ignorance as something whose essential nature is to undergo transformation that requires new denotations. *Anṛta* defined as certain types of actions (*karma*), *tamas* as unmanifest matter, and so on do not support ignorance as Rāmānuja defines it. His interpretation of *tamas* only loosely points to the detail that will be provided by the VP and in the last example that discusses *māyā*, he even utilizes VP 1.9.20 to argue his perspective. As we shall see, without the evidence from the VP, his task is not yet complete.

VP (2.12.36–46) support

In the Major Objection, the Advaitin argues that:

> the Highest Brahman, who is of the essence of sentience alone (*cinmātra*), the manifestation of this whole world which is made up of

> distinctions such as gods, animals, men, etc. assumed to exist in Brahman, is unreal (*mithyā*). And the defect, which is endless ignorance (*avidyā*) is inexpressible as either existence or non-existence, causes the varied and wonderful superimpositions that veil (*tirodhāna*) the true nature of Brahman.[113]

To support this point of view the śruti discussed above were cited, and now VP 2.12.39–40, 43–45 are provided as evidence. Rāmānuja claims that if the context of these VP passages is rightly understood they, in fact, reject such a conception of ignorance. In a sense, then, this is the second reclamation of the VP that Rāmānuja undertakes in ŚBh 1.1.1. The first instance of such extensive re-interpretation of the VP we saw in the section on the essential nature of the individual self. In contrast to the *prima facie* view, which begins the sequence of citations from the VP 2.12.38, he begins his analysis in the Major Conclusion with 2.12.36–37:

> And their regions and those who inhabit them,
> their essential nature has been explained, Listen as I briefly reiterate.[114]
>
> (VP 2.12.36)

> From the waters which constitute the body of Viṣṇu, was produced the lotus-shaped earth, together with its mountains and seas.[115]
>
> (VP 2.12.37)

Chapters 1–12 of Book Two of the VP describe the world as a lotus bud (*bhuvanakośa*). Passages 2.12.1–2.12.35, provide a description of the various planets, constellations, and regions inhabited by the progenitors and so on. In 2.12.36, the sage Parāśara having described the various regions of the cosmos to Maitreya claims that the following passages (37ff) present that very information in a summary (*saṃkṣepa*) format. But it is noteworthy that this world with its various regions and beings is affirmed as a manifestation of Viṣṇu's body (*aṃbu*). For Rāmānuja this supports his soul–body doctrine. Thus these passages that set the context for the verses that follow have not been taken into account in the Major Objection as the sequence of VP citations begins with 2.12.38. The fact that VP 2.12.37 supports, according to Rāmānuja, the soul–body paradigm allows him to re-interpret 2.12.38 quite differently than the Advaitin:

> O' Best among Brahmins, the stars are Viṣṇu, the worlds are Viṣṇu, the forests are Viṣṇu, the mountains, directions, rivers, and seas are Viṣṇu; He alone is all that exists (*asti*) and all that does not exist (*nāsti*).[116]

While the Advaitin reads this verse as affirming the sole reality that is Brahman and all else as a result of ignorance (*avidyā*), Rāmānuja argues that it in fact articulates an identity based on the soul–body relationship that was already posited in 2.12.37. He elaborates:

> In the world which is a combination of sentient and insentient beings, the sentient (*cid*) part (*aṃśa*) has an essential nature that is self-knowing and inexpressible by speech and the mind, is entirely of the nature of knowledge, is untouched by materiality (*prākṛtatva*), and, because it is indestructible, is denoted by the word 'existence'. On the other hand, the insentient (*acid*) part undergoes modifications due to the karma of the sentient part, is destructible, and is denoted by the word 'non-existence'. However, both these parts are the body of Vāsudeva, the highest Brahman, and therefore both are His.[117]

Brahman encompasses the whole world as its soul with the sentient individual selves as existence and insentient matter as non-existence comprise his body (*śarīra*). Having defined existence and non-existence, ignorance is discussed not in terms of sublation, but rather in terms of change or transformation. As the commentator notes:

> Do the words 'non-existence' and 'unreal' relate to sublation of knowledge during creation and dissolution, or do the terms relate to the view that Brahman is subject to modifications, a view similar to Bhedābheda [Vedānta]? Moreover, the word 'ignorance' does not indicate something that is inexpressible; on the contrary, it refers to karma only.[118]

The juxtaposition of both the Advaita and Bhedābheda view of the doctrine of causality suggests the importance of the VP in articulating a Vedānta that is quite distinct from these existing schools of thought. Rāmānuja utilizing the VP in the *Vedārthasaṃgraha* has argued the metaphysical reality of ignorance (*avidyā*) as a real power of Brahman. For him the relation between "existence" (*sat*) and "non-existence" (*asat*) is dependent on the capacity for transformation—"the words 'existence' and 'non-existence' mean 'that which changes', and 'that which does not'; they do not mean sublation or non-sublation of knowledge."[119] Viṣṇu as the inner self of the individual selves and matter is both existence and non-existence, "as the body of Brahman, the *cid* and *acid* forms come together and disassociate."[120] In the discussion of śruti provided as support Rāmānuja does not consider the interpretation of the terms "existence" and "non-existence" such as Ch Up 8.3.1 and R.V. 10.129.1–3.

As we noted in the earlier section on the discussion of śruti, the individual self as metaphysically real is a major concern for Rāmānuja. Here he comments:

> the *acid* part is explained as of the nature of non-existence only; this is the essence of the discussion. Indeed, the doubt that the *acid* part could

> be illusion must be excluded. Therefore, because the *acid* part is subject to modification, it is of the nature of non-existence only; this is the meaning.[121]

On the other hand, "because the *cid* part is not subject to modification it would follow that it is of the nature of existence."[122] Thus VP 2.12.38 is crucial in allowing Rāmānuja to interpret existence and non-existence quite differently, to refute the Advaita claim of sublation and the Bhedābheda view of transformation. Rāmānuja also provides additional passages from other chapters of the VP to support this reading of the world as the body of Viṣṇu, such as *they are all His body* (VP 1.22.84), *the whole of that is the body of Hari* (VP 1.22.36), *being indestructible, He alone is the self of all and has the universe as His form*[123] (VP 1.2.68), which reinforce a Viśiṣṭādvaita reading of the VP verses thus far.

Not only has the Advaitin failed to take the complete context of VP 2.12 into account, according to Rāmānuja, he also mistakes the passages that address the individual self as referring to Brahman. Thus, while in the Major Objection VP 2.12.39 and 40 are understood as articulating the nature of Brahman, Rāmānuja understands the individual self and not Brahman as the subject matter of these verses. This is an exegetical move we have come across in the section on the nature of the individual self. The soul–body paradigm that Rāmānuja was able to establish based on VP 2.12.37 can in fact support such a reading of these passages:

> the Lord, whose essential nature is knowledge, He is without form, but is not an entity.
> Therefore, know that the distinctions such as mountains, oceans etc. are indeed due to illusion of apprehension.[124]
>
> (VP 2.12.39)

> But, when knowledge is pure, in its true form, devoid of karma, and dis-associated from faults,
> then the tree of desire bears fruit: the distinctions of things, no longer exist.[125]
>
> (VP 2.12.40)

Contrary to Śaṅkara, for whom individuation results due to "the connection of immutable consciousness with superimposed adjuncts" (Alston 1981, Vol. III: 1), Rāmānuja takes "the Lord" referred to here as the individual self whose essential nature is knowledge. However, in the state of embodiment the individual self associates with various physical forms that are a result of the endless cycle of karma. This is how karma and matter (*prakṛti*) are related and in some instances Rāmānuja refers to these two terms indiscriminately as ignorance (*avidyā*). "Thus the material thing is the seat of modifications in proportion with the karma of the individual self, therefore, it has been rightly said to be denoted as 'non-existence' and everything else as 'existence'."[126] The illusion spoken of in this purāṇic verse relates to the erroneous identification of the individual self with the body it inhabits as a result of the karma that is accrued. The fact that Rāmānuja makes such a distinction between the individual self and Brahman is not only significant for his theology, but is only possible through his reading of the VP.

The next two verses, VP 2.12.41–42, elaborate on the distinction between the individual self and matter rather than Brahman and the empirical world as the Advaitin claims:

> What and where is the thing that is devoid of beginning, middle, end, and forever of a uniform nature?
> For how can reality be attested to that which is subject to change and that which does not possess its original character anymore? O' twice-born one!
>
> (VP 2.12.41)

> Earth is made into a pot, the pot is broken into pieces, and the pieces ground to dust, the dust to atoms.
> Tell me, is there any object in this, though it is thus understood by man whose self-knowledge is restricted by his own actions?[127]
>
> (VP 2.12.42)

While the Advaitin reads phrases such as "uniform nature" and "subject to change" as related to change in cognitions for Rāmānuja due to karma, which is real, the attributive knowledge of the individual self is restricted (see Chapter 2). The commentator elaborates: "Those who through their own karma exist as gods, men and so on, and consequently are incapable of having the correct ideas regarding the sentient thing (self), they experience the insentient thing (matter), which is an object of their enjoyment, as changing every moment."[128] Therefore, karma restricts correct understanding of the true nature of the individual self because karma affects the kind of embodiment one must experience. For Rāmānuja the reference to the destruction of the pot made of clay down to atoms illustrates constant physical transformation that matter undergoes as it is its essential nature to be so.

In the Major Objection, the last three passages, VP 2.12.43–45 are understood to "sum-up the already stated idea that anything other than Brahman is unreal" and "it is made clear that one's own karma alone is the cause of the ignorance, which in turn is the cause of the perception of difference in Brahman, whose essential nature is knowledge."[129] Note that though both Śaṅkara and Rāmānuja admit that karma leads to ignorance, for the latter karma is a power of Brahman himself. In the following VP passages the Advaitic tenor has to be explained:

> Therefore, O' twice-born one, without *vijñāna*, none of the many entities exist anywhere, at anytime.
> The one discriminative knowledge is understood as manifold by those whose minds are scattered by distinction created by their own karma.
> (VP 2.12.43)

> Knowledge, perfect, pure, stainless, free from suffering, and unattached to desires such as endless greed;
> single, always one, it is the supreme highest Lord, Vāsudeva other than whom there is nothing else.[130]
> (VP 2.12.44)

> Thus has the truth been stated to you, by me: how that knowledge is real[131] and all else unreal;
> however, that which is of a temporal and worldly nature has also been taught to you.[132]
> (VP 2.12.45)

Based on the soul–body paradigm of VP 2.12.37, Rāmānuja reads these passages as addressing the individual self rather than Brahman. The distinctions such as gods, men, and so on "are not due to anything in the essential nature of the self" since it is "free from karma, and for this very reason is untouched by matter (*prakṛti*) in the form of faults."[133] The individual self is referred to as Brahman here:

> because it is one, it is not subject to increase and decrease and for this very reason always of one form, and forms the body of Vāsudeva, and therefore has Him for its self.[134] The world which in this way is made up of *cid* and *acid* forms the body of Vāsudeva, and has Him for its self.[135]

As the body of Vāsudeva, the individual self can be denoted as Vāsudeva as in these passages. Moreover, since the individual self shares consciousness and an eternal nature with Brahman compared to matter, denoting the individual self as Brahman is also acceptable. On the whole then, it is easier for Rāmānuja to interpret the entity spoken of in these passages as Brahman, based on the soul-body paradigm articulated in VP 2.12.37.

Rāmānuja, utilizing the VP,[136] affirms the world as real and "knowledge of the reality of the world is to induce the effort to secure the means of liberation."[137] Moreover, "the whole world denoted by the words existence and non-existence, made up of sentient and insentient things, constitutes the body of the most high, highest lord, Viṣṇu, who is their self."[138] Rāmānuja's main goal in discussing these VP passages is to establish the distinction between existence and non-existence and the rejection of the sublation of knowledge, which is a distinguishing feature of his Vedānta from the *prima facie* view:

> The words non-existence and unreality are opposites (of existence and reality). Therefore they indicate unreality; but they really mean destructibility. In VP 2.12.41 and VP 2.12.42 also only destructability is declared, but not that they cannot be proved, or that they are set aside by knowledge.[139]

The VP, then, according to Rāmānuja, does not present us with any vocabulary or context that can be used to denote a Brahman completely devoid of attributes nor indicate the world as a result of ignorance (*avidyā*).

He concludes this section by providing support for his interpretation of these verses from other chapters of the VP to prove that his interpretation of these passages is in line with the rest of the purāṇa:

> O King! What is that entity that, even at other times does not go by another name, corresponding to its alterations (*pariṇāma*) etc.?
>
> (VP 2.13.96)

> The ultimate truth (*paramārtha*) is understood by the wise to be eternal; however, it would be impermanent if it were obtained through imperishable things.[140]
>
> (VP 2.14.24)

These passages that occur subsequent to the discussion of VP 2.12.36–46 are meant to illustrate that there is a continuity of meaning through the various chapters of the purāṇa contra the Advaitin if understood according to Viśiṣṭādvaita. To further support his interpretation as the correct one, Rāmānuja uses verses from the commencement of the very next chapter, VP 2.13, as well:

> You have told me how the three worlds exist supported (*ādhāra*) by Viṣṇu Please tell me now, how the one you called *paramārtha* is essentially knowledge.[141]
>
> (VP 2.13.2)

With this verse also a concrete relationship between the Brahman and the world is posited as he is affirmed as the supporter (*ādhāra*) of the latter. We have already seen that the *ādhāra/ādheya* relationship is a significant aspect of the soul–body relationship that Rāmānuja envisions. Therefore, the passage the *stars are Viṣṇu* (2.12.38) is not meant to denote identity in essential nature, but rather an identity based on the soul–body relationship.

Conclusion

ŚBh 1.1.1 presents a unique case of the exegetical use of the VP. As we noted earlier in the chapter, the sections that present scripture as valid means of knowledge (*śabdapramāṇa*) in the Major Objection mirror Rāmānuja's response in the Major Conclusion. He takes up the very scriptural passages presented as support for the *prima facie* view and re-interprets them in the Major Conclusion. There are however important differences. For instance, though Rāmānuja does address most of the scriptural passages cited in the Major Objection, he however breaks up the sequence of the passages in his re-interpretation of them to introduce additional scripture, especially the VP. The Major Objection cites śruti and VP as evidence for an attribute-less Brahman, which alone is claimed as real; all plurality is claimed as unreal and as due to the effect of adjuncts (*upādhi*).

Rāmānuja first takes up the refutation of these śruti while he includes thirty VP passages to redefine the nature of Brahman. As for the VP passages cited in the Major Objection as further evidence for an attribute-less Brahman, Rāmānuja claims these purāṇa passages in fact address the individual self and not Brahman. Through such an exegetical move, he makes a case for the metaphysical reality of the individual self based on scripture, something that does not concern the Advaitin in the Major Objection. So, whereas in the Major Objection, śruti, BhG, and VP are presented seamlessly as support for the Advaita view, Rāmānuja in his Major Conclusion introduces additional topics such as the discussion of the individual self in its embodied and liberated state that is so important for his Vedānta.

In the section on the nature of Brahman, Rāmānuja re-interprets the śruti utilized in the Major Objection by imposing certain ontological frameworks to read these passages. He uses the soul–body (*śarīraśarīri*/*lipner*) paradigm and the concept of the dual nature of Brahman (*ubhayaliṅgatva*) to reach very different interpretations of śruti than the objector on the nature of Brahman. He also utilizes the concept of scriptural harmony (*samanvaya*) to argue his re-reading of śruti. However, the additional citations from the VP that accompany the re-interpretation of śruti provide support for the very frameworks that Rāmānuja utilizes to reinterpret śruti, such as the soul–body relationship and so on. Thus the VP is the source text that supports Rāmānuja's view of Brahman and the world providing evidence for the very doctrines that are utilized to re-interpret śruti contra-Advaita.

Having refuted the Advaita interpretation of śruti, Rāmānuja turns to the VP passages cited in the Major Objection as evidence for an attribute-less Brahman. In the Major Conclusion, however, these passages are understood as addressing the individual self. This section which argues the metaphysical reality of the individual self and its distinction from Brahman, in its embodied and liberated states is extensive. The section on the essential nature of the individual self and its distinction from Brahman is solely supported by the very same VP passages utilized in the Major Objection. The re-interpretation of these VP passages is a reclamation of this purāṇa as a Viśiṣṭādvaitic text, where large sections of the VP are re-read to refute Advaita. We see this kind of exegetical strategy in the section on ignorance as well. In addition to refuting the Advaita interpretation of the VP, Rāmānuja introduces scriptural passages from śruti and VP to establish the distinction between Brahman and the individual self even in its liberated state. As we see in these sections, the VP is invariably called on to interpret śruti.

To counter the Advaita claim that ignorance (*avidyā*) that cannot be defined as either existence (*sat*) or non-existence (*asat*) is a cognition sublatable by true knowledge, Rāmānuja resorts to the VP. His main task is to re-define the concepts of existence and non-existence and also to refute the cognitive context of ignorance as the Advaitin understands it. In this section in the Major Objection, the Advaitin provides śruti and VP examples to support his claim. In the Major Conclusion, then, Rāmānuja re-interprets ignorance as karma, as not simply a cognitive error, but as physical transformation. As is traditional, the *prima facie* view cites śruti and then smṛti. His refutation of the Advaita interpretation of the VP, in the Major Conclusion, then, is the second reclamation of this purāṇa as a Viśiṣṭādvaita text in ŚBh 1.1.1. The VP is called on to provide detail on ignorance as karma, a power (*śakti*) and form (*rūpa*) of Brahman, and to define a type of relationship between ignorance and Brahman that does not depend on the concept of sublation. For both, Rāmānuja utilizes the same VP passages as the Advatin in the Major Objection. The significant difference and indeed his critique of the Advaita reading of the VP is that the entire context of VP 2.12 is not taken into account. Specifically VP 2.12.37, which states that *from the waters which constitute the body of Viṣṇu, was produced the lotus-shaped earth*. This passage Rāmānuja understands as affirming the soul–body relationship which is then utilized to read the rest of VP 2.12.37ff and facilitates the Viśiṣṭādvaita view of ignorance.

Notes

1 One of the reasons for this two-fold division is that the "Minor" and "Major" sections are said to address different aspects of Br Sū 1.1.1. The sūtra under consideration reads *then therefore the enquiry into Brahman* (*athato brahmajijñāsā*). Traditionally, it is believed that the Minor Objection and Conclusion (*Laghupūrvapakṣa* and *Laghusiddhānta*) address the different interpretations of the term *then*, whereas, the Major Objection and Conclusion (*Mahāpūrvapakṣa* and *Mahāsiddhānta*) examine the analysis of the word *therefore* (Carman 1974: 55). Thibaut's division of the SBh 1.1.1 (20–129).

2 Rāmānuja does not address this passage.

3 Also Kaṭh Up 4.10.

4 Also Bṛ Up 4.5.15.

5 Rāmānuja does not address this passage.

6 He also refers to the *Vedārthasaṃgraha* that discusses Ch Up 6 in detail.

7 Also in Ch Up 6.2.3.

8 For the purposes of this study, I define interpretive community as proficients of expert knowledge (*śāstra*) of a particular tradition that are actively engaged in creation of new texts whilst depending on prior textual traditions. These expositions are usually directed towards similar experts in rival traditions (Olivelle 2004; Ganeri 2010).

9 yadapy āhur aśeṣaviśeṣapratyanīkacinmātram brahmaiva paramārthaḥ. tadatireki nānāvidhajñātṛajñeyatatkṛtajñānabhedādi sarvam tasminneva parikalpitam mithyābhūtam. (ŚBh 13, cf Thibaut 1996: 20)
10 Abhyankar 69, fn 9.
11 This concept of co-ordinate predication, *sāmānādhikaraṇya,* has both grammatical and ontological significance for the Vedāntins. Grammatically, in Sanskrit, it means that non-synonymous terms having the same case-ending can be applied to one particular thing. So, in the statement, *Brahman is reality, knowlegde, infinity* (Taitt Up 2.1.1), all three terms, being in the same case-ending are at the same level, that is, are applied to the one entity, Brahman. Ontologically, for Rāmānuja, this means that Brahman, though one, is a differentiated entity (Lipner 1986: 29).
12 paraṃ brahma svabhāvata eva nirastanikhiladoṣagandhaṃ samastakalyāṇaguṇātmakaṃ jagadutpattisthitisamhārāntaḥpraveśaniyamanādilīlaṃ pratipādya kṛtsnasya cidacidvastunaḥ sarvāvasthāvashtitasya pāramārthikasyaiva parasya brahmaṇaḥ śarīratayā rūpatvaṃ śarīrarūpatanvaṃśaśaktivibhūtyādiśabdais tattacchabdasāmānādhikaraṇyena cābhidhāya tadvibhūtibhūtasya cidvastunaḥ svarūpeṇāvasthitaṃ acinmiśratayā kṣetrajñarūpeṇāvasthiti coktvā kṣetrajñāvasthāyāṃ puṇyapāpātmakakarmarūpāvidyāveṣṭitatvena svābhāvikajñānarūpatvān anusandhānaṃ acidrūpārthākāratayānusandhānaṃ ca partipāditam iti paraṃ brahma saviśeṣaṃ tadvibhūtibhūtaṃ jagadapi pāramārthikameveti jñāyate. (ŚBh 69; cf Thibaut 1996: 88–89)
13 VS #42. Rāmānuja uses only VP 6.5.72, 79, 76, and 77.
14 Rāmānuja does not address this passage.
15 Also Kaṭh Up 4.10.
16 Also Bṛ Up 4.5.15.
17 Rāmānuja does not address this passage.
18 Since I examine Rāmānuja's exegetical strategies thematically I do not address his interpretation of all the śruti discussed in the Major Objection and the Major Conclusion as some fall into the categories of exegesis that are already mentioned.
19 He refers to his discussion of this in the VS, where the soul–body paradigm is utilized to interpret this upaniṣad and states that he addresses it yet again in his commentary on Br Sū 2.1.15.
20 Also Kaṭh Up 4.10.
21 Also Bṛ Up 2.4.14.
22 tatkṛtsnasya jagato brahmakāryatayā tadantaryāmikatayā ca tadātmakatvena aikyāt tatpratyanīkanānātvam pratiṣidhyate. (ŚBh 63; cf Thibaut 1996: 84–85)
23 atha parā yayā tad akṣaram adhigamyate yat taddreśyam agrāhyam agotram avarṇam acakṣuḥśrotraṃ tad apāṇipādam nityaṃ vibhuṃ sarvagataṃ susūkṣmaṃ tadavyayam yadbhūtayoniṃ paripaśyanti dhīrāḥ. (Muṇḍ Up 1.1.5–6)
24 ŚBh 58–59; cf Thibaut 1996: 78–79.
25 *Jalān* is a hapax. See Olivelle 1998: 544.
26 I do not discuss Br Sū 3.2.3 as this *sūtra* is a discussion of the individual self in the dream and waking states and though important does not add to our discussion here on exegetical strategies and would be too tangential of a topic to address at this juncture.
27 yo mām ajam anādim ca vetti lokamaheśvaram. (BhG 10.3ab)
28 On the meaning of the term *bhāvana* see van Buitenen 1955.
29 matsthāni sarvabhūtāni na cāham teṣvavasthitaḥ. (BhG 9.4cd)
na ca matsthāni bhūtāni paśya me yogam aiśvaram
bhūtabhṛnna ca bhūtastho mamātmā bhūtabhāvanaḥ.
(BhG 9.5; ŚBh 65; cf Thibaut 1996: 86)
30 Except 10.42, which is also connected to the VP in that Rāmānuja utilizes VP 1.9.53 to interpret this verse in his *Bhagavadgītābhāṣya.*
31 VP 6.5.83ab in the critical edition has *vikāram* instead of *vikārān.*

32 VP 6.5.84ab in the critical edition has *samastakalyāṇaguṇātmako hi svaśaktileśāvṛtabhūtasargaḥ.*

33 sa sarvabhūtaprakṛtiṃ vikārān guṇādidoṣāṃśca mune vyatītaḥ
atītasarvāvaraṇo' khilātmā tenā'stṛtaṃ yad bhuvanāntarāle.
(VP 6.5.83)

34 samastakalyāṇaguṇātmakosau hi svaśaktileśoddhṛtabhūtasargaḥ
icchāgṛhītābhimatorudehaḥ saṃsādhitāśeṣajagaddhitosau.
(VP 6.5.84)

35 tejobalaiśvaryamahāvabodhasuvīryaśaktyādiguṇaikarāśiḥ
paraḥ parāṇām sakalā na yatra kleśādayaḥ santi parāvareśe.
(VP 6.5.85; ŚBh 65–66; cf Thibaut 1996: 86–87)

36 sa īśvaro vyaṣṭisamaṣṭirūpo'vyaktasvarūpo prakaṭasvarūpaḥ
sarveśvaraḥ sarvadṛksarvavettā samastaśaktiḥ parameśvarākhyaḥ.
(VP 6.5.86, ŚBh 66; cf Thibaut 1996: 86–87)

37 saṃjñāyate yena tad astadoṣaṃ śuddhaṃ paraṃ nirmalamekarūpam
samdṛśyate vā'pyavagamyate vā tajjñānamajñānam ato'nyad uktam.
(VP 6.5.87; ŚBh 66; cf Thibaut 1996: 86–87)

38 athāvatāradvāreṇa sādhyaṃ vigrahaprayojanamāha saṃsādhiteti. (ŚP Vol. I 212)

39 vyaṣṭisamaṣṭiśabdābhyāṃ kāryakāraṇāvasthaś cetanavargocyate. rūpaṃ śarīram. svarūpaṃ svāsādhāraṇaṃ śarīram. śarīrilakṣaṇaṃ sūcayati sarveśvareti. īśvara niyantā. anena niyāmyatvaṃ śarīratvaṃ siddham. (ŚP Vol. I 212)

40 bhuvanāntarāle ubhayavibhūtyantarāle. (ŚP Vol. I 211)

41 For the historical development of this term in the BhG, VP, and Śaṅkara's works, see Oberhammer 2000: 11–41.

42 In the critical edition, VP 6.7.70 cd reads: *tadviśvarūparūpaṃ vai rūpam anyad dharer mahat.*

43 samastāḥ śaktayaś caitā nṛpa yatra pratiṣṭhitāḥ
tadviśvarūpavairūpyaṃ rūpam anyad dharer mahat.
(VP 6.7.70)

44 samastaśaktirūpāṇi tatkaroti janeśvara
devatiryaṅmanuṣyādiceṣṭāvanti svalīlayā.
(VP 6.7.71; ŚBh 67; cf Thibaut 1996: 87)

45 I skip 1.2.11 as it does not add to the discussion at hand.

46 paraḥ parāṇām paramaḥ paramātmātmasamsthitaḥ
rūpavarṇādinirdeśaviśeṣaṇavivarjitaḥ.
(VP 1.2.10; ŚBh 67; cf Thibaut 1996: 87)

47 sarvatrāsau samastam ca vastyatreti vai yataḥ
tataḥ sa vāsudeveti vidvadbhiḥ paripaṭhyate.
(VP 1.2.12)

48 tadbrahma paramam nityam ajam akṣayam avyayam
ekasvarūpaṃ ca sadā heyābhāvācca nirmalam.
(VP 1.2.13; ŚBh 67; Thibaut 1996: 87–88)

49 tadeva sarvam evaitad vyaktāvyaktasvarūpavat
tathā puruṣarūpeṇa kālarūpeṇa ca sthitam.
(VP 1.2.14; ŚBh 67; cf Thibaut 1996: 88)

50 ŚP 216–17.

51 I do not discuss VP 1.2.11, which reaffirms the śruti claims that Brahman alone always is (*sad*).

52 This is also stated in VP 6.4.39–40. These passages are not discussed as they do not add anything significant to the discussion at hand.

53 VP 1.22.53 cd in the critical edition reads: *kṣarākṣarasvarūpe te sarvabhūteṣvavasthite.*

54 dve rūpe brahmaṇastasya mūrtam cāmūrtam eva ca
kṣarākṣarasvarūpe te sarvabhūteṣu ca sthite.
(VP 1.22.53)

akṣaram tatparam brahma kṣaram sarvamidaṃ jagat
ekadeśasthitasyāgner jyotsnā vistāriṇī yathā
parasya brahmaṇaḥ śaktis tathedam akhilaṃ jagat.
(VP 1.22.54; ŚBh 68; cf Thibaut 1996: 88)

55 viṣṇuśaktyā mahābuddhe vṛtau samśrayadharmiṇau.
(VP 2.7.29 cd)
tayoḥ saiva pṛthagbhāvakāraṇam saṃśrayasya ca.
(VP 2.7.30ab; ŚBh 68; cf Thibaut 1996: 88)

56 The VP critical edition has *saktam* instead of *sakto* in VP 2.7.31ab.

57 *pradhānam ca pumāmścaiva sarvabhūtātmabhūtayā and pradhānapuruṣātmakam* instead of *pradhānapuruṣātmanaḥ* in VP 2.7.31 cd.
yathā sakto jale vāto bibharti kaṇikāśatam
śaktiḥ sāpi tathā viṣṇoḥ pradhānapuruṣātmanaḥ.
(VP 2.7.31)
tad etad akṣayam nityaṃ jaganmunivarākhilam
āvirbhāvatirobhāvajanmanāśavikalpavat.
(VP 1.22.58; ŚBh 68–69; cf Thibaut 1996: 88)

58 kāraṇāt kāryasya vibhāge dṛṣṭāntaḥ. jalasya kaṇikāḥ tasmādbhedena bibharti vāyuḥ. saṃyojakatvaviyojakatvayor vā dṛṣṭāntaḥ. parasparaṃ saṅkalitāsaṅkalitāśca bibharti vāyuḥ. yadvā prakṛtipuruṣagatadoṣaleśarāhitye dṛṣṭāntaḥ. vāyur hi kaṇikāśataṃ tatsvabhāvāspṛṣṭo bibharti. pradhānapuruṣātmanaḥ pradhānapuruṣayor ātmanaḥ. (ŚP 220)

59 Subsequent to the discussion of the essential nature of the individual self, Rāmānuja using VP 1.4.38–41 argues that Brahman is the inner self of the individual self. However, since we have already considered this to a certain extent in the section on the nature of Brahman, I will not do so here.

60 pratyastamitabhedam yat sattāmātram agocaram
vacasām ātmasaṃvedyam, tajjñānam brahmasaṃjñitam.
(VP 6.7.53)

61 The discussion on the worthy object of meditation begins with verse 6.7.28 in the purāṇa.

62 pratyastamitabhedam ityatra devamanuṣādiprakṛtipariṇāmaviśeṣasaṃsṛṣṭasyāpyātmanaḥ svarūpam tadgatabhedarahitvena tadbhedavācidevādiśabdāgocaram jñānasattaikalakṣaṇam svasaṃvedyam yogayuṅmanaso na gocara ityucyata iti anena na prapañcāpalāpaḥ. (ŚBh 69; cf Thibaut 1996: 89)

63 Rāmānuja concludes this discussion by citing from the *Viṣṇudharmottara Purāṇa* 114.23–26 that explains that both the embodied and unembodied selves are not worthy as objects for meditation because of the association with karma of the former and as far as the latter is concerned its knowledge is derived from another source and is not intrinsic to it as in the case of the Highest Brahman.

64 jñānasvarūpamatyantanirmalam paramārthaḥ
tamevārthasvarūpeṇa bhrāntidarśanataḥ sthitam.
(VP 1.2.6)

65 asmiñ chāstre parasya brahmaṇo viṣṇornirastājñānādinikhiladoṣagandhasya samastakalyāṇaguṇātmakasya mahāvibhūteḥ pratipannatayā tasya bhrāntidarśanāsambhavāt. sāmānādhikaraṇyena aikyapratipādanamca bādhāsahamaviruddham cetyanantaram evopapādayiṣyate. (ŚBh 71; cf Thibaut 1996: 91)

66 yato vā imāni bhūtāni jāyante, yena jātāni jīvanti yat pratyantyabhismaviśanti tadvijiñāsatva tadbrahmeti. (Taitt Up 3.1.1; Olivelle 1998 translation)

67 Introduction, fn 8; Also see ŚBh 72; cf Thibaut 1996: 91–92.

68 so'ham icchāmi dharmajña śrotum tvatto yathā jagat
babhūva bhūyaśca yathā mahābhāga bhaviṣyati.
(VP 1.1.4).
yanmayam ca jagad brahman yataścaitaccarācaram

līnamāsīd yathā yatra layameṣyati yatra ca.
(VP 1.1.5; ŚBh 72; cf Thibaut 1996: 92–93)

69 jagacca sa VP 1.1.31.

70 For instance, in the question *what does the world consist of* (*yanmayam ca jagad*), the *mayaṭa* affix in *yanmayam* does not denote modification. That is, the question is not how does the world come about or transform because if this was the case then this question would be redundant as Maitreya already previously questions *how this world came into existence and what will it become again?* The *mayaṭa* affix in *yanmayam* also does not designate the sense of the word to which it is attached such as *prāṇa-maya* means "*prāṇa* only." For in that case the answer should have been "Viṣṇu only" rather than *the world is Brahman* (1.1.31), which implies a difference between Brahman and the world. Thus the most appropriate meaning according to *Pāṇini Sūtras* 5.4.21 is that the affix-*maya* denotes abundance and the answer to the question, what does the world consist of, as the world is Brahman is appropriate as it suggests that the world is abundantly present in the world. Thus through some grammatical maneuvers Rāmānuja argues that the world is a positive manifestation of Brahman and is identical to the latter in so far as it is His body.

71 yadi nirviśeṣajñānarūpabrahmādhiṣṭhānabhramapratipādanaparam śāstram tarhi—
nirguṇasyāprameyasya śuddhasyāmalātmanaḥ
katham sargādikartṛtvam brahmaṇo'bhyupagamyate. (VP 1.3.1)
iti codyam,
śaktyaḥ sarvabhāvānām acintyajñānagocarāḥ
yato'to brahmaṇastāstu sargadyā bhāvaśaktyaḥ
bhavanti taptām śreṣtha pāvakasya yathoṣṇatā. (VP 1.3.2–3ab)
iti parihāraśca na ghaṭate. (ŚBh 73–74; cf Thibaut 1996: 94)

72 tasyātmaparadeheṣu sato'pyekamayam hi yat
vijñānam paramārtho 'sau dvaitino' tathvadarśinaḥ.
(VP 2.14.31)

73 'tasyātmaparadeheṣu sato'pyekamayam' ityatra sarveṣvātmasu jñānaikākāratayā samāneṣu satsu devamanuṣyādiprakṛtipariṇāmaviśeṣarūpapiṇḍasamsargakṛtam-ātmasu devādyākāreṇa dvaitadarśaṇamatathyamityucyate. (ŚBh 75–76; cf Thibaut 1996: 96)

74 piṇḍagatam ātmagatamapi dvaitam na pratiṣidhyate. devamanuṣyādivivibhavicitrapiṇḍeṣu vartamānam sarvātmavastu samam ityarthaḥ. (ŚBh 76; cf Thibaut 1996: 96)

75 yadyanyosti paraḥ kopi mattaḥ pārthivasattam
tadaiṣo'hamayam cānyo vaktumevamapīṣyate.
(VP 2.13.86)

76 etaduktam bhavati yadi madvyatiriktaḥ ko'pyātmā madākārabhūtajñānākārād anyākāro'sti tadāhamevam ākāroyam cānyādṛśākāraḥ' iti śakyate vyapadeṣṭum. na caivamasti; sarveṣām jñānaikākāratvena samānatvādeveti. (ŚBh 76; cf Thibaut 1996: 97)

77 'yadyanyo'sti paraḥ ko' pi' ityatrāpi nātmaikyam pratīyate; 'yadi mattaḥ paraḥ ko'py anya' iti ekasminnarthe paraśabdānyaśabdayoḥ prayogāyogāt. tatra paraśabdaḥ svavyatiriktātmavacanaḥ anyaśabdastasyāpi jñānaikākāratvādanyākāratvapratiṣedhārthaḥ. (ŚBh 76; cf Thibaut 1996: 97)

78 veṇurandhravibhedena bhedaḥ ṣaḍjādisamjñitaḥ
abhedavyāpino vāyostathā'sau paramātmanaḥ.
(VP 2.14.32)
VP critical edition reads: *vāyostathā tasya mahātmanaḥ.*

79 dṛṣṭānte cānekarandhravartinām vāyvamśānām na svarūpaikyam api tvākārasāmyameva teṣām. vāyutvenaikākārāṇām randhrabhedaniṣkramaṇakṛto hi ṣaḍjādisañjñābhedaḥ; evamātmanām devādisamjñābhedaḥ. (ŚBh 76; cf Thibaut 1996: 97)

80 ākāravaiṣamyam ātmanām na svarūpakṛtam, api tu devādipiṇḍapraveśakṛtamityupadiśyate; nātmaikyam. (ŚBh 76; cf Thibaut 1996: 95)
81 The commentary irons out the grammatical problems of such an interpretation by utilizing VP 2.13.86 (ŚP Vol. I. 241–42).
82 so'ham sa ca tvam sa ca sarvam etad ātmasvarūpam tyaja bhedamoham
itīritas tena sa rājavaryastatyāja bhedam paramārthadṛṣṭiḥ.
(VP 2.16.23cd–24ab)
83 tacca 'piṇḍaḥ pṛthag yataḥ pumsaḥ śiraḥpāṇyādilakṣaṇaḥ' (VP 2.13.89) iti prakramāt (ŚBh 77; cf Thibaut 1996: 97).
84 vibhedajanake'jñāne nāśamātyantikam gate
ātmano brahmaṇo bhedam asantam kaḥ kariṣyati.
(VP 6.7.96; ŚBh 77; cf Thibaut 1996: 97)
85 Prior to the discussion on the distinction between the liberated individual self and Brahman, Rāmānuja once again cites from various śruti, VP, and Br Sū to establish that the individual self is distinct from Brahman. Since, we have covered this topic in some depth in earlier sections of this chapter and the chapter on the *Vedārthasaṃgraha*, I do not examine these scriptural citations here. Rāmānuja cites, Muṇḍa Up 3.1.1, Kaṭh Up 3.1, Taitt Āra 3.21, VP 6.5.83–85, VP 6.7.61–62, Br Sū 1.2.21, Br Sū 1.1.22, Br Sū 2.1.22, Bṛ Up Mādh 3.7.22, Bṛ Up 4.3.21, Bṛ Up 4.3.35 (ŚBh 77–78; cf Thibaut 1996: 98).
86 nāpi sādhanānuṣṭhānena nirmuktāvidyasya pareṇa svarūpaikyasaṃbhavaḥ, avidyāśrayatvayogyasya tadanarhatvāsaṃbhavāt (ŚBh 78; cf Thibaut 1996: 98).
87 paramātmātmanor yogaḥ paramārtha itīṣyate
mithyaitad anyad dravyaṃ hi naiti taddravyatāṃ yataḥ.
(VP 2.14.27)
idaṃ jñānam upāśritya mama sādharmyam āgatāḥ
sarge'pi nopajāyante pralaye na vyathanti ca.
(BhG 14.2)
ātmabhāvaṃ nayaty enaṃ tad brahma dhyāyinam mune
vikāryamātmanaḥ śaktyā loham ākarṣako yathā.
(VP 6.7.30) (ŚBh 78–79; cf Thibaut 1996: 98–99)
88 atha brahma veda brahmaiva bhavatītyādi vākyāni hṛdi nidhāya asyānyathāsiddhiṃ śaṅkate (ŚP. Vol I. 247).
89 Subsequent to the VP 2.14.27, 6.7.30 and BhG 13.2, Rāmānuja cites the *Brahma Sūtras* (4.4.17, 4.4.21, 1.3.2) and former Vedānta commentators such as Bodhāyana and Dramiḍa to illustrate that though the liberated selves may share qualities such as enjoyment and bliss with Brahman, their new found powers do not include the capability of the creative act. Rāmānuja cites a series of śruti passages. He reads these śruti passages in the context of the information arrived at with the VP passages. Some of these passages claim that the liberated self acquires "freedom of movement" (Ch Up 8.1.6), "attains all his desires" (Taitt Up 2.1.1), "moves about there" (Ch Up 8.12.3), "attains bliss" (Taitt Up 2.7.1), and can take on whatever form he likes (Taitt Up 3.10.5). The Advaitin would read all these passages as referring to the Supreme Self, but since Rāmānuja has cited the VP he takes liberation to be the realization of the highest identity as the servant (*śeṣa*) of Brahman. He also utilizes the concept of scriptural harmony (*samanvaya*) to reconcile certain contradictory śruti such as Muṇḍ Up 3.2.9, 3.2.8, 3.1.3, and Ch Up 8.3.4. All this does not grant us any new information as to his exegetical strategy at this point.
90 Van Buitenen 1955.
91 vijñānam prāpakam prāpye pare brahmaṇi pārthiva
prāpaṇīyastathaivātmā prakṣīṇāśeṣabhāvanaḥ.
(VP 6.7.92)
92 kṣetrajñaḥ karaṇī jñānam karaṇam tena tasya tat

niṣpādya muktikāryam vai kṛtakṛtyam nivartate.
(VP 6.7.93)

93 In the VP critical edition 6.7.94 ab ends with *tathā' sau.*

94 tadbhāvabhāvam āpannas tadāsau paramātmanā
bhavaty abhedī bhedaś ca tasyājñānakṛto bhavet.
(VP 6.7.94) (ŚBh 81; cf Thibaut 1996: 100).

95 muktasya svarūpam āha tadbhāvo brahmaṇo bhāvaḥ svabhāvaḥ; na tu svarūpaikyam. tadbhāvabhāvam āpanna iti dvitīyabhāvaśabdānanvayāt; pūrvoktārthavirodhācca (ŚBh 81; cf Thibaut 1996: 100).

96 jñānaikākāratayā paramātmanaikaprakārasyāsya tasmād bhedo devādirūpaḥ. tadanvayo'sya karmarūpājñānamūlo na svarūpakṛtaḥ. sa tu devādibhedaḥ parabrahmadhyānena mūlabhūtājñānarūpe karmaṇi vinaṣṭe hetvabhāvān nivartata ityabhedī bhavati (ŚBh 81; cf Thibaut 1996: 100).

97 ajñānaśabdasya anirvacanīyaparatvam lokataḥ śāstrataś ca na vyutpannam. karma vācitvavyutpattir asmin prabandha eva darśitā (ŚP. Vol I. 255).

98 VP 2.14.33 ab in the critical edition reads: *ekatvam rūpabhedaśca bāhyakarmapravṛttiprajaḥ.*

99 ekatvasvarūpabhedas tu bāhyakarmapravṛttiprajaḥ
devādibhede'padhvaste nāsty evāvaraṇo hi saḥ.
(VP 2.14.33)
vibhedajanake'jñāne nāśam ātyantikaṃ gate
ātmano brahmaṇo bhedam asantaṃ kaḥ kariṣyati.
(VP 6.7.95) (ŚBh 81; cf Thibaut 1996: 100)

100 ŚP. Vol I. 255.

101 In addition to these passages, Rāmānuja also cites BhG 15.16–17, 18.61, 15.15, 10.41–42. All verses are meant to be read through the soul–body framework. Chapter 4 discusses the importance of the VP for 15.16–17, 15.15, and BhG 10.

102 For more on this see Grimes 1990.

103 etam brahmalokaṃ na vindati anṛtena hi pratyuḍhāḥ (Ch. Up 8.3.2).
teṣāṃ satyānāṃ satām anṛtam apidhānam (Ch Up 8.3.1).

104 The *daharavidyādhikaraṇa* in Rāmānuja's commentary comprises *sūtra* 1.3.13–1.3.22. In Śaṅkara's commentary the numbering is 1.3.14–1.3.21.

105 Śaṅkara of course does not mean that the world of Brahman is a place to be obtained. As he comments on this upaniṣad in the Br Su Bh 1.3.15, he does not take the terms in the compound *brahmaloka* in the sense of the sixth-case ending, but rather in the sense of *sāmānādhikaraṇa* (co-ordination), that is, he reads *brahmaloka* not as "world of Brahman", but as "the world that is Brahman".

106 nāsadāsīnno sadāsīt tadānīm … tamāsīt. tamasā gūḍhamagre praketam (RV 10.129.1–3).

107 ŚBh 1.2.27

108 māyāṃ tu prakṛtim vidyān māyinam tu maheśvaram (Śve Up 4.10).

109 Olivelle 1998 translation.

110 anādimāyayā supto yadā jīvaḥ prabudhyate (Māṇḍ Up 2.21).
indro māyābhiḥ purarūpa īyate (Bṛ Up 2.5.19) (ŚBh 102; cf Thibaut 1996: 125–26).

111 Tvaṣṭṛ is the divine architect of the gods in Hindu mythology.

112 tavaṣṭeha rājati (R.V. 6.47.19).
mama māyā duratyayā (BhG 7.14).

113 evam cinmātravapuṣi pare brahmaṇi doṣaparikalpitam idam devatiryaṅmanuṣyasthāvarādibhedam sarvam jagad yathāvasthitabrahmasvarūpāvabodhabādhyam mithyārūpam. doṣaśca svarūpatirodhānavividhavicitravikṣepakarī sadasadsnirvacanīyā anādyavidyā (ŚBh 15–16; cf Thibaut 1996: 22–23).

114 varṣāṇāñ ca nadīnāñ ca ye ca teṣu vasanti vai
teṣām svarūpamākhyātam saṃksepāśrūyatām punaḥ.
(VP 2.12.36)

115 yadambu vaiṣṇavaḥ kāyastato vipra vasundharā
padmākārā samudbhūtā parvatābdhyādisamyutā.
(VP 2.12.37)

116 jyotīṃṣi viṣṇurbhuvanāni viṣṇur vanāni viṣṇurgirayo diśaśca
nadyaḥ samudrāśca sa eva sarvam yadasti yannāsti ca vipravarya.
(VP 2.12.38)

117 cidacinmiśre jagati cidaṃśo vāṅmanasāgocarasvasaṃvedyasvarūpabhedo jñānaikākāratayā aspṛṣṭaprākṛtabhedo vināśitvenāstiśabdavācyaḥ. acidaṃśas tu cidaṃśakarmanimittapariṇāmabhedo vināśīti nāstiśabdābhidheyaḥ. ubhayaṃ tu parabrahmabhūtavāsudevaśarīratayā tadātmakam ity etadrūpaṃ saṃṣkepeṇātrābhihitam (ŚBh 104; cf Thibaut 1996: 127).

118 tatra nāstyasatyaśabdayoḥ kiṃ jñānabādhyatvaṃ pravṛttinimittam, uta pariṇāmitvam iti vicāre pariṇāmitvapakṣe svārasyam asti; *mahīghaṭatvam* (VP 2.12.42) ityupapādanāt. ajñānaśabdasya ca nānirvacanīyaparatvam; api tu karmaparatvameva. (ŚP. Vol I. avidyā section. 42).

119 pariṇāmitvāpariṇāmitve eva nāstyasatyādiśabdarthāḥ; na tu jñānabādhyatvābādhyatve (ŚP. Vol I. avidyā section. 43).

120 cidacidrūpam anyonyasamsṛṣṭam niṣkṛṣṭam ca bhagavaccharīram ityarthaḥ (ŚP. Vol I. avidyā section. 43).

121 acidamśasya nāstyātmakatvanibandhanameva tātparyaviṣayaḥ. acidamśasya hi mithyātvaśankā vyudasanīyā. atastasya pariṇāmitvāt nāstyātmakatva eva tātparyam (ŚP. Vol I. avidyā section. 44).

122 cidamśasya ... apariṇāmitvādstyātmakatvam phalitam syād (ŚP. Vol I. avidyā section. 44).

123 asmiñcchāstre pūrvam apy etad asakṛd uktaṃ *tāni sarvāṇi tadvapuḥ* (VP 1.22.84) *tat sarvam vai hares tanuḥ* (VP 1.22.36), *sa eva sarvabhūtāmā viśvarūpo yato'vyayaḥ* (VP 1.2.68) iti (ŚBh 104; cf Thibaut 1996: 127).

124 jñānasvarūpo bhagavān yato'sāviśeṣamūrtina tu vastubhūtaḥ
tato hi śailābdhidharādibhedāñ jānīhi vijñānavijṛmbhitāni.
(VP 2.12.39)

125 yadā tu śuddham nijarūpi sarvam karmakṣaye jñānamapāstadoṣam.
tadā hi samkalpataroḥ phalāni bhavanti no vastuṣu vastubhedāḥ.
(VP 2.12.40)

126 aśeṣakṣetrajñātmanāvasthitasya bhagavato jñānam eva svābhāvikam rūpam; na devamanuṣyādivasturūpam. yata evam tata evācidrūpadevamanuṣyaśailābdhidharādayaśca tadvijñānavijṛmbhitāḥ. tasya jñānaikākārasya sato devādyākāreṇa svātmavaividhyānusandhānamūlāḥ devādyākārānusandhānamūlakarmamūlā ityarthaḥ. yataścācidvastu kṣetrakjñakarmānuguṇam pariṇāmāspadam, tatas tan nāstiśabdābhidheyam itaradastiśabdābhidheyam ityarthāduktam bhavati (ŚBh 105; cf Thibaut 1996: 126–27).

127 vastvasti kim kutracid ādimadhyaparyantahīnam satataikarūpam
yaccānyathātvam dvija yāti bhūyo na tattathā kutra kuto hi tattvam.
(VP 2.12.41)
mahī ghaṭatvam ghaṭataḥ kapālikā kapālikā cūrṇarajasyato' ṇuḥ
janaiḥ svakarmastimitātmaniścayairālakṣyate brūhi kimatra vastu.
(VP 2.12.42)

128 svakarmaṇā devamanuṣyādibhāvena stimitātmaniścayaiḥ svabhogyabhūtamacidvastu pratikṣaṇam anyathābhūtamālakṣyate anubhūyata ityarthaḥ. (ŚBh 106; cf Thibaut 1996: 127)

129 'tasmānna vijñānamṛtam' (VP 2.12.43) iti pratijñātam brahmavyatiriktasyāsatyatvam upasamhṛtya 'vijñānamekam' (VP 2.12.43) iti jñānasvarūpe brahmaṇi bhedadarśananimittājñānamūlam nijakarmaiveti sphuṭīkṛtya (ŚBh 103; cf Thibaut 1996: 127).

130 tasmān na vijñānam ṛte'sti kiñcit kvacit kadācid dvija vastujātam
vijñānam ekam nijakarmabhedavibhinnacittair bahudhā'bhyupetam.
(VP 2.12.43)
jñānam viśuddham vimalam viśokam aśeṣalobhādinirastasaṅgam
ekam sadaikam paramaḥ pareśaḥ sa vāsudevo na yato'nyad·asti.
(VP 2.12.44)

131 VP 2.12.45 ab in the critical edition has *eṣo* instead of *evam*.

132 sadbhāva evaṃ bhavato mayokto jñānaṃ yathā satyamastyamanyat.
etat tu yat saṃvyavahārabhūtaṃ tatrāpi coktaṃ bhuvanāśritam te.
(VP 2.12.45)

133 tadbhedānusandhānam nātmasvarūpaprayuktamityāha'vijñānamekam' (VP 2.12.43) iti. ātmasvarūpam tu karmarahitam tat eva malarūpaprakṛtisparśarahitam (ŚBh 107; cf Thibaut 1996: 128).

134 upacayāpamcayānarhatayaikam tata eva sadikarūpam. tacca vāśudevasarīramiti tadātmakam (ŚBh 107; cf Thibaut 1996: 129).

135 evamrūpamcidacidātmakam jagad vāsudevaśarīram tadātmakamiti jadagyāthātmyam (ŚBh 107; cf Thibaut 1996: 129).

136 Rāmānuja also cites VP 2.12.46, which reinforces the individual self and matter as his body.

137 jagadyāthātmyajñānaprayojanaṃ mokṣopāyatanam (ŚBh 107; cf Thibaut 1996: 127).

138 astināstiśabdābhidheyaṃ cidacidātmakaṃ kṛtsnaṃ jagatparamasya pareśasya parasya brahmaṇo viṣṇoḥ kāyatvena tadātmakam (ŚBh 108; cf Thibaut 1996: 129).

139 nāstyasatyaśabdāvastisatyaśabdavirodhinau. ataś caitābhyām asattvaṃ hi pratīyate na nirvacanīyatvam. api tu vināśitvaparau. *vasvasti kim* (VP 2.12.41) *mahī ghaṭatvam* (VP 2.12.42) ityatrāpi vināśitvameva hy upapāditam; na niṣpramāṇakatvaṃ jñānabādhyatvaṃ vā (ŚBh 108; cf Thibaut 1996: 129).

140 yattu kālāntareṇāpi nānyām samjñāmupaitu vai
pariṇāmādisambhūtām tadvastu nṛpa tacca kim.
(VP 2.13.96)
anāśī paramārthastu prājñāirabhyupagamyate
tattu nāśi na sandeho nāśidravyopapāditam.
(VP 2.14.24)
VP 2.14.24ab critical edition reads paramārthaśca.

141 viṣṇavādhāram yathā caitat trailokyam samavasthitam
paramārthastu tenokto yathājñānam pradhānataḥ.
(VP 2.13.2)
VP 2.13.cd critical edition states *paramārthaśca me proktā …*

4 Sāṃkhya-Yoga, Kṛṣṇa, and the foremost devotee in the *Bhagavadgītābhāṣya*

Rāmānuja's commentary on the *Bhagavadgītā* (BhG), the *Bhagavadgītābhāṣya* (RBhGBh), is thought to have been written after the *Śrībhāṣya* (ŚBh) (Carman 1974: 60). In this commentary Rāmānuja does not quote scripture as evidence for his arguments as liberally as he does in his other writings. A plausible reason for this sparing use of scripture is that the RBhGBh may have been his last work and, as such, he takes for granted a number of concepts established in his two earlier expositions, the *Vedārthasaṃgraha* (VS) and the ŚBh (van Buitenen 1956: 12–15). Furthermore, the BhG was perhaps theologically closer to Rāmānuja's own Vedānta and thus it did not need the support of the *Viṣṇu Purāṇa* (VP) as often, as there are some commonalities between the BhG's reaction to the monism of the upaniṣads and Rāmānuja's response to the monism of Advaita (van Buitenen 1956: 4). Regardless of this sparing use of the VP, Rāmānuja does utilize it in discussions salient to his theology. In the exegetical instances that are explored in this chapter, both Rāmānuja and his commentator Vedānta Deśika take Śaṅkara's commentary on the BhG as representative of the Advaita perspective. So, in this chapter the terms "Advaita Vedānta" and "Śaṅkara's Vedānta" are used indiscriminately.

Rāmānuja utilizes the VP as support to clarify his interpretation on the following issues: the question of Being and Non-being (2.16), the man of steady wisdom (2.61), the two natures of Kṛṣṇa (7.6), the field and the field-knower (13.4), Kṛṣṇa's *māyā* (7.14), and the foremost devotee (7.17).[1] Structurally, these passages are crucial in their respective chapters and as such the use of VP in their interpretation is significant. Not only is the VP important in Rāmānuja's interpretation of these verses, it is essential to refute the Advaita perspective on the same verses, in order to establish the BhG as a Viśiṣṭādvaita text. In a sense then, the VP is an exegetical link, a kind of intertextual connection between the two Vedānta commentaries, whilst it also differentiates them. This chapter is concerned only with Śaṅkara's and Rāmānuja's interpretion of the BhG; it is neither a study of the philology nor the doctrines and contexts of the BhG as such, unless they are applicable to the discussion at hand.[2]

Defining Sāṃkhya and Yoga

Arjuna's reluctance to fight his kinsmen in Chapter 1 of the BhG and the opening verses of Chapter 2 (BhG 2.1–10), prompt Kṛṣṇa's instruction on Sāṃkhya and Yoga. These speculations, of course, are not those of the *darśanas*, but rather proto-classical forms.[3] In the BhG, Sāṃkhya refers to the discipline of knowledge and Yoga is disciplined activity rooted in the realization that the body is distinct from the individual self.[4] Verses 11–37 of BhG 2 affirm the immortal individual self as distinct from the body in 2.16–18, and the VP is utilized as support in 2.16. The latter portion of Chapter 2 of the BhG (39–72) addresses Yoga and the man of steady wisdom[5] and Rāmānuja also relies on this purāṇa in his commentary on 2.61. As we shall see in both these strategically important verses, 2.16 and 2.61, the role of the VP in their interpretation is important.

Being (*sat*) and Non-being (*asat*)

Verses, 2.16–2.18, on the immortality of the soul are meant as an antidote to Arjuna's misplaced grief, but for Śaṅkara and Rāmānuja, this discussion is only relevant within the larger interpretive contexts of Advaita and Viśiṣṭādvaita respectively. Defining discrimination as knowledge that discerns the soul from the body, Kṛṣṇa mentions several terms such as, *sat*,[6] *asat*, *bhāva* and *abhāva*, which due to their semantic polyvalence problematize the translation of BhG 2.16.[7] We first address Śaṅkara's interpretation of this verse and then evaluate the contribution of the VP in Rāmānuja's refutation of the Advaitin.

Śaṅkara reads BhG 2.16 as follows: *there is no coming to be* (bhāva) *of the non-existent/unreal* (asat)*, there is no ceasing to be* (abhāva) *of the existent/real* (sat). *However, the correct conclusion of both is seen by those who see reality*[8] (*tattva*).[9] Commenting on this passage he states "indeed, cold, heat, and so on and their causes evaluated by the valid means of knowledge are not absolutely real (*vastusat*); for they are transformations (*vikāra*), and transformations are not continuous."[10] According to Śaṅkara, BhG 2.16 refers to *satkāryavāda*, the doctrine that the effect is pre-existent in the cause. Citing the illustration of the clay and its transformations into pots and so on, he remarks that every effect is unreal because it is not perceived as different from its cause. That is, the pot, which is a transformation of clay, is not seen to exist before its creation and also after its destruction. Moreover, the same is the case with the cause of pots and so on, such as clay, for those causes are also not perceived apart from their causes.[11] Here, Śaṅkara identifies true reality (*vastusat*) with cognitive unchangeableness. For him "that is real or true, of which the consciousness is never negated; that is unreal or untrue, of which the consciousness can be negated" (De Smet 1953: 44).

His rationale in introducing the concept of causality is to ultimately deny the reality of anything that is caused. The significance of the doctrine of causality does not lie in its factual framework, but rather in the suggestion that nothing new is ever produced. It also intimates that cause and effect are non-different, and that only the cause is real while "all effects not cognizable apart from the cause are unreal."[12] Thus far, Śaṅkara has grounded his analysis of the real and unreal in the context of cause and its effects utilizing illustrations of clay and its transformations. But though he claims clay as real and its transformations as unreal, he also refrains from labelling clay as ultimately real, because even clay is dependent on its own causes. Though clay is real in comparison to a pot (made of clay) which is unreal, it is only an illustration that is meant to point the seeker to what is ultimately real—the Self or Brahman.

Śaṅkara's discussion transitions from the context of cause-effect to the distinction between the Self and non-Self, where he employs the method of *anvayavyatireka*. Cardona (1981: 93) remarks that Śaṅkara utilizes this mode of reasoning "to discriminate between what is and is not the Self as well as to show what meanings may be attributed to given words."Typically, *anvayavyatireka* for Śaṅkara allows for the cognition of continuity-and-discontinuity as a means of achieving discrimination (Halbfass 1991: 166–67). What continues without disruption is real and all else is unreal. He states:

> always, two cognitions obtain, the cognition of the real (*sadbuddhi*) and the cognition of the unreal (*asadbuddhi*). The cognition of that object which does not discontinue (*avyabhicarati*) that is real, that cognition which discontinues (*vyabhicarati*) is unreal. Therefore, the distinction of real and unreal depends on the issue of cognition ... hence the cognition of a pot because it is discontinuous is unreal; not so, the cognition of the 'real' because it is continuous.[13]

"Śaṅkara is not seeking to investigate the nature of objects, that is to say, how one distinguishes between different elements of the order of things" rather "he draws the line between Being and non-Being, not by way of subjective and objective states, but by distinguishing between the changeful and the permanent"(Ram-Prasad 2013: 2–4). Because for him "what is essential never 'deviates' or 'departs' (*vyabhicar*), while what is 'accidental' may always be discontinued and cease to accompany what is essential."[14] "Thus there is no existence of unreal and caused entities like bodies or dual entities (like heat and cold), nor does the real—the Self—ever cease to exist because it is said to be present everywhere (*avyabhicar*)."[15] So, in the subsequent verse when Kṛṣṇa in 2.17 states *however, know that to be imperishable, by which this whole universe was spun. No one can bring destruction to that which is imperishable,*[16] Śaṅkara comments that this whole world is pervaded by Brahman just as pots are pervaded by the sky, and in fact "this Brahman, known as *sat*, does not change its own nature."[17]

Having suggested the distinction between real and unreal as one dependent on the characteristic of perishability and destruction in BhG 2.17, Kṛṣṇa in 2.18 illustrates this distinction:

> Those bodies of the self (*śarīrin*) have an end while the self itself is eternal, indestructible, and incomprehensible, therefore, fight O' Arjuna.[18]
>
> (BhG 2.18)

For Kṛṣṇa, the perishable–imperishable distinction is the soul–body opposition. Śaṅkara recasts this distinction as an epistemological one. The perishable–imperishable dichotomy that the BhG utilizes to distinguish the body as opposed to the Self is not according to him, one of physical destruction or change. He compares physical bodies to the bodies one finds in dreams—(which are) just as unreal and just as perishable:

> The meaning is, just as the cognition of the reality in mirage and so on continues until it is interrupted at the conclusion of investigation by valid means of knowledge (*pramāṇa*)—this is the end of it. So also, these bodies of the impermanent, eternal soul are like bodies of the indestructible, imperishable self as seen in a dream or due to illusion (*māyā*), men of discrimination affirm this.[19]

Thus *sat-asat* denotes Self and non-Self not based just on perishable (*vināśi*) nature (as in the individual self and the body), but on discontinuing cognitions, even though Kṛṣṇa in 2.18 seems to suggest that the perishable (*vināśi*)-imperishable (*avināśi*) distinction denotes the body and the individual self, for Śaṅkara this distinction is one between Brahman, the true Self and all that is other than this, which is evident in the doctrine of causality which is introduced in 2.16 itself.

To refute Śaṅkara's interpretation of BhG 2.16 based on the doctrine of causality (*satkāryavāda*), Rāmānuja explicitly states in his commentary on 2.16 that "this verse has no reference to *satkāryavāda* and as such this doctrine has no relevance here."[20] Because it is reading these BhG passages using the doctrine of causality that has led Śaṅkara to address the distinction articulated here as one between Brahman and the world that is ultimately a sublatable cognition. Unlike Śaṅkara, Rāmānuja reads the *sat–asat* distinction as ontologically real and as a distinction between the individual self and the body—not as different orders of being, but categories of being (Ram-Prasad 2013: 43). To understand the role of the VP in Rāmānuja's refutation of Śaṅkara's definition of these terms, we begin with the his interpretation of BhG 2.16:

> [t]he non-being (*asat*) has no existence/reality (*bhāva*), the being (*sat*) no non-existence (*abhāva*);
> however, those who see the true nature of both see this conclusion (*anta*).[21]
>
> (BhG 2.16)

New concepts are introduced from the VP, to establish Being and Non-being as the individual self (*ātman*) and the physical body (*deha*):

> [t]he non-being (*asat*), the body, has no existence/reality, whereas (*ca*) the being (*sat*), the self, has no non-existence. When they observe both, the body and the self, those who see their true nature as they observe it, see this conclusion … that means: they see the conclusion that the true nature of the body, an insentient object, is complete (*eva*) non-being, whereas, the true nature of the self, a sentient element, is pure being. Indeed, the true nature of non-being is that it is perishable, whereas the true nature of being is that it is imperishable.[22]

The attribute of consciousness (*cetana*) differentiates existence from non-existence. Whereas, the individual self possesses consciousness the body does not. The latter is understood as non-existence in that it is purely unreal (*asattvam eva*) because it is an insentient object (*acidvastu*) lacking consciousness (*cetana*). Thus non-being (*asat*) is equated with the body which is said to be unreal because it has insentience as its property. *Sat* or Being is the individual self (*jīvātman*) that is sentient. First, Rāmānuja does not take *asat* to mean caused entities. Second, he defines non-being (*asat*) as possessing an inherently perishable (*vināśasvabhāva*) nature and being (*sat*) as characterized by eternal or imperishable nature (*avināśasvabhāva*). His interpretation echoes BhG 2.18 and he in fact claims that his reading of 2.16 is more in line with the rest of the BhG passages, namely 2.17 and 2.18.

As support for his interpretation he utilizes four VP passages: VP 2.12.43ab, 2.12.45ab, 2.14.24, and 2.13.96.[23] Each of these passages provides scriptural evidence for Rāmānuja's claim that the 'unreal' refers to the body and 'real' to the individual self. According to him, one of the defining characteristics of the 'real' is sentience and perishability denotes destruction, change, transformation unrelated to the issue of sublatable or unsublatable cognitions. VP 2.12.43ab and 2.12.45ab provide the scriptural support to distinguish the 'real' and 'unreal' based on the characteristic of sentience:

> Therefore, O' twice-born One, of all possible objects (*vastujāta*) none, anywhere, at any time exists (*asti*), except for discriminative knowledge (*vijñāna*).[24]
>
> (VP 2.12.43ab)

> I have told you this about existence: knowledge (*jñāna*) is being (*satya*), all else is non-being (*asatya*).[25]
>
> (VP 2.12.45ab)

Rāmānuja skips 2.12.43cd and 2.12.44 here and the significance of this is explained shortly. For now, in these two passages, the dichotomy of *asti–nāsti* and *satya–asatya* is drawn along the lines of insentient objects (*vastu*) and consciousness (*vijñāna*/*jñāna*) not based on the distinction between cause and its effects. 2.12.45ab explicitly identifies knowledge as Being (*satya*) or what really exists, and everything else that exists, as Non-being (*asatya*). This is an important distinction that Rāmānuja finds in the VP only, to refute Śaṅkara. In addition to delineating Being and Non-being along the lines of sentience and insentience, the next VP passage introduces the additional characteristic of perishability. The discussion of perishability has come up in BhG 2.18 and we saw that Śaṅkara takes it to denote sublatability. With the use of the VP, Rāmānuja reaches a different conclusion:

> The wise regard the highest reality (*paramārtha*) as imperishable (*avināśi*), whereas there is no doubt that anything derived from perishable matter (*nāśidravya*) is perishable (*nāśi*).[26]
>
> (VP 2.14.24)

This verse provides evidence that Being is a higher reality that is imperishable and is of the nature of consciousness (*vijñāna*/*jñāna*), in contrast to the worldly perishable existence, which though it exists, is not real in this sense. Deśika commenting on Rāmānuja's interpretation in the *Tātparyacandrikā* (TC), notes that:

> the words *sat* and *asat* have to do with being worthy or unworthy of practical use. If the doubt arises as to how these words *satya* and *asatya* are concerned with empirical and ultimate reality, destruction and non-destruction alone as the cause for the use of the terms 'empirical' and 'ultimate' are stated in sage Parāśara's VP verse 2.14.24.[27]

That is, ultimate/highest and empirical reality is distinguished by the issue of physical transformation and change and not by sublation, as Śaṅkara would have it. Rāmānuja claims:

> It is also said in the *Bhagavadgītā*—
> those bodies have an end (BhG 2.18); however know that to be imperishable (BhG 2.17).[28] It is seen that this (perishability of body and imperishability of self) alone is the reason for the designations 'being' and 'non-being'.[29]

Deśika notes:

> in the BhG, this alone is the meaning of the two later verses (2.17 and 2.18). The claim is that even though the word *sat* is used to indicate sentient being, it is only in regard to the particular state of giving up name and form such as gods etc. But strictly speaking, essential nature without modification is denoted by the word *sat.*[30]

This further characterization of *sat* as sentient being but in the context of its association with matter is a reason as to why *sat* here does not refer to Brahman, though the supreme reality is also characterized by sentience and whose essential nature is not subject to change or transformation.

The last VP verse, 2.13.96, defines higher reality (*paramārtha*), Being, as not subject to modification, that warrants a new designation:

> O' King, that which even at different times does not come to have different names (*saṃjña*)
> brought about by being transformed (*pariṇāma*) and the like, what is that?[31]
>
> (VP 2.13.96)

Matter which is perishable (*nāśidravya*) mentioned in VP 2.14.24 is read together with the physical transformations it undergoes that signal a change in denotation. As Deśika comments:

> that which is characterized by aging, change, and destruction, is characterized by relinquishing a previous condition, due to the difference in denotation alone is denoted by the word *acidvastu* and what is not that is denoted by the word *vastu*. That this meaning is articulated clearly, Rāmānuja shows with VP 2.13.96.[32]

These VP passages decisively recast the Advaita interpretation of BhG 2.16–2.18 adding a new dimension to perishability as transformation and change rather than sublatability. As a result, the entities spoken of in BhG 2.16–18 are now understood as the individual self and the body contrary to Śaṅkara's interpretation.

We mentioned earlier that Rāmānuja does not cite VP 2.12.43 cd and 2.14.44. These passages have a clear Advaitic tenor in that they affirm discriminative knowledge (*vijñāna*) mentioned in 2.12.43ab as one (*eka*), is said to be perfect, pure, and free from pain and afflictions, single, eternal and is declared to be the supreme Vāsudeva, apart from which nothing else exists.[33] Perhaps Rāmānuja omits these verses because of their monistic sensibility. He may also omit them because, from the perspective of the VP context, these stanzas address the Supreme Self, Viṣṇu, and not the individual self, which is contrary to his perspective. However, we have seen in the previous chapter on the ŚBh that he undertakes a detailed interpretation of these very VP verses, from 2.12, 2.13, and 2.14, to establish the topic of discussion as the individual self and not Brahman. Hence, even though these particular VP passages may support Śaṅkara, they are re-interpreted by Rāmānuja.

Deśika remarks in Rāmānuja's commentary on BhG 2.16 that:

> by ten verses, in the middle of the commentary on the *Brahma Sūtras* [ŚBh] with the beginning and concluding sections of the purāṇa, and in accord with perception and the various śruti and smṛti, the meaning of the words thing, no-thing, existence and non-existence is established with VP 2.12.42 and so on as based on modification and non-modification alone.[34]

So as far as Rāmānuja is concerned the VP passages, and now BhG 2.16–18, denote Being and Non-being as the individual self and the body.

Realization of Brahman (*samyagdarśana*) and realization of the individual self (*ātmadarśana*)

The VP is utilized in Chapter 2 of the BhG a second time in the discussion of Yoga,[35] specifically, to address the man of steady wisdom (2.61) who according to Kṛṣṇa successfully implements the teaching of this chapter.[36] In addition, to the different perceptions of the discipline of knowledge and discipline of action and their relationship, Śaṅkara and Rāmānuja also disagree on the path to achieving the goal and the definition of that goal itself. For Śaṅkara, the man of discipline through renunciation of actions, control of senses, thinking Brahman to be the inner self of all, attains the experience of the absolute—*samyagdarśana*. On the other hand, for Rāmānuja, the man of steady wisdom conquers his senses and his desires for objects through meditation on a form of Viṣṇu. His argument is rooted in scriptural evidence from the VP.

Śaṅkara views the paths of Sāmkhya and Yoga, presented by Kṛṣṇa, as different and incompatible since the discipline of knowledge (*sāṃkhya*) and the discipline of action (*yoga*) are rooted in two different types of understanding (*buddhidvayāśraya*).[37] As the path of knowledge, Sāmkhya, a kind of meditative reflection teaches that "the self because it is free (*abhāva*) from the six-fold transformation like birth and so on (*janmādiṣaḍvikriya*), is a non-agent (*akartā*)".[38] Whereas, Yoga is the performance of actions based on the understanding of *dharma* and *adharma* (*dharmādharmaviveka*) is based on the view that the Self is other than the body (*dehādivyatirikta*). The Self is understood as an agent of actions (*kartṛ*) an enjoyer (*bhoktṛ*) of results and so on.[39] Thus Sāṃkhya, the path of knowledge and Yoga, the path of action are two different paths, rooted in two different concepts of non-agency (*akartṛtva*) and agency (*kartṛtva*) of the Self and the understanding of unity (*ekatva*) and plurality (*anekatva*) respectively.[40] Given such an understanding of the relationship of Sāṃkhya to Yoga, the man of steady wisdom, one who has correctly understood the teaching of BhG 2, according to Śaṅkara follows Sāṃkhya and not Yoga.

BhG 2.61 characterizes the man of steady wisdom as follows: controlling all of them (senses), let him be intent upon Me as the supreme (*matpara*); for, he who has his senses under control has his knowledge firmly established (*sthitaprajña*).[41] For Śaṅkara, the one who is "established firmly in the wisdom 'I am the Supreme Brahman' is a *sthitaprajña*".[42] However, one who desires such knowledge characterized as *samyagdarśana* (*samyagdarśana-lakṣaṇa*), must first control his senses. How is this to be accomplished? Śaṅkara understands this to mean that one must sit in concentration thinking "I am not different from Him" (*na anyo'ham tasmāt*), that is Vāsudeva, who is the inner self of all. Furthermore, it is through force of such repeated practice (*abhyāsabala*) that the senses are brought under control. This then is how Śaṅkara portrays the man of steady wisdom, as one who engages in the practice of Sāṃkhya, but not Yoga.

Contrary to Śaṅkara, Rāmānuja defines the man of steady wisdom as one who integrates the Sāṃkhya teaching of the difference in essential natures of the body and the soul and applies it in his spiritual practice (*Yoga*).[43] The man of steady wisdom engaged in devotion to knowledge perfects the goal of visualizing the essential nature of the self. His mind depends on only the self within himself (*manasā ātmaikāvalambana*) and expels all desires. Rāmānuja calls this the highest devotion to knowledge (*jñānaniṣṭhākāṣṭhā*).[44] The differences between Śaṅkara's and Rāmānuja's understanding of the goal of the *sthitaprajña*, whether it is *ātmadarśana* or *samyagdarśana*, is reflected in the nature and extent to which the aspirant depends on Kṛṣṇa. For scriptural support for this view, Rāmānuja turns to the VP. Commenting on BhG 2.61, he states:

> [d]esiring to abandon all faults, restraining the senses, which are difficult to conquer because of their attachment to objects, fixing the mind on me, the auspicious object of meditation (*śubhāśraya*), he should remain composed. When the mind has me [Kṛṣṇa] as its object, then such a mind, purified because of the burning away of all impurities and without attachment to sense-objects, brings the senses under its control. Then the mind, restraining the senses, will be able to see the self.[45]

The mind requires an auspicious object of meditation (*śubhāśraya*) in order to control the senses and gain the true realization of the individual self (*ātmadarśana*). Restraint of senses alone is not enough:

> for one who is restrained without the experience of the self, the passion for objects does not cease, when the longing for objects does not end, the troubling senses of even a wise man, whose mind is restrained, prove strong, that is, carry away the mind by force. Thus the overpowering of the senses depends on experiencing the self, and the experiencing of the self is dependent on the overpowering of the senses; thus, firm establishment in knowledge is difficult to achieve.[46]

The uncontrollable hankering of the senses, even for one whose mind is restrained, is due to the accumulation of karma from innumerable previous births. This deposit of karma is what needs to be consumed allowing for the unrestricted reflection on the true nature of the individual self. This then is the complete definition of subduing the senses—not simply turning away from external objects but curbing the inner temptation that continually leads the mind astray from the vision of the self. Whereas, Śaṅkara understands "focusing of the mind on Viṣṇu" as contemplation of "I am Vāsudeva", for Rāmānuja it is a form of Viṣṇu, the object of meditation is the sole aid. VP

6.7 traditionally referred to as the *Treatise on the Auspicious Object of Meditation* (*Śubhāśrayaprakaraṇa*) provided scriptural evidence to support the view that Viṣṇu alone can be an efficient object of meditation.

We have come across VP 6.7, a section that is very important to Rāmānuja in the earlier chapters on the VS and the ŚBh. The context of VP 6.7 is a dialogue between the brothers Keśidhvaja and Khāṇḍikya. The former teaches the latter the path of Yoga just as Kṛṣṇa imparts his teaching to Arjuna. Though the VP does not mention the term "Sāṃkhya", the spiritual practice presented as an antidote to ignorance (VP 6.7.11–16.7.25) prior to the path of Yoga (VP 6.7.26–6.7.104) is remarkably similar to Kṛṣṇa's teaching in the BhG 2. According to Keśidhvaja, the path of Yoga begins with the knowledge that the body is distinct from the self and that the properties of matter (*prakṛti*), which comprises the body do not taint the self. The purification of the mind by the knowledge that the self is not the body is a precursor to the practice entailed in subsequent stages of Yoga.

The Yoga described in the VP is of course not the Yoga of BhG 2. However, the fact that the VP charts a spiritual path called "Yoga" that begins with awareness of the knowledge of the distinction of body and self mirrors the structure of Chapter 2 of the BhG itself. According to Rāmānuja, just as Kṛṣṇa begins by praising Sāṃkhya and then Yoga, which are to be integrated in the man of steady wisdom, so too, the VP presents a regimen that integrates the discrimination of the self from the body with further spiritual practice.

In addition to the structural similarities between Chapter 2 of the BhG and VP 6.7, when Kṛṣṇa in BhG 2.61 claims one must be intent upon me (Kṛṣṇa) as the supreme (*matpara*), he takes this literally. As Ram-Prasad remarks:

> Śaṅkara does not see Kṛṣṇa as a creator god, a being whole and distinct before there is creation, bringing beings into creation—*ex nihilo*—and continuing to be a being distinct from creation. ... [instead he] reads Kṛṣṇa's statements about his power in relation to being and things in a way that does not challenge Kṛṣṇa's divinity, yet subtly re-presents it within a metaphysics of non-duality.[47]

So, when Kṛṣṇa in 2.61 claims that He ought to be the object of devotion, for Rāmānuja this is to love the Supreme Being who is the controller and supporter of the world and not in the non-dual sense as Śaṅkara interprets it.

The VP passage that Rāmānuja utilizes is part of the section of the VP that recommends the yogin to mediate on the "great form of Hari", which is the origin of all the incarnations, similar to the one seen by Arjuna in the BhG, that are assumed by Him in sport (VP 6.7.70) and it is this very form, which as an object of purification in the elimination of sins and it is this passage that Rāmānuja utilizes in his commentary on BhG 2.61:

> just as the rising flames of fire, fanned by wind burns away a forest of dry trees

so also, Viṣṇu, who is established in the minds of all yogis, (destroys) all sins.[48]

When Kṛṣṇa claims in BhG 2.61 "be intent upon me", Rāmānuja interprets this to mean that the supreme person, Viṣṇu, is to be understood as the auspicious object (*śubhāśraya*) of meditation as mentioned in the VP.

But in what sense is Viṣṇu the object of meditation in the VP? It seems that the VP itself oscillates between different ontologies, never clearly advocating one view or the other. In one instance, the end result of such yogic behavior is defined as the absorption into Brahman (*brahmalaya*, 6.7.27).[49] However, the purāṇa says a few stanzas later that if the person is steeped in this kind of meditation, Brahman attracts the individual self to himself, like a magnet attracts iron. This analogy is anything, but monistic. It speaks of a closer connection between the individual self and Brahman, but does not suggest a convergence of the two (VP 6.7.30).[50] The next verse is even more explicit in its non-Advaitic perspective, when Yoga is defined as union (*samyoga*) in Brahman (VP 6.7.31).[51] However, the term *śubhāśraya* utilized by Rāmānuja as the object of meditation, occurs in VP 6.7.54, where begins the description of the stages of meditation focusing on forms of Viṣṇu including incarnated form such as the Kṛṣṇa of the BhG. That Rāmānuja considers this section of the VP as analogous to the BhG teaching is also reflected in the sole use of this purāṇa as scriptural evidence. In the next section the VP's role in characterizing the nature of Kṛṣṇa as discussed in BhG 7 and BhG 13 is examined.

Kṛṣṇa's nature

Two of the most important instances in the BhG where the nature of Kṛṣṇa vis-à-vis his relationship to the world is addressed is in chapters 7 and 13. Within these chapters, passages 7.4–6 and 13.2–4 are significant. Rāmānuja utilizes the VP in both these contexts (7.6 and 13.4) to establish the Viśiṣṭādvaita view of Brahman's relationship to creation. Here too, Rāmānuja turns to the VP to refute Śaṅkara's reading of these BhG passages. We first examine the interpretation of Śaṅkara and then address Rāmānuja's response, but first a brief comment on the structural importance of these passages within their respective chapters.

Chapter 7 of the BhG marks the beginning of a comprehensive Kṛṣṇa theology that continues into the rest of the chapters. This self-revelation of Kṛṣṇa in a monotheistic context differs from older revealed literature and hence Chapter 7 marks a crucial juncture in the BhG narrative (van Buitenen 1981: 6–13). Kṛṣṇa presented as the creator, the maintainer of dharma, is also the liberator from *saṃsāra* for those who knowing his true nature are devoted to him (Malinar 2007: 128–29). Within this broader context, an exposition of Kṛṣṇa's nature is begun where his lower nature and higher nature are defined (7.5) and then through these He declares Himself the womb (*yoṇi*) of all beings (7.6). It is in the commentary on 7.6 that Rāmānuja utilizes the VP as scriptural support for his interpretation of Kṛṣṇa's nature and His relationship to the created world. This very topic is explored further in Chapter 13 also and in some ways it is a continuation of what was begun in Chapter 7.[52]

In Chapter 13, the two constituents of being—the field (*kṣetra*) and the knower of the field (*kṣetrajña*), and their relationship to Kṛṣṇa are explored and Kṛṣṇa assumes "the role of the *kṣetrajña* in all fields of consciousness, in all bodies" (13.2). What is problematic here is the interpretation of the field-knower (*kṣetrajña*) and its connection to the field (*kṣetra*). The BhG references the field-knower twice, once to refer to Kṛṣṇa's higher nature (BhG 7.5) and once to claim that he himself is the *kṣetrajña* in all beings (BhG13.2). Śaṅkara interprets the field-knower as one's true Self/Brahman. For Rāmānuja the field-knower is the individual self not ultimately Brahman. BhG 13.2 is interpreted from the Advaita perspective much more easily as the field-knower is ultimately Brahman limited by adjuncts. Nevertheless, for Rāmānuja BhG 13.2 and 13.4 affirm the distinction between the Brahman and the individual self. To read the BhG 13.2–13.4 in this way, he relies on the VP. First, we evaluate the function of the VP in Rāmānuja's commentary on BhG 7.5–6 and BhG 13.2–4.

The two natures (*prakṛti*) of Kṛṣṇa

At the beginning of Chapter 7 Kṛṣṇa articulates his relationship to the world through a discussion of His two natures—a lower (*apara*) nature constituting the eight elements and their evolutes that comprise matter and a higher (*para*) nature, the *jīvabhūta*, the soul, which supports the world.[53] Then, these two natures are declared to be the source of the entire world:[54]

> Keep in mind that all beings originate out of these (*prakṛti*-s)
> I am the origin (*yoni*) of the entire universe and its dissolution as well.[55]

Śaṅkara understands the lower nature of Kṛṣṇa as impure and inferior. Its essential nature is one of bondage in *saṃsāra* (*saṃsārabandhanātmikā*)[56] and as the illusory-power belonging to Īśvara (*aiśvarī māyāśakti*) that is eightfold.[57] Since, Śaṅkara uses *māyā* in different senses in his commentaries,[58] to understand his interpretation of matter as *māyā* we turn to BhG 4.6, where Kṛṣṇa claims *even though I am unborn, being the imperishable self, though I am the lord of all beings, still, controlling my material nature (prakṛti), I come into being by my own supernatural power (ātmamāyayā)*.[59] The context of the discussion here is Kṛṣṇa's incarnations, however, it gives us a glimpse of how Śaṅkara views *prakṛti*. In the BhG context he comments that Kṛṣṇa, being the Īśvara of all beings, from Brahmā down to the blade of grass, controls his own nature (*prakṛti*), which is Viṣṇu's *māyā* (*vaiṣṇavī māyā*), composed of the three qualities (*guṇa*). It is on this power (*vaśa*) that this whole world rests and being deluded by it, the world does not know its own self as Vāsudeva.[60]

Prakṛti as creative energy essentially deludes, because it prevents the recognition of one's true self as Brahman.

If Śaṅkara defines the lower nature, matter, as an illusory power, he understands the higher nature as Kṛṣṇa's very self (*mama ātmabhutam*) that penetrates (*antaḥpraviṣṭa*) and supports (*dharyate*) the world. Śaṅkara understands the *jīva* as Brahman with adjuncts, and thus the *kṣetrjña* is ultimately Brahman itself, the Self of all; any discussion of the two *prakṛti*-s is rooted in ignorance. The connection of the Supreme Self to adjuncts is due to ignorance that results from past experiences and presents itself as the *kṣetrajña* and "which is a consequence of our psychophysical limitation a cognitive failure" (Alston 1980, Vol III: 1–3; Ram-Prasad 2013: 106). Basically, Rāmānuja needs to prove the metaphysical reality of the individual self in relation to Brahman. Furthermore, though Rāmānuja would agree with Śaṅkara that *prakṛti* can be deluding, he would not agree with its characterization as delusion/*māyā*.

In BhG 7.4, commenting on Kṛṣṇa's lower nature Rāmānuja claims:

> this *prakṛti* of this universe which exists in the form of different and limitless objects of enjoyment, means of enjoyment and places of enjoyment, is divided eight-fold in the forms of earth, water, fire, ether, and so on, which have smell and other characteristic qualities, in the form of mind (*manas*) and other organs of sense, and in the form of principles such as *mahat* and *ahaṃkāra*—it belongs to me.[61]

This is essentially similar to Śaṅkara's view of *prakṛti* and though Kṛṣṇa asserts that this lower *prakṛti* encompasses all the qualities and faults of an impermanent nature, it belongs to Kṛṣṇa. The higher *prakṛti* is the animating principle of this whole world:

> whose nature is different from this inanimate *prakṛti*, which is the object of enjoyment for animate beings. It is higher, i.e., more pre-eminent compared to the lower *prakṛti* which is constituted only of inanimate substances. My higher *prakṛti*, is the individual self; know this as my higher *prakṛti* by which the whole inanimate universe is supported.[62]

Commenting on the two natures of Kṛṣṇa as the womb of all beings, he states:

> keep in mind that all beings, from Brahmā to a blade of grass, situated at higher or lower levels, mixtures of spirit and matter, originate out of these, my two natures involving an aggregate of *cetana* and *acetana*; they are mine. Indeed, since they originate out of my two natures, they belong to me alone. So, keep in mind that, since the entire universe originates from my two natures, and since both (all beings and the universe) originate from me and are mine, I alone am the origin of the entire universe,

> that I alone am its dissolution, and that I alone am the master (*śeṣin*). The fact that both *prakṛti* and *puruṣa*, which are an aggregate of sentience and insentience, originate out of the Supreme person, is established in śruti and smṛti.[63]

In this comment the world comprised of matter and individual selves is repeatedly affirmed as belonging to Kṛṣṇa for instance—my two natures involving an aggregate of *cetana* and *acetana*, they are mine; they originate out of my two natures, they (matter and individual selves) belong to me alone; since both (all beings and the universe) originate from me and are mine. Having affirmed that the world belongs to Krsna, Rāmānuja decisively rejects the Advaita perspective by claiming the relationship between Kṛṣṇa and his two natures as that between master–servant (*śeṣa–śeṣin*), which is an important aspect of the soul–body paradigm. In fact, in his commentary on 7.7, Rāmānuja claims that just as the individual self is the *śeṣin* over physical bodies, so also Kṛṣṇa is the *śeṣin* in all individual selves. Whereas, the field-knower, for Śaṅkara, is ultimately Brahman himself, for Rāmānuja, it is the individual self. The former distinguishes Brahman (field-knower) from the world (field) while Rāmānuja differentiates between the world (field), the individual self (field-knower), and Brahman. Rāmānuja reads these three BhG verses (7.4–7.6) as articulating the body – soul relationship between Kṛṣṇa and his two *prakṛti*-s in contrast to Śaṅkara for whom the world, including the field-knower, is only provisionally real.

Rāmānuja turns to the *Subāla Upaniṣad* and the VP for scriptural support to counter the Advaita claim. Although, it may seem that he utilizes śruti first and then resorts to smṛti for corroboration, the concept of master–servant (*śeṣa–śeṣi*), which is used to interpret BhG 7.4–7.6, is not articulated in the upaniṣad, but is drawn from the VP. But first, the śruti support:

> The *mahat* is absorbed into the unmanifest (*avyakta*), the unmanifest is absorbed into the imperishable (*akṣara*), the imperishable is absorbed into darkness (*tamas*), the darkness becomes one with the supreme lord.[64]
>
> (Sub Up 2)

The section of the *Subāla Upaniṣad* from which this passage is taken addresses the origin of the world and the creation of beings. Here, it is cited to support the view that creation manifests out of Viṣṇu and is reabsorned into Him. This upaniṣad is a synthesis of the various upaniṣad teachings on creation such as, "that one which was neither existence nor non-existence", the concept of the primordial egg, the sacrifice of the divine primordial being (*puruṣa*),[65] and a type of Sāṃkhyan theory of evolutes that eventually gives rise to the manifest world (Radhakrishnan 1996: 863–65). The passage that Rāmānuja utilizes teaches the latter, where all creation is reabsorbed into the Supreme Being—proceeding from *mahat* to the unmanifest to the imperishable to darkness to Brahman. *Tamas* here is not one of the qualities (*guṇa*) of *prakṛti*, but it is the unmanifest darkness from which all the subtle elements such as air, water, and so on are meant to evolve. By stating that *mahat* is eventually reabsorbed into Viṣṇu, the *Subāla* passage does not clarify the issue of distinction of the world from Viṣṇu.

Though, it clearly supports the concept of Viṣṇu as the source of all creation, but the fact that it is reabsorbed into Viṣṇu suggests His close association with the vicissitudes of matter, which is contrary to the perfections that characterize Him. The main reason for the use of *Subāla Upaniṣad* seems to be to support the view that Brahman as the cause of creation is source of manifestation and reabsorption of the world.

Perhaps, Rāmānuja cannot at this point cite any of the upaniṣad passages on creation such as *Chāndogya Upaniṣad* 6 on *sadvidyā* without creating further exegetical complications; besides those passages do not address creation in terms of *puruṣa* and *prakṛti*. One upaniṣad that could support Rāmānuja's view is *Śvetasvatara* 4.10—*One unborn male [billy-goat], burning with passion, covers one unborn female [nanny-goat] colored red, white, and black, and giving birth to numerous offspring with the same colo[u]rs as hers.*[66] Though Rāmānuja himself does not cite this passage, Deśika comments that the VP passage 1.2.24 that is utilized does support the *Śvetāśvatara Upaniṣad*:

> Because the essential nature of substance is eternal, by this, there is no contradiction with passages such as Śve Up 4.5 etc. This he illustrates with VP 1.2.24.[67]

But note also that Śaṅkara reads matter as a *māyā*, an illusory power of Īśvara and this upaniṣad passage might complicate Rāmānuja's assertion that matter (*prakṛti*) is real.

Regardless of whether Rāmānuja had this upaniṣad in mind, he does not cite it and relies instead on the VP, and the purāṇic vocabulary is more suitable to the BhG discussion. Subsequent to Sub Up 2, three VP passages are utilized to counter Śaṅkara's Advaitic interpretation of the field-knower as Brahman associated with adjuncts. The context of VP 1.2 is the evolution of creation. Here, it is stated that *prakṛti* in its manifest and unmanifest state, *puruṣa*, and time are the three aspects that comprise the supreme Viṣṇu.[68] Furthermore, Hari of His own will is said to enter *prakṛti* and *puruṣa*, which commences the process of creation:[69]

> O' sage (Maitreya) different from the essence of Viṣṇu are the two forms *puruṣa* and *pradhāna*.[70]
>
> (VP 1.2.24ab)

This gives Rāmānuja the necessary context to establish the distinction and unity between Kṛṣṇa and his two natures and at the same time affirm their reality. That the VP provides the necessary evidence is reflected in Deśika's comment that the next two VP passages utilized as support [by Rāmānuja] are "for the sake of clearly articulating our position":[71]

> the *prakṛti* which was spoken of, by me, as having the nature of manifest and unmanifest
> and *puruṣa* they are both absorbed into the supreme self.
>
> (VP 6.4.39)
>
> the supreme lord is the support (*ādhāra*) of all and the supreme self,
> he is praised by the name Viṣṇu in the Veda and the upaniṣads.[72]
>
> (VP 6.4.40)

In VP 1.2.24ab the relationship between Brahman, matter, and individual selves is established as matter (*pradhāna*) and individual selves (*puruṣa*) are affirmed as forms [Rāmānuja reads modes] of Viṣṇu. Here, in VP 6.4.39–40, Viṣṇu is declared as not only the source, but the supporter and lord of all even during after the dissolution of creation. Rāmānuja notes that matter and individual selves exist as modes of the Supreme Reality eternally:

> Thus, since everything constitutes the body of the supreme person and is only a mode of the supreme person who is their self, the supreme person alone exists; all words denote him only. The four-armed one (Viṣṇu), teaches this here, by *sāmānādhikaraṇya.*[73]

Though reabsorbed into Viṣṇu, matter and individual selves remain as modes even in the unmanifest state, distinct yet dependent on Him. The commentator remarks that the "dissolution of *prakṛti* and *puruṣa* in the supreme self is just as water in milk, the nature of their union or connection is unworthy of distinction [though there is a distinction]."[74] This interpretation of *puruṣa* and *prakṛti* as modes is not supported by the upaniṣad passage, while the VP passage is more conducive to this interpretation.

What follows from BhG 7.8 to 7.13 is an elaboration of this nature of the Supeme Being as the mode-possessor (*prakārin*) (van Buitenen 1974: 101). Thus BhG 7.7 is crucial in guiding the interpretation of subsequent verses through the Viśiṣṭādvaita perspective. The VP verses provide a much more detailed picture of the process of creation and the Supreme Being's relationship to it, which supports more effectively Rāmānuja's interepretation of the BhG. Utilizing the same terminology of the *prakṛti* and *puruṣa* as in the BhG, the VP clearly differentiates between these entities and Brahman, while articulating the connection amongst them as one of unity. At the same time, the VP also counters Śaṅkara's interpretation of the world as simply *māyā*.

The field (*kṣetra*) and the field-knower (*kṣetrajña*)

The topic of Kṛṣṇa's nature, particularly his relationship to the created world in terms of his lower *prakṛti* (kṣetra) and higher *prakṛti* (*kṣetrajña*), is explored not only in Chapter 7, but in Chapter 13 of the BhG as well.[75] However, in this chapter, the issue is complicated by Kṛṣṇa's claim that he is also the field-knower (*kṣetrajña*) in all beings: "and know me also as the field-knower in all fields, O' Arjuna. In my view, the knowledge of the field and its knower, is the highest knowledge."[76] The BhG is clear that the knowledge of the distinction between the two entities, the field and the field-knower is true knowledge. However, who is the field-knower? Is it simply the individual self or ultimately Brahman as Śaṅkara understands this verse? The discussion begins in 13.2 and is summarized in 13.4. It is in his commentary on the latter verse that Rāmānuja turns to the VP. We will first examine Śaṅkara's commentary and then Rāmānuja's response to this Advaita interpretation.

For Śaṅkara, Chapter 13 of the BhG is a continuation of Chapter 7 as both address the relationship of the field (*kṣetra*) and the field-knower (*kṣetrajña*):

> In Chapter Seven, the two *prakṛti*-s of Īśvara were mentioned. The inferior *prakṛti* is of the nature of the three qualities (*guṇa*), which divides eight-fold; this is the cause of *saṃsāra*; the superior *prakṛti*, existing as the individual self (*jīva*), named *kṣetrajña,* is of the nature of Īśvara. By these two *prakṛti*-s, Īśvara is the cause of world creation, sustenance, and dissolution. The chapter on *kṣetra* (13) is begun to determine the truth of Īśvara by means of an investigation of the two *prakṛti*-s called *kṣetra* and *kṣetrajña,* which he possesses.[77]

In the previous section on BhG 7.4–7, we saw that for Śaṅkara the knower is one who knows the truth of Viṣṇu (*viṣṇos tattvavit*), that is, knows that Vāsudeva is his own Self. Knowing this he seeks to gain knowledge by contemplating "I myself am the Lord Vāsudeva, I am none else" (7.18). Thus though a plurality of transmigrating individual sleves may be real empirically, there is only Vāsudeva, the Supreme Brahman. His discussion of *kṣetra* and *kṣetrajña* in the present chapter (13) is also in line with such a reading. What strengthens Śaṅkara's interpretation is Kṛṣṇa's claim in 13.2, "know me also as the field-knower present in all fields" (*kṣetrajñam cāpi mām viddhi sarvakṣetreṣu*). His comment on this BhG verse is as follows: "For this reason, the field-knower who in reality is Īśvara, due to difference of adjuncts created by *avidyā*, becomes as it were a transmigrator, just as the nature of the body is identified with that of the self."[78]

The error of personhood is a cognitive error. Due to the influence of adjuncts "the *puruṣa*, *jīva*, field-knower, enjoyer are all synonyms" that come to denote the Self.[79] However, according to Śaṅkara, any discussion of the field-knower is not of importance as is the attempt to differentiate between the field and the field-knower:

> The union characterized by the reciprocal superimposition of the attributes of field and field-knower, subject and object and their different essential natures, this union resembles the superimposition of the rope and shell-silver etc. and that of the snake and silver etc. due to the lack of

knowledge of their difference. For him who discriminates between the field and field-knower, this union which is of the nature of superimposition is called ignorance.[80]

The apparent association between the field and the field-knower is in fact "essentially superimposition [which is] of the nature of wrong knowledge (*mithyājñāna*)" (Sarasvati 1989: 46–47). According to Śaṅkara 13.2 affirms the distinction between the field and the field-knower, but is relevant only in the context of ignorance (*avidyā*). BhG 13.4 is a reiteration of 13.2. So, when Kṛṣṇa claims in 13.4 "it is this truth about the field and field-knower that has been sung manifold by the sages, separately with various chants, and with words from the *Brahma Sūtras*, having valid reasons, and drawing the right conclusions,"[81] the *truth* mentioned here is the illusory nature of the association between the field and field-knower, which results from ignorance as discussed in 13.2.

Before we discuss Śaṅkara's interpretation of 13.4, a brief comment here on the translation of this verse is needed. According to Rāmānuja, BhG 13.4 articulates three different genres of literature—those sung by the sages, hymns, and the *Brahma Sūtras.*[82] However, this verse can also be interpreted as referring to two types of texts only—the hymns sung by various seers and the *Brahma Sūtras* (Zaehner 1969: 355). Śaṅkara opts for the latter interpretation. Interpreting *brahmasūtrapada* as statements regarding Brahman, i.e., upaniṣad passages, Śaṅkara only cites Br Up 1.4.7 "one should consider them as simply his self."[83] This upaniṣad echoes Kṛṣṇa's claim that He is the Self in all beings. In summary, Śaṅkara does not cite scripture to differentiate the relationship between the field and the field-knower, because such a conjunction itself is unreal. In BhG 13.4 he couches the discussion in the context of knowledge and ignorance, which is the only distinction that is important for him. To affirm the difference between field (*kṣetra*) and field-knower (*kṣetrajña*) as real, Rāmānuja utilizes the VP. His use of the VP facilitates his refutation of Śaṅkara's interpretation of the apparent association between the field and the field-knower.

As mentioned earlier, Rāmānuja interprets BhG 13.4 as speaking of three genres of texts. He understands "sung by sages" to refer to smṛti, and "by hymns (*chandas*)" to mean upaniṣads, and so in his commentary he cites from the VP and the *Mahābhārata* (*Śāntiparvan*), and then concludes with the-*Taittirīya Upaniṣad.*[84] The interpretation that BhG 13.4 refers to three types of texts rather than two, gives Rāmānuja the opportunity to utilize the VP and the MBh, which broaden the context of the BhG. The inclusion of smṛti literature as relevant in these matters is a distinctively Viśiṣṭādvaitic position. The commentator, Vedānta Deśika notes, by means of smṛti passages that are clear (*viśadopabṛṃhaṇavākyānusāreṇa*) Rāmānuja determines the meaning of unclear Vedic passages (*aviśadavedavākyārthaniścaya*).[85]

The VP episode that Rāmānuja turns to once again is the narrative of Bharata, who though a devotee of Viṣṇu, because of his attachment to a mother-less fawn succumbs to repeated births. He ultimately understands the distinction between the body and the soul that allows him to overcome all attachments. Born as a palanquin-bearer for a local king, in one of his births, Bharata imparts this discriminative knowledge to him. This section of the VP is also cited in the ŚBh to establish the metaphysical reality of the individual self and in the discussion on the plurality of selves. Overall, VP 2.13 is dedicated to the recognition of the distinction between the body and self and the result of such an understanding as liberating. Thus to a certain degree, Rāmānuja is justified in utilizing these verses to support his interpretation of BhG 13.4. Yet, there are passages in this section of the purāṇa that seem to support the Advaita perspective. For instance, VP 2.13.91 mentions that only one soul is dispersed in all bodies (*samasta deheṣu pumān eko*). In the ŚBh, Rāmānuja undertakes an extended re-interpretation of VP 2.12, 2.13, and 2.14 to argue that it is indeed the relationship of Brahman to the world and individual selves as one of soul to body that is articulated. We have already discussed this in Chapter 2 in the section on the nature of the individual self and also the section on ignorance. I do not restate that entire argument here, but instead note that, for Rāmānuja, VP 2.13 exemplifies the soul–body relationship, with the Supreme Being as the supporter (*ādhāra*) of the individual selves and matter. Thus 2.13.91 is re-interpreted from the Viśiṣṭādvaita view rather than from that of Advaita.

Coming back to the commentary on BhG 13.4, Rāmānuja utilizes the following VP quotes to support the distinction between the body and the individual self:

> It, the true nature (*yāthātmya*) of the field and the field-knower, has been sung manifold, in various ways, by the sages, Parāśara and others—
> O' King, I, you, and others as well, are borne by elements
> this group of elements in turn moves, moving along in the stream of qualities.
>
> (VP 2.13.65)

> Now these qualities, goodness and the rest, depend on acts. O' King
> and those acts are obstructed by *avidyā* in all living beings.
>
> (VP 2.13.66)

> The self is pure, imperishable, tranquil, quality-less and higher than matter (*prakṛti*)
> it alone does neither increase nor decrease in any living being.[86]
>
> (VP 2.13.67)[87]

Here the material body is stated as comprised of *guṇas* (the three qualities that comprise matter/*prakṛti*) and that it functions according to their respective predispositions. The flow of these qualities in the cycle of *saṃsāra* is dictated by one's karma. To such a description of the body is contrasted the definition of the self as higher than matter (*prakṛti*) and as eternal, free from *guṇas* and peaceful. Though Rāmānuja does not reiterate his discussion from the ŚBh on the interpretation of VP 2.13, Vedānta Deśika commenting on Rāmānuja's interpretation of BhG 13.4 remarks that VP 2.13.65 opposes the meaning that the non-difference of the self and body is the non-difference between the palanquin-bearer (Bharata) and the king who is to be carried, which is precisely what Śaṅkara would claim.[88]

The distinction between matter (*kṣetra*) and the individual self (*kṣetrajña*) is further elaborated in the subsequent discussion on the topic of what constitutes "I". Bharata poses the following questions to the king:

> Since the body of a man is characterized severally by his head, hands and so on,
> to what shall I attach the term 'I' O' King.
>
> (VP 2.13.85)
>
> Is this head of yours 'you', or your neck, or stomach?[89]
> are your feet etc. 'you'? what part of you is 'you' O' King?
> You are actually distinct from all your parts O' King
> O' King think seriously about the question 'who am I'.[90]
>
> (VP 2.13.98–99)

The individual identity one derives based solely on the physical body is erroneous. The true "I", which is one's individual self, is distinct from all anatomical parts, indeed the body as a whole. Bharata urges the king to re-consider individuality that a person takes for granted, which derives from the misidentification of the self with the body.

Though for Rāmānuja, the VP passages discriminate the individual conscious self and the physical body, the risk of an Advaita interpretation of these purāṇa passages remains, as is evident from Deśika's comment mentioned earlier. In the ŚBh, Rāmānuja's extended polemic counters such rival interpretations of these VP passages by arguing the soul–body paradigm. Here in his commentary on BhG 13.4 he cites a MBh passage instead as evidence of the soul–body relationship between Brahman and the world:

> They say that the senses, mind, intellect, vigor, splendor, strength, and constancy,
> have Vāsudeva as their self, and so do the field and the knower of the field.[91]
>
> (MBh Śāntiparvan 13.135.136)

Vāsudeva as the self of both the matter and individual selves validates the soul–body connection so important to refute the Advaitin. This verse also denotes matter and individual selves as field and field-knower, the terms utilized in BhG 13.4 as well. The VP and MBh verses support all aspects of Rāmānuja's

Vedānta necessary to establish the distinction between the individual self and matter as real.

Subsequent to the VP and MBh passages, Rāmānuja also cites from the upaniṣads. He glosses the phrase in 13.4, "by various Vedic hymns" as a reference to the Vedānta portion of the Veda and utilizes the *Taittirīya Upaniṣad* 2. Chapter 2 of this upaniṣad is called the "chapter on bliss" (*ānandavallī*) wherein the nature of the self as food, mind, breath, and finally bliss is addressed.[92] This text is also discussed in the *Ānadamayādhikaraṇa* (1.1.13–20)[93] of Bādarāyana's *Brahma Sūtras*. For Vedāntins this text is a scriptural source for the doctrine of Brahman and, "various schools of Vedānta ... invest a great deal of energy in arguing, on the basis of *Taittirīya Upaniṣad* 2, the relationship of *brahman* and the human self."[94] Śaṅkara's commentary for instance, concludes that ultimately this upaniṣad does not refer to Brahman as the self consisting of bliss (*ānandamaya*), it in fact suggests that Brahman cannot be an object of knowledge to be known.[95] According to Rāmānuja in the *Taittirīya Upaniṣad*:

> the nature of the body is described thus:
> From this very self (*ātman*) space was produced, from space wind, from wind fire, from fire water, from water earth, from earth plants, from plants food, from food man (*puruṣa*). Surely the essence of man is food (*annamaya*).
> (Taitt Up 2.1)
>
> after this is described another self (*ātman*) different from this,
> the essence of which is breath (*prāṇamaya*), and one different from this, the essence of which is the mind (*manomaya*).
> (Taitt Up 2.3–4)
>
> and after describing the nature of the knower-of-the field (*kṣetrajña*), this is said:
> Surely, different from this self (*ātman*) the essence of which is mind, there is another interior self (*antarātman*) that consists of *vijñāna* (*vijñānamaya*).
> (Taitt Up 2.4)
>
> The knower-of-the-field (*kṣetrajña*) being the inner self (*antarātman*), the text describes the highest self (*paramātman*) consisting of bliss:
> There is another inner self, different from the one that consists of *vijñāna*, and which consists of bliss (*ānandamaya*).[96]
> (Taitt Up 2.5)

In his reading, Rāmānuja distinguishes the body (2.1), the individual self (*ksetrajña* or *anatarātman*) which consists of knowledge (*vijñānamaya*) (2.4), and the *paramātman* which consists of bliss (*ānandamaya*) (2.5). However, the connection of these three entities to each other is not stated; the soul–body relationship is understood based on evidence from the VP and MBh verses.

The significance of these smṛti is underscored when we examine another instance of Rāmānuja's engagement with the Taitt Up.

In ŚBh 1.1.13–20, where he discusses these Taitt Up passages, Rāmānuja:

> inserts a lengthy exposition of the claim that the *Taittiriya* text cannot be read as equating the self consisting of bliss with *Brahman* on the grounds that from scripture and reason we (already) know that *Brahman* and the human self are not identical. The *adhikaraṇa* thus becomes the place where Rāmānuja chooses to detail his position on the difference between [B]rahman and the human self.[97]

Additionally, whereas, there he imposes the soul–body paradigm to interpret these very passages, here, in BhG 13.4, that ontological framework is provided by the VP and MBh passages. Thus smṛti serves the same function as this "lengthy exposition" in the Br Sū commentary.[98] Taitt Up is not adequate as support, in the sense that it only supports the differentiation between Brahman, the individual self, and the world, and neglects to explain their relation to each other. The nature of the soul–body relationship amongst them is not evident in the Taitt Up passages Rāmānuja has cited. In conclusion, though this upaniṣad garners enough evidence to distinguish the individual self, matter, and Brahman, the VP and MBh mentioned earlier, need to be taken into account to complete the reading of this upaniṣad as validating the soul–body association. Only when read together with the VP and MBh does this upaniṣad affirm the differentiation and the modal relation between Brahman, individual selves, and matter.

Bondage and liberation

In Chapter 7 of the BhG, Kṛṣṇa not only claims that he is the creator through his higher and lower natures (*prakṛti*), but that he is also the liberator. Due to the delusory nature of his creative nature denoted by the term *māyā*, refuge in Kṛṣṇa is the only antidote to the bondage of *saṃsāra* (Malinar 2007: 131). In the discussion of the path to liberation, Kṛṣṇa mentions four types of devotees of Kṛṣṇa and among them the true seeker, the knower or *jñānīn*, is deemed the best. This type of devotee alone, is the one who knows Kṛṣṇa's true nature, is solely dedicated to Him and thus worthy of liberation (7.16–17). The "knower" however, has different connotations for Śaṅkara and Rāmānuja. In his commentary on both BhG verses (7.14 and 7.17), which concern the deceptive nature of Kṛṣṇa's *māyā*, and the devotee truly worthy of being saved from it, Rāmānuja utilizes the VP once again to distinguish his interpretation from that of Śaṅkara. If we take into consideration the beginning of the chapter (7.1–2), where Kṛṣṇa proclaims that through knowledge and its realization, Arjuna will know Him without any doubt whatsoever, then BhG 7.14 and 7.17 are key passages that provide a road map to understanding the nature of ignorance and overcoming it. The fact that Rāmānuja utilizes the

VP in the commentary on these passages is thus significant. In the previous section to interpret the knowledge of the two natures of Kṛṣṇa, Rāmānuja utilizes the VP and the next two sections demonstrate this purāṇa's importance in solidifying the path to Kṛṣṇa-realization as interpreted by Rāmānuja. We will first address the concept of *māyā* and then the means to transcend it as stated by Kṛṣṇa and as understood by the two Vedāntins.

Kṛṣṇa's māyā

Both Rāmānuja and Śaṅkara invoke Viṣṇu's *māyā* as an explanation for bondage in *saṃsāra*, however, their interpretations of it are quite different. As noted earlier in the section that discusses BhG 7.6, Śaṅkara's understanding of *māyā* vacillates between a few different meanings ranging from magical illusion to the magical power of God.[99] In the BhG, he does not directly take up *māyā*'s metaphysical status as less than real (*mithyā*),[100] but describes it as the wonderful power of god, which is also deceptive. This is the same connotation of *māyā* found in the *Śvestāśvatara Upaniṣad*, the *Mahābhārata*, and the purāṇas, where "the power of the Lord to undergo manifestation in manifold form is objectivized as the world of nature (*prakṛti*) giving birth to three constituents, bodies and so on."[101] So how does Śaṇkara's understanding of *māyā* differ from that of Rāmānuja in the BhG? In the discussion of the three qualities of *prakṛti* and their effects, Kṛṣṇa claims that:

> by these three conditions composed of qualities (*guṇa*), the whole world is deluded and does not know me as the highest, as the immutable.[102]

For Śaṅkara, this means that modifications of these qualities (*guṇavikāra*) lead to states such as delusion (*moha*), hatred (*dveṣa*), passion (*rāga*), and so on.[103] Deluded by these they cannot discriminate, cannot attain the absolute (*sat*). Kṛṣṇa clearly equates his lower nature, *prakṛti*, with his magical power or divine *māyā*, but offers a solution to end delusion:

> For this divine *māyā* of mine, consisting of qualities, is difficult to traverse
> He who seeks refuge in me alone, cross over this *māyā*.[104]

If Kṛṣṇa's *māyā* is hard to navigate, the only antidote is surrender to Him. According to Śaṅkara taking refuge in Kṛṣṇa entails having renounced all *dharma*-s (*sarvadharmān parityājya*) whole-heartedly to Him. For He who is the wielder of *māyā* is the devotee's very self.[105] As Ram-Prasad remarks, "Kṛṣṇa is not the culminating point of [Śaṅkara's] inquiry; nor is a devotional love of God the ultimate human mode of fulfillment" and "God understood in the language of prayer and poetry is for Śaṅkara a God described through contingent limiting adjuncts."[106] Renunciation of all actions is essential because the Self is not a knower, a doer, or an agent. Thus with the notion that one's Self is the very Vāsudeva, one must seek refuge from bondage. This is Śaṅkara's understanding of surrender to Kṛṣṇa.

Rāmānuja also agrees with the claim that divine *māyā* is deluding but characterizes delusion and surrender to Kṛṣṇa differently. Though *prakṛti* can be read as divine *māyā*, it does not have the same sense of delusion that Śaṅkara's interpretation conveys. To distinguish his definition of *māyā* from that of Śaṅkara, Rāmānuja utilizes the VP:

> Since, this *māyā* of mine consisting of qualities, ie., composed of *sattva, rajas*, and *tamas*, is divine, made by a god, made by me alone, while engaged in sport, it is difficult to overcome, difficult to traverse, by anyone. Even as the weapons of the āsuras and rākṣasas, and the like, bears the name *māyā* because it produces wonderful effects. Compare verses such as these—
>
> > Then the excellent discus, Sudarśana, commanded by the Lord, approached blazing, for his (Prahlāda) protection. Shielding the body of the boy, moving quickly it destroyed those thousand weapons (*māyā*) of Śaṃbara one after other.
> >
> > (VP 1.19.19–20)[107]

The VP example is taken from the narrative of Prahlāda, who is besieged by his father Hiraṇyakaśipu's minion, Śaṃbara. The VP passage uses *māyā* in a context that counters Śaṅkara's understanding of the term. Even the rākṣasa's weapons, which the VP denotes by the word *māyā*, do not signify illusion because "truthfully even in the case of the weapons of the āsuras, the use of the word *māyā* does not support illusion … for it is not possible to harm with weapons that are illusory in nature":[108]

> hence the word *māyā* does not mean something that is false. On the other hand, the word *māyāvin* is used for jugglers and the like, because with the help of spells, herbs, and the like, they evoke knowledge which, though based on things that are false, is perfectly real. Thus, in that case, *māyā* is nothing but spells, herbs, and so on, because a word has only one meaning, adapted to its various usages. In that case the use of the word *māyā* for things that are false is metaphorical, in so far as it refers to knowledge that is the result of *māyā*, as in the expression, "the benches scream".[109]

Māyā according to Rāmānuja is that which has the power of creating real impressions and is applicable as illusion only in the metaphorical sense. Deśika comments that even those "who practice *indrajāla* or illusionist magic create real knowledge in the minds of the spectators, even though the object of the knowledge is unreal … the incantations and the herbs are … real things having the power of producing wonderful effects."[110] Since even the knowledge that comes about by deceptive means is real, Viṣṇu is compelled to aid

Prahlāda who is terrified by the weaponry generated by the demon's *māyā*. Rāmānuja concludes his commentary on BhG 7.14 citing Śvet Up 4.10:

> *This māyā* of the Lord, *consisting of qualities* (*guṇas*) is true (in BhG 7.14), is addressed in texts such as this
> However, know that *māyā* is *prakṛti* and the possessor of *māyā* is Maheśvara.
>
> (Śve Up 4.10)
>
> Its purpose is to obscure the true nature of the Lord and create a state of mind that one should enjoy one's own nature. As a result, the entire universe is deluded by the *māyā* of the Lord and does not recognize that the true nature of the Lord is the limitless highest bliss.[111]

In this context, *māyā* identified as *prakṛti* obscures the essential nature of Kṛṣṇa but also creates a mind-set that makes the world enjoyable and as independent of Him. As a means of freeing oneself of *māyā*, the text says— those who seek refuge in me alone, who wills the truth, the most compassionate, the refuge of people without regard to their differences, they cross over this *māyā* of mine which is composed of *guṇa*s. That means: they cast forth *māyā* and worship Me alone.[112]

As we saw earlier, Śvet Up 4.10 is utilized in the discussion of ignorance in the Major Objection to support *māyā* as the unmanifest, *avyakta*, which cannot be determined to be real or as unreal. *Māyā* is a limiting adjunct (*upādhi*) that brings about the state of personhood. Consequently, matter (*prakṛti*) as *māyā* is something unreal. In the Major Conclusion, Rāmānuja cites this very VP passage (1.19.20) to counter the Adviata claim. In a way then, Śvet Up 4.10 cannot be read without the VP and this is evident throughout Rāmānuja's Vedānta expositons. Immediately following this verse Kṛṣṇa elaborates on the types of people who surrender to Him and those who do not, and in verse BhG 7.17 the model of perfect devotion is Prahlāda. In a way even in BhG 7.14 Rāmānuja has the Prahlāda narrative in mind to define Viṣṇu's *māyā* and also to characterize the perfect devotee.

The foremost devotee (jñānin)

If right knowledge is the correct understanding of Kṛṣṇa's *māyā*, then the one who comes to know and realize this knowledge is the knower (*jñānin*). BhG 7.16 enumerates four types of devotees:

> the men of good deeds who worship me, are four-fold, O' Arjuna
> these are the afflicted, seekers of knowledge, seekers of wealth, and men of wisdom.[113]

Among them, the afflicted (*ārta*), the seekers of knowledge (*jijñāsu*), the seekers of wealth (*arthārthin*), and the man of wisdom (*jñānin*), the *jñānin* is deemed the foremost devotee of Kṛṣṇa. Śaṅkara defines these four types of aspirants as follows:

> the afflicted are those who are in the grasp of suffering, attacked by bandits, tigers, or succumbing to ill health. The seeker of knowledge is one who desires to know the truth of the Lord (*Bhagavan*). The seeker of wealth desires prosperity. The knower is he who knows the truth of Viṣṇu.[114]

That is the knower thinks, "my self is Vāsudeva's self and as such he is exceedingly dear to me."[115] "Indeed the knower, begins to ascend the peak of knowledge resorting to the truth that 'I myself am the Lord Vāsudeva, I am none else.'"[116] Such wisdom requires renunciation of all *dharma* and the notion that the self is an agent. Even the seeker of knowledge still operates according to Śaṅkara, in the realm of ignorance, wishing to understand Īśvara as the supreme deity, the creator of the world, while the knower achieves true discrimination.

For Rāmānuja, the man of wisdom (*jñānin*) is the foremost devotee who correctly realizes the true delusory nature of matter. Juxtaposing the knowledge-seeker and the knower he argues contra-Śaṅkara:

> The seeker of knowledge is one who desires to realize the real nature of the self, as different from *prakṛti*. A knower, is one who knows that it is the essential nature of the self to find joy solely as the servant (*śeṣa*) of the Lord, as taught in the text beginning with *but know that which is other than this (lower prakṛti) to be the higher prakṛti* (BhG 7.5). Without concluding with the knowledge of self as different from *prakṛti*, he desires to attain the Lord. He considers the Lord alone as the highest object to be attained.[117]

Whereas, Śaṅkara understands the knowledge-seeker (*jijñāsu*) as simply submitting to an all-powerful Īśvara, for Rāmānuja such a person discriminates between the body and soul and, though important, discontinues his spiritual practice at this stage. The knower (*jñānin*), on the other hand, is superior to the seeker of knowledge because he goes a step beyond simply realizing the distinction between the individual self and the physical body; he yearns to attain Kṛṣṇa as his master (*śeṣin*); this is his highest aim. Kṛṣṇa claims in BhG 7.18 "indeed, I am exceedingly dear to the man of wisdom and he is dear to me".[118] Rāmānuja elaborates:

> Among them (devotees) the knower is special. Why? Because He is constantly attached, his devotion is single-minded. Indeed, he, for whom I am the only one to be reached, is constantly attached to me, whereas the other two (types of devotees) are attached to me until they obtain what they desire. Also, the knower is devoted to me alone, whereas the other

> two[119] (are devoted to me) in regard to what they desire, and as a means of obtaining it.[120]

As for the other devotees their connection with Kṛṣṇa lasts as long as their desires are obtained. Their attachment to Kṛṣṇa is a way to fulfill their own desires. Not so the man of knowledge. Rāmānuja goes on to say:

> Moreover, I am infinitely dear to the knower. Here the word 'infinitely' means something that cannot be expressed in words. That means: the way in which I am dear to the man of wisdom even I the all-powerful one am unable to express in words, because there is no limitation on love.[121]

Carman discussing this section of Rāmānuja's commentary on the BhG notes that Kṛṣṇa reciprocates the exclusive devotion of the knower, when he says "Rāmānuja understands Lord Krishna to be teaching in the Gita that he is similarly dependent upon his exclusive devotees" (Carman 1974: 191). In fact in the commentary on 7.18 Rāmānuja writes that just as the devotee is utterly dependent on Kṛṣṇa and cannot support himself without the lord, so also Kṛṣṇa finds it impossible to be without the devotee. In this sense, Rāmānuja understands Kṛṣṇa as saying "thus verily he is my very self" (*tato mama api ātmā hi sa*). To support this interpretation of the man of knowledge, in contrast to Śaṅkara he turns to the VP:

> Just as in the case of Prahlāda,[122] the foremost among the men of knowledge
>
> > But, he while being bitten by great serpents, his mind fixed on Kṛṣṇa,
> > was not conscious of his body, absorbed in the joy of recollecting him.
> > (VP 1.17.39)
>
> He (man of knowledge) in return is equally dear to me.[123]

As an ideal devotee, a *jñānin*, Prahlāda is immersed in constant recollection of Viṣṇu. The passage cited by Rāmānuja is in reference to the incident where the young boy is bound by serpents and thrown into the sea, but he is oblivious to the serpents striking him as he is engrossed in recollections of Viṣṇu (VP 1.19.55). Biardeau (1975) notes that the state of bondage of Prahlāda is akin to the image of beings striving in the ocean of *saṃsāra* bound by karma. Only Viṣṇu is the liberator from these cosmic constraints.[124] Rāmānuja understands Kṛṣṇa as saying that regardless of birth or status, when one surrenders to Kṛṣṇa, abides in Kṛṣṇa, the Lord also abides in the devotee as though he/she is His superior.[125] Thus, when Prahlāda though an *āsura* seeks refuge, Viṣṇu cannot refuse.

Though the VP presents Prahlāda as a devotee of Viṣṇu, the nature of devotion (*bhakti*) and the characterization of liberation are sometimes in stark contrast to that of Rāmānuja's interpretation of these concepts. For instance, on the one hand, Prahlāda is presented as meditating on Viṣṇu as identical with his own self and is said to have become one with Viṣṇu regarding himself as the deity (VP 1.20.1–3). On the other hand, Viṣṇu is said to have appeared to the young boy in response to his intense devotion. Moreover, this ambiguity in the VP version of this narrative leads Hacker (1959) to comment that once Prahlāda realizes his own self as identical with that of Kṛṣṇa, this type of intellectual devotion (*bhakti*) that privileges liberation undermines the purpose of the incarnation (*avatāra*) in the sense that the whole narrative of Narasiṃha as an incarnation that descends to uphold *dharma* and protect the good loses its importance.[126] Soifer (1991: 98) however, notes that "in the VP we find a *bhakti* that transcends and perhaps transgresses or ignores *dharma*. Therefore the incarnation, which the BhG inextricably binds to *dharma*, is … not an integral part of the VP."[127] In the case of Rāmānuja too, Arjuna's *dhārmic* dilemma is mapped onto the prominence given to liberation in the Vedānta system and though Rāmānuja also claims that the man of wisdom is Brahman's own self he is quite clear on the qualitative distinction between Brahman and the individual self and the latter as the *śeṣa* of the Lord. Indeed, Prahlāda has a long history in the Śrīvaiṣṇava tradition as an embodiment of true devotion (*bhakti*), an ideal devotee clearly not in the Advaitic sense (Clooney 1988: 247).

Rāmānuja is aware of this ambiguity in the VP, and puts it in perspective in the *Vedārthasaṃgraha*, citing VP 1.19.85, where Prahlāda claims he is the infinite one, the primeval one, all-pervading and that all things arise out of him and dwell in him.[128] According to Rāmānuja, Prahlāda can say that he *is* Viṣṇu since all beings form His body. The identity between Viṣṇu and Prahlāda is due to the fact that the young devotee constitutes a mode of the Supreme Being. Through *sāmānādhikaraṇya*, the attribute or mode can be identified with the substrate or mode-possessor. Prahlāda as interpreted by Rāmānuja is in stark contrast to Śaṅkara's renunciant scaling the peak of knowledge thinking "I myself am Lord Vāsudeva, I am none else" (ŚBhGBh 7.18). What the Prahlāda narrative allows Rāmānuja is a way to underscore his interpretation of *māyā* and the dependence of the individual self on Brahman, its servant-hood (*śeṣatva*) that cannot be transcended even after liberation.

Conclusion

We have mentioned in the earlier chapters on the VS and ŚBh that a majority of the BhG passages that Rāmānuja utilizes as support for his arguments in those commentaries depend on the VP for scriptural evidence. That is, to interpret many of the BhG passages themselves the use the VP is crucial as we see in this chapter on the *Bhagavadgītābhāṣya* (RBhGBh). An interesting aspect of VP use in RBhGBh is that he relies on the VP to not only interpret Kṛṣṇa's teaching in terms of Viśiṣṭādvaita Vedānta, but also to consistently refute the Advaita interpretation alluding to Śaṅkara's commentary on the

BhG (ŚBhGBh). So, whereas the Advaita "presence" is evident as the Major Objection of the ŚBh 1.1.1, in the RBhGBh, Rāmānuja's reference to Śaṅkara's commentary and his use of the VP go hand in hand.

In this chapter the exegetical use of the VP in RBhGBh is evaluated in the discussion of three topics: the teaching of Sāṃkhya-Yoga, Kṛṣṇa's nature in relation to creation, and the nature of bondage and path to liberation. The teaching of Sāṃkhya-Yoga in Chapter 2 of the BhG is important as one of the first teachings of Kṛṣṇa, but it also sets the tone for interpreting the rest of the BhG consonant with a particular Vedānta system. In the teaching of Sāṃkhya (BhG 2.16) the VP is important in clarifying the meaning of the terms Being (*sat*) and Non-Being (*asat*). Relying solely on the VP, Rāmānuja introduces the concept of sentience (*cetana*) from the purāṇa, to argue that *sat* and *asat* refer to a sentient thing (*cidvastu*) and an insentient thing (*acid-vastu*) respectively. This counters the Advaita interpretation of *sat* and *asat* as simply cognition of the real (*sadbuddhi*) and cognition of the unreal (*asad-buddhi*). To further define Non-being as unreal Rāmānuja draws on the VP's definition of the unreal as based on transformation and change (*vikāra*), rather than sublatability of cognition. Similarly, in the discussion of Yoga in BhG 2.61, VP 6.7, titled the *Śubhāśrayaprakaraṇa*, is utilized to argue that it is in fact the realization of the individual self that is stated in BhG 2.39–72 and not Brahman realization as Śaṅkara claims. Exploiting some of the structural and conceptual similarities between VP 6.7 and BhG 2, Rāmānuja argues that the realization at the end of the teaching of Chapter 2 of the BhG is not that one's innermost self is Vāsudeva, but rather that the individual self which is distinct from the body exists in a dependent (soul–body) relationship with Him.

Kṛṣṇa's nature in relation to the world is taught in Chapter 7 and Chapter 13 of the BhG. To articulate Brahman's association with his creation in 7.6 and 13.4, Rāmānuja turns to the VP. While Śaṅkara takes the higher and lower nature of Kṛṣṇa to be the individual self and the body, his perspective is that ultimately both exist due to cognitive misconceptions. Rāmānuja needs to prove that individual selves (higher nature of Kṛṣṇa) and matter (the lower nature of Kṛṣṇa) are real and comprise His body. Though as scriptural support, *Subāla Upaniṣad* 2 is mentioned first, the context of that passage which is world dissolution only affirms that the Supreme Self is the source of unmanifest matter which later evolves into manifest creation. This affirms the claim of BhG 7.6 that matter is the lower nature of Kṛṣṇa. However, this passage lacks the kind of detail that is required to counter Śaṅkara's interpretation. For the Advaitin too can use the *Subāla Upaniṣad* passage as support for his Vedānta. Compare the following phrases from the VP passages cited as corroborative evidence after the upaniṣad that clearly articulate the distinction between the individual selves and matter existing in an inseparable relationship with Brahman: "different from the essence of Viṣṇu are the two forms, matter (*prakṛti*) and individual self (*puruṣa*); *prakṛti* and *puruṣa* are absorbed into the Supreme Self," and the Supreme Self is "the support of all."

The individual self and matter as forms of Viṣṇu, which Rāmānuja is able to interpret as modes of Viṣṇu though when reabsorbed into Him do not affect His perfections.

The discussion of the two natures of Kṛṣṇa continues in Chapter 13 of the BhG though the terminology used to denote matter (*prakṛti*) and the individual self (*puruṣa*) here are *kṣetra* and *kṣetrajña*. What complicates matters for Rāmānuja is that in BhG 13.2 Kṛṣṇa declares himself as the field-knower in all fields. He goes on to claim in BhG 13.4 that this distinction between the field and field-knower has been professed in scripture in many ways. Śaṅkara reads BhG 13.2 and 13.4 together and understands the distinction mentioned here as the one between the individual self and Brahman. Rāmānuja on the other hand, interprets the distinction as a reference to the difference between matter and individual selves. The scriptural passage cited by Śaṅkara as support in ŚBhGBh 13.4 is Bṛ Up 1.4.7, *one should consider them simply as his self*. To counter this Advaitic perspective Rāmānuja cites the VP, the MBh, and the Taitt Up. This is one of the clearest examples where, because of the sequence of citations dictated by the BhG verse 13.4, we discern how the purāṇa cited first is used to read the śruti that follows. The VP according to Rāmānuja articulates the distinction between the individual self and the body in a way that is consonant with his Vedānta. Utilizing VP passages such as "the self is pure, imperishable, tranquil, quality-less and higher than matter (*prakṛti*) it alone does neither increase nor decrease in any living being"; "since the body of a man is characterized severally by his head, hands and so on, to what shall I attach the term 'I'"; "is this head of yours 'you', or your neck, or stomach? are your feet etc 'you'? what part of you is 'you'"; "you are actually distinct from all your parts O' King" he argues the metaphysical reality of the self and its relation to matter, while affirming their dependence on Kṛṣṇa. Having established that such a distinction is real, Rāmānuja re-interprets the very important *Taittirīya Upaniṣad* 2 also, quite differently from the Advaitin.

On the topic of bondage and liberation in the BhG, Rāmānuja yet again relies on the VP. In the discussion of Kṛṣṇa's *māyā* (7.14) and the devotee who successfully overcomes this (7.17) he turns to the Prahlāda narrative from the VP. Śaṅkara understands Kṛṣṇa's *māyā* as illusory, unreal, and a cognitive deception. To counter this view of *māyā*, Rāmānuja cites from the VP where *māyā* does not denote delusion but rather fantastical or wonderful creations. For Rāmānuja though *māyā* may be delusory, the knowledge it produces is real. VP 1.19.19–20 refers to the demon Śaṃbara's many weapons that torture the young boy Prahlāda as *māyā*. Having interpreted *māyā* according to the VP, he then cites Śvet Up 4.10, where *māyā* is also used to denote matter (*prakṛti*). Śaṅkara identifies *māyā* in this upaniṣad passage with ignorance (*avidyā*) that is illusory. However, based on the understanding of *māyā* in VP 1.19.19–20, Rāmānuja counters this rival claim. The Prahlāda narrative is also important as he is identified as the foremost devotee that Kṛṣṇa mentions in BhG 7.17, who successfully traverses His *māyā*. No śruti, only the VP is cited here as evidence, to characterize the foremost devotee in the BhG. Though, the Prahlāda narrative in the VP reflects a type of Advaita devotion (*bhakti*) that is not really consonant with Viśiṣṭādvaita, we see that Rāmānuja and the commentator make great effort to translate it into the Śrī vaiṣṇava context.

Notes

1 Rāmānuja utilizes the VP in the following BhG verses: 2.16, 2.61, 4.14, 6.6, 7.4, 7.14, 7.17, 10.42, 11.50, 13.4, 15.15, 15.18, 16.8, and 18.11. Among these only 2.16, 2.61, 7.4, 7.14, 7.17, and 13.4 are examined as a representative sample.
2 For such studies, the reader may consult sources such as Malinar 2007, Edgerton 1964, and Zaehner 1969.
3 For discussions on the historical development of these systems of thought see Burley 2005: 15–35 and Larson 1998: 73–153.
4 Malinar 2007: 62–75; Edgerton 1964: 165ff; Zaehner 1969: 120–22.
5 Zaehner 1969: 120–21.
6 Historically, the study of Being (*sat*), *sadvidyā*, has been an important pre-occupation of Indian thought since the Vedas. It is of particular importance in the Sāṃkhya and Vedānta systems, although it assumes different meanings in each of these two philosophies, "[f]or Vedānta as a whole *sat* is the transcendent and immaterial, for Sāṃkhya the immanent and material first cause of the world" (van Buitenen 1956: 3).
7 Zaehner 1969: 127–29; Edgerton 1964: 10; Hill 1953: 85; Sargeant 1979: 113 for variant translations.
8 Śaṅkara interprets *tattva* in the term *tattvadarśibhiḥ* as the "all", "ultimate reality", or Brahman (ŚBhGBh 2.16).
9 na asato vidyate bhāvo na abhāvo vidyate sataḥ
ubhayor api dṛṣṭo 'ntas tv anayos tattvadarśibhiḥ.
(BhG 2.16)
10 na hi śītoṣṇādi sakāraṇaṃ pramāṇair nirūpyamānam vastu sat bhavati. vikāro hi so, vikāraśca vyabhicarati (ŚBhGBh 2.16).
11 ŚBhGBh 2.16.
12 sarvo vikāraḥ kāraṇavyatirekeṇa anupalabhdher asan (ŚBhGBh 2.16).
13 sarvatra buddhidvayopalabdheḥ sadbuddhir asadbuddhir iti. yadviṣayā buddhir na vyabhicarati, tat sat, yadviṣayā buddhir vyabhicarati tad asat iti sadasadvibhāge buddhitantre sthite...tasmād ghaṭādibuddhi-viṣayo' san vyabhicārāt na tu sadbuddhiviṣayo' vyabhicārāt. (ŚBhGBh 2.16)
14 Halbfass 1991: 167.
15 tathā sataś ca ātmano' bhāvo' vidyamānatā na vidyate, sarvatra avyabhicārāt avocām (ŚBhGBh 2.16).
16 avināśi tu tadviddhi yena sarvamidaṃ tatam
vināśamavyayasyāsya na kaścitkartumarhati.
(BhG 2.17)
17 na etat sadākhyam brahma svena rūpeṇa vyeti (ŚBhGBh 2.17).
18 antavant ime dehā nityasyoktāḥ śarīriṇaḥ
anāśino'prameyasya tasmādyudhyasva bhārata.
(BhG 2.18)
19 yathā mṛgatṛṣṇikādau sadbuddhiḥ anuvṛttā pramāṇanirūpaṇānte vicchidyate, sa tasya antaḥ; tathā ime dehāḥ svapnamāyādehādivacca antavantaḥ nityasya śarī riṇaḥ śarīravataḥ anāśinaḥ aprameyasya ātmanaḥ antavanta iti uktāḥ vivekibhir ityarthaḥ. (ŚBhGBh 2.18).
20 atra tu satkāryavādasya asaṅgatvān na tatparo'yam ślokaḥ (RBhGBh 2.16).
21 na asato vidyate bhāvo na abhāvo vidyate sataḥ

ubhayor api dṛṣṭo 'ntas tv anayos tattvadarśibhiḥ.
(BhG 2.16)
This translation is based on Rāmānuja's commentary on this verse.

22 asato dehasya sadbhāvo na vidyate sataś ca ātmano na asadbhāvaḥ. ubhayor dehātmanor upalabhyamānayor yathopalabdhitattvadarśibhir anto dṛṣṭaḥ ... dehasyācidvastuno' sattvameva svarūpam ātmanaś cetanasya sattvam eva svarūpamiti nirṇayo dṛṣṭetyarthaḥ. vināśasvabhāvo hyasattvam, avināśasvabhāvaśca sattvam (RBhGBh 2.16).

23 The passages from VP 2.12, 2.13, and 2.14, as mentioned in the Introduction, discuss the legend of Bharata who is cursed to undergo several rebirths because of his attachment to a fawn. He ultimately achieves liberation after expounding the true nature of existence to a certain king.

24 tasmānna vijñānam ṛte'sti kiṃcit kvacit kadācid dvija vastujātam (VP 2.12.43ab).

25 sadbhava evaṃ bhavato mayokto jñanaṃ yathasatyam asatyam anyat (VP 2.12.45ab) (RBhGBh 2.16).

26 anāśī paramārthaśca prājñair abhyupagamyate
tattu nāśi na sandeho nāśidravyopapāditam.
(VP 2.14.24) (RBhGBh 2.16)

27 vyavahārārhatvānārhatvādiviṣayau sadasacchabdau tayoḥ paramārthāparamārthaviṣayasatyāsatyaśabdābhyām katham aikārthyam iti śaṅkāyām nāśānāśayor eva paramārthāparamārthādiśabdaprayogahetutve maharṣivacanam upadatte anāśīti. (TC 2.16)

28 However, know that to be imperishable, by which this whole universe was spun. No one can bring destruction to that which is imperishable (BhG 2.17).

29 atrāpi *antavanta ime dehāḥ* (BhG 2.18) *avināśi tu tadviddhi* (BhG 2.17) ity ucyate. tadeva sattvāsattvavyapadeśahetur iti gamyate (RBhGBh 2.16).

30 atra uttaraślokadvayaikyārthācca ayam evārthaityāha atrāpīti etena kvaciccetanaviṣayāsacchabdo' pi devādināmarūpaprahāṇādyavasthāviśeṣāpekṣayetyuktam bhavati. svarūpatastu nirvikāratvāt sacchabdvācyatvam eva. (TC 2.16)

31 yattu kālāntareṇāpi nānyasamjñām upaiti vai
pariṇāmādisambhūtāṃ tadvastu nṛpa tacca kim.
(VP 2.13.96) (RBhGBh 2.16)

32 vināśopalakśitanpariṇāmavṛddhyādibhiḥ pūrvāsthāprahāṇena saṃjñāntarayogādeva avastuśabdavācyatvam, tadabhāvācca vastuśabdavācyatvam ityasminarthe spaṣṭoktim darśayati yattviti (TC 2.16).

33 jñānaṃ viśuddhaṃ vimalaṃ viśokamaśeṣalobhādinirastasaṅgam
ekaṃ sadaikaṃ paramaḥ pareśaḥ sa vāsudevo na yato'nyadasti.
(VP 2.12.44)

34 daśaślokyām vastvavastvastināstisatyāsatyaśabdānām śārīrakabhāṣye purāṇopakramopasaṃhārādinā tatprakaraṇopakramopasaṃhārādinā madhye 'mahī ghaṭatvam ghaṭataḥ kapālikā' (VP 2.15.41) ityādinā ca savikāratvenaivāvastutvopapādanāt śrutismṛtyantarapratyakṣādyanurodhācca nirvikārasavikāratayā nityānityacetanācetanaviṣayatvam sthāpitam (TC 2.16).

35 For more on the connections between Yoga as defined by Rāmānuja and the system of Patañjali see Lester 1976.

36 Zaehner 1969: 120–21; Malinar 2007: 69–77.

37 ŚBhGBh 2.11.

38 ātmanaḥ janmādiṣaḍvikriyābhāvāt akartā ātmā (ŚBhGBh 2.11).

39 Ibid.

40 Ibid.

41 tāni sarvāṇi saṃyamya yukta āsīt matparaḥ
vaśe hi yasyendriyāṇi tasya prajñā pratiṣṭhitā.
(BhG 2.61)

42 sthitā pratiṣṭhitā 'aham asmi param brahma' iti prajñā yasya sa sthitaprajñaḥ (ŚBhGBh 2.54).
43 Van Buitenen 1974: 59.
44 RBhGBh 2.55.
45 asya sarvasya doṣasya parijihīrṣayā viṣayānurāgayuktatayā durjayāni indriyāṇi saṃyamya cetasaḥ śubhāśrayabhūte mayi mano' vasthāpya samāhita āsīta. manasi madviṣaye sati nirdagdhāśeṣakalmaṣatayā nirmalīkṛtam viṣayānurāgarahitam mana indriyāṇi svavaśāni karoti. tato vaśyendriyam mana ātmadarśanāya prabhavati (RBhGBh 2.61).
46 ātmadarśanena vinā viṣayarāgo na nivartate, anivṛtte viṣayarāge vipaścito yatamānasya api puruṣasya indriyāṇi pramāthīni balavanti manaḥ prasahya haranti. evam indriyajaya ātmadarśanādhīnaḥ ātmadarśanam indriyajayādhīnam; iti jñānaniṣṭhā duṣprāpyā (RBhGBh 2.60).
47 Ram-Prasad 2013: 12.
48 yathāgnir uddhataśikaḥ kakṣam dahati sānilaḥ
tathā cittasthito viṣṇur yogināṃ sarvakilbiṣam (VP 6.7.74) iti (RBhGBh 2.61).
49 yogasvarūpam khāṇḍikya śrūyatām gadato mama
yatra sthito na cyavate prāpya brahmalayam muniḥ.
(VP 6.7.27)
50 ātmabhāvam nayatyenam tadbrahma dhyāyinam mune
vikāryyamātmanaḥ śaktyā lohamākarṣako yathā.
(VP 6.7.30)
51 ātmaprayatnasāpekṣā viśiṣṭā yā manogatiḥ
tasyā brahmaṇi samyogo yoga ityabhidhīyate.
(VP 6.7.31)
See also verses 53, 94. However, in the ŚBh on the section of the individual self, Rāmānuja argues that these verses refer to the individual self and not Brahman. This is examined in Chapter 3.
52 Malinar 2007: 192–93.
53 BhG 7.4–5.
54 Zaehner 1964: 246 "etad—in compounds can be taken as either singular or plural. S[ankara] and R[amanuja] take it to refer to both natures of God". That is, it could refer to either of the natures individually or both together.
55 etadyonīni bhūtāni sarvāṇītyupadhāraya
aham kṛtsnasya jagataḥ prabhavaḥ pralayastathā.
(BhG 7.6)
56 ŚBhGBh 7.5.
57 ŚBhGBh 7.4.
58 Halbfass 1995: 78–81; Alston 1981 Vol. III: 69–85.
59 ajo'pi sannvyayātmā bhūtānāmīśvaro' pi san
prakṛtim svāmadhiṣṭhāya sambhavāmy ātmamāyayā.
(BhG 4.6)
60 ŚBhGBh 4.6.
61 asya vicitrānandabhogyabhogopakaraṇabhogasthānarūpeṇa avasthitasya jagataḥ prakṛtir iyaṃ gandhādiguṇakapṛthivyaptejovāyvākāśādirūpeṇa manaḥ prabhṛtī ndriyarūpeṇa ca mahadahamkārarūpeṇa ca aṣṭadhā bhinnā madīyeti vidhi (RBhGBh 7.4).
62 itas tu anyām ito' cetanāyāś cetanabhogyabhūtāyāḥ prakṛter visajātīyākārāṃ jī vabhūtāṃ paraṃ tasyā bhoktṛtvena pradhānabhūtāṃ cetanarūpāṃ madīyāṃ prakṛtiṃ vidhi yayā idam acetanaṃ kṛtsnaṃ jagad dhāryate (RBhGBh 7.5).
63 etaccetanācetanasamaṣṭirūpamadīyaprakṛtidvayayoṇīni brahmādistambaparyantāni uccāvacabhāvenāvasthitāni cidacinmiśrāṇi madīyāni sarvāṇi bhūtānīty upadhāraya. madīyaprakṛtidvayayoṇīni hi tāni madīyāny eva. tathā prakṛtidvayayonitvena kṛtsnasya jagataḥ. tayor dvayor api madyoṇitvena madīyatvena ca kṛtsnasya jagato'

ham eva prabhavo' ham eva pralayo 'ham eva ca śeṣīty upadhāraya. tayoś cidacitsamaṣṭibhūtayoḥ prakṛtipuruṣayor api paramapuruṣayoṇitvam śrutismṛtisiddham (RBhGBh 7.6).

64 mahānavyakte līyate avayktamakṣare līyate akṣaram tamasi līyate tamaḥ pare deve ekībhavati (Sub Up 2).

65 He is the primordial being sacrificed by the gods to create the universe. Later *puruṣa* is identified with Viṣṇu.

66 Olivelle 1998 translation.

67 tena dravyasvarūpasya nityatvāt ajāmityāder avirodhaḥ. uktārther smṛtim udāharati viṣṇoriti (TC 7.6).

68 VP 1.2.13 ff.

69 pradhānam puruṣam cāpi praviśyātmecchayā hariḥ
kṣobhayāmāsa samprāpte sargakāle vyayāvyayau.
(VP 1.2.29)

70 VP 1.2.24 ab: viṣṇoḥ svarūpāt parato hi te' nye rūpe pradhānaṃ puruṣaś ca vipra.

71 svābhimatārthe sphuṭārtham vacanam udāharati prakṛtir iti (TC 7.6).

72 viṣṇoḥ svarūpātparatodite dve rūpe pradhānaṃ puruṣaś ca vipra (VP 1.2.24 ab). Critical edition reads:
viṣṇoḥ svarūpātparato bi te'nye ...
prakṛitir yā mayā khyātā vyaktāvyaktasvarūpiṇī.
puruṣaś cāpyubhāvetau līyete paramātmani.
paramātmā ca sarveṣāmādhāraḥ parameśvaraḥ.
viṣṇur nāmnā sa vedeṣu vedānteṣu ca gīyate.
(VP 6.4.39–40) (RBhGBh 7.6)

73 sarvaiḥ śabdaiḥ tasyaivābhidhānam iti tattatsāmānādhikaraṇyena āha raso' ham iti caturbhiḥ (RBh GBh 7.8).

74 prakṛtipuruṣayoḥ paramātmani layo nāma kṣīre nīrasyeva vibhāgānarhasaṃśleṣaviśeṣaḥ (TC 7.6).

75 For a history of the use of these two terms in the upaniṣads, see Zaehner 1969: 333–35.

76 kṣetrajñaṃ cāpi māṃ viddhi sarva kṣetreṣu bhārata
kṣetrakṣetrajñayor jñānaṃ yattajjñānaṃ mataṃ mama.
(BhG 13.2; 13.3 in Sadhale 1935)

77 saptame adhyāye dve prakṛtī sūcite īśvarasya triguṇātmikā aṣṭadhā bhinn' parā samsārahetutvāt, parā ca anyā jīvabhūtā kṣetrajñalakṣaṇā īśvarātmikā; yābhyām prakṛtibhyām īśvaraḥ jagadutpattisthitilayahetutvam pratipadyate. tatra kṣetrakṣetrajñalakṣaṇaprakṛtidvayanirūpaṇadvāreṇa tadvataḥ īśvarasya tattvanirdhāraṇāya kṣetrādhyāyaḥ ārabhyate (ŚBhGBh13.0).

78 tatra evam sati kṣetrajñasya īśvarasya eva sato' vidyākṛtopādhibhedataḥ samsāritvam iva bhavati, yathā dehādyātmatvam ātmanaḥ (ŚBhGBh 13.2; 13.3 in Sadhale 1935).

79 puruṣo jīvaḥ ksetrjño bhoktā iti paryāyaḥ (ŚBhGBh 13.20; 13.21 in Sahale 1935).

80 kṣetrakṣetrajñayor viṣayaviṣayiṇor bhinnasvabhāvayoḥ itaretarataddharmādhyāsalakṣaṇaḥ samyogaḥ kṣetrakṣetrajñasvarūpavivekābhāvanibandhanaḥ, rajjuśuktikādīnām tadvivekajñānābhāvād adhyāropitasarparajatādisamyogavat. so'yam adhyāsasvarūpaḥ kṣetrakṣetrajñayoḥ samyogo mithyājñānalakṣaṇaḥ (ŚBhGBh 13.26; 13.27 in Sadhale 1935).

81 ṛṣibhirbahudhā gītaṃ chandobhirvividhaiḥ pṛthak brahmasūtrapadaiścaiva hetumadbhirviniścitaiḥ (BhG 13.4; 13.5 in Sadhale 1935).

82 Rāmānuja takes the phrase *brahmasūtrapadaiścaiva* to mean in the "'*Brahma Sūtras* as well." Although an alternate translation could be "also in the aphoristic verses concerning Brahman." Regardless of whether this verse is specifically referring to the *Brahma Sūtras* or the upaniṣads, it does affect our reading here (Zaehner 1969: 335).

83 Though Śaṅkara has cited other scriptural passages in 13.2 in his discussion on the field and the field-knower, those passages are in support of the knowledge over ignorance and the benefits thereof. Śaṅkara cites Kaṭha Up 2.4, 2.2, 2.5; Taitt Āraṇ 3.12; Śvet Up 3.8; Taitt Up 2.4, 2.7; Muṇ Up 3.2.9; Bṛ Up 1.4.10; Śvet Up 6.20. He also cites smṛti passages such as MBh 12.240.6; BhG 5.15, 5.19, and 13.28 etc. Rāmānuja in his commentary on BhG 13.2 also utilizes śruti to prove that the individual self is not identical to Brahman. However, in the context of this discussion, he also mentions the distinction between the field and the field-knower and cites support from śruti.

84 Chapter 4, fn 94.

85 TC 13.4.

86 tadidaṃ kṣetrakṣtrajñayāthātmyaṃ ṛiṣibhiḥ parāśarādibhiḥ bahudhā bahuprakāraṃ gītam—
aham tvam ca tathānye ca bhūtairuhyāṃ pārthiva
guṇapravāhapatito bhūtavargo'pi yātyayam.
karmavaśyā guṇā hy ete sattvādyāḥ pṛthivīpate
avidyāsañcitaṃ karma taccāśeṣeṣu jantuṣu.
ātmā śuddho'kṣaraḥ śānto nirguṇaḥ prakṛteḥ paraḥ
pravṛdddhyapacayau nāsya ekasyākhilajantuṣu.
(VP 2.13.65–67) (RBhGBh 13.4; 13.5 in Sadhale 1935)

87 VP 2.13.67 cd is note quoted by Rāmānuja.

88 aviviktadehātmasvarūpasya rājño vāhyavāhakatvoktipratikṣepārtham vākyam aham tvam ca iti (TC 13.4; 13.5 in Sadhale 1935).

89 In critical edition VP 2.13.98 ab reads: *tvaṃ kimetacchiraḥ kiṃ nu śrastava tathodaram.*

90 piṇḍaḥ pṛthagyataḥ puṃsaḥ śiraḥpāṇyādilakśaṇaḥ
tatho'hamiti kutraitāṃ saṃjñāṃ rājankaromyaham.
(VP 2.13.85).
kiṃ tvametacchiraḥ kiṃ nu śiras tava tathodaram
kimupādādikaṃ tvaṃ vai tavaitattkiṃ mahīpate.
samastāvayavebhyastvaṃ pṛthag bhūpa vyavasthitaḥ
ko'hamityeva nipuṇo bhūtvā cintyaṃ pārthiva.
(RBhGBh 13.4; 13.5 in Sadhale 1935).

91 evaṃ vivikatayor dvayoḥ vāsudevātmakatvaṃ cāhuḥ: indriyāṇi mano buddhiḥ sattvaṃ tejobalaṃ dhṛtiḥ. vāsudevātmakānyāhuḥ kṣetram kṣetrajñameva ca (RBhGBh 13.4; 13.5 in Sadhale 1935).

92 This upaniṣad addresses the nature of the self (*ātman*) in the different ways mentioned such as food, mind and so on (Olivelle 1998: 300–303).

93 The numbering of the sūtras differs from one Vedānta commentary to the next. The corresponding *sūtra* numbers in Śaṅkara's version are Br Sū 1.1.12–19.

94 Clooney 1994: 150.

95 Clooney 1994: 151–53.

96 chandobhir vividhaiḥ pṛthak pṛthagvidhaiś chandobhiś ca ṛgyajus sāmātharvabhiḥ dehātmanoḥ svarūpaṃ pṛthaggītam—tasmādvā etasmād ātmana ākāśaḥ sambhūtaḥ ākāśād vāyuḥ vāyoragniḥ agnerāpaḥ adbhyaḥ pṛthivī pṛthivyā auṣadhayaḥ auṣadhībhyo'annam annāt puruṣaḥ sa vā eṣa puruṣo'annarasamayaḥ (Taitt Up 2.5) iti śarīrasvarūpam abhidhāya tasmād antaraṃ prāṇamayaṃ tasmāc ca antaraṃ manomayam abhidhāya tasmādvaitasmān manomayādanyo 'ntara ātmā vijñānamayaḥ (Taitt Up 2.4) iti kṣetrajñasvarūpam abhidhāya tasmād vā etasmād vijñānamayāt anyo'ntara ātmānandamayaḥ (Taitt Up 2.5) iti kṣetrajñasyāpi antarātmatayā ānandamayaḥ paramātmā ābhihitaḥ (RBhGBh 13.4; 13.5 in Sadhale 1935). My own translation of the Taitt Up passages.

97 Clooney 1994: 154.

98 Br Sū 2.3.1, 18, and 40 are also cited to support the true nature of the field, field-knower, and Brahman. Their contribution is to underscore the nature of individual selves and matter as modes of Brahman, although this is adequately covered by the VP and MBh citations.
99 Halbfass 1995: 78–85 and Alston 1980: Vol. II: 60–69.
100 Ram-Prasad 2013: 13.
101 Alston 1980: Vol. II: 69.
102 tribhir guṇamayair bhāvair ebhiḥ sarvamidam jagat
mohitam nābhijānāti mām ebhyaḥ paramavyayam.
(BhG 7.13)
103 ŚBhGBh 7.13.
104 daivī hi eṣā guṇamayī mama māyā duratyayā
māmeva ye prapadyante māyāmetām taranti te.
(BhG 7.14)
105 ŚBhGBh 7.14.
106 Ram-Prasad 2013: 13, 14.
107 mama eṣā guṇamayī sattvarajastamomayī māyā yasmād daivī devena krīḍāpravṛttena mayā eva nirmitā tasmāt sarvair duratyayā duratikramā. asyā māyāśabdavācyatvam āsurarākṣasāstrādīnām iva vicitrakāryakaratvena yathā ca tato bhagavatā tasya rakśārtham cakramuttamam. ājagāma samājñaptam jvālāmāli sudarśanam tena māyāsahasram, tacchambarasyāśugāminā. bālasya rakśatā dehamekaikāṅkśena sūditam (VP 1.19.19–20) ityādau (RBhGBh 7.14).
108 satyeṣu eva āsurarākṣasāstrādiṣu māyāśabdaprayogo na mithyātvanibandhana itybhāvaḥ ... mithyābhūtasya śastrasya niṣūdanīyatvābhāvād (TC 7.14).
109 ato māyāśabdo na mithyārthavācī. aindrajālikādiṣv api kenacin mantrauṣadhādinā mithyārthaviṣayāyāḥ pāramārthikyā eva buddheḥ utpādakatvena māyāvīti prayogaḥ. tathā mantrauṣadhādir eva ca tatra māyā sarvaprayogeṣu anugatasya ekasya eva śabdārthatvāt. tatra mithyārtheṣu māyāśabdaprayogo māyākāryabuddhiviṣayatvena aupacārikaḥ 'mañcāḥ krośanti' itivat (RBhGBh 7.14).
110 Sampatkumaran 1985: 187.
111 eṣā guṇamayī pāramārthikī bhagavanmāyā eva māyām tu prakṛtim vidyānmāyinam tu maheśvaram (Śve Up 4.10) ityādiṣu abhidhīyate. asyāḥ kāryam bhagavatsvarūpatirodhānam svasvarūpabhogyatvabuddhiś ca ato bhagavanmāyayā mohitam sarvam jagad bhagavantam anavadhikātiśayānandasvarūpam na abhijānāti (RBhGBh 7.14).
112 māyāvimocanopāyam āha—mām eva iti. mámeva satyasamkalpam paramakāruṇikam anālocitaviśeṣāśeṣalokaśaraṇyam ye śaraṇam prapadyante ta etām madīyām guṇamayīm māyām taranti. māyām utsṛjya mām eva upāsata ityarthaḥ (RBhGBh 7.14).
113 caturvidhā bhajante mām janāḥ sukṛtino'rjuna
ārto jijñāsurarthārthī jñānī ca bharatarṣabha.
(BhG 7.16)
114 ārta ārtiparigṛhītaḥ taskaravyāghrarogādinā' bhibhūta āpannaḥ. jijñāsur bhagavattattvam jñātum icchati yaḥ ... jñānī viṣṇoḥ tattvavit (ŚBhGBh 7.16).
He who desires to know the truth about the Lord is the seeker of knowledge. A knower knows the true nature of Viṣṇu.
115 sa ca jñānī mama vāsudevasya ātmā eva iti mama atyartham priyaḥ (ŚBhGBh 7.17).
116 āsthita ārodhum pravṛttaḥ saḥ jñānī hi yasmād 'aham eva bhagavān vāsudevo na anyo' smi' iti (ŚBhGBh 7.18).
117 jijñāsur prakṛtiviyuktātmasvarūpāvātpīcchuḥ jñānam eva asya svarūpam iti jijñāsur iti uktam. jñānī ca itas tv anyām prakṛtim vidhi me parām (BhG 7.5) ityādinā abhihitabhagavaccheṣataikarasātmasvarūpavit prakṛtiviyuktakevalātmani aparyavasyan bhagavantam prepsuḥ bhagavantam paramaprāpyam manvānaḥ. (RBhGBh 7.16).

118 priyo hi jñānino'tyartham aham sa ca mama priyaḥ (BhG 7.17cd).

119 Rāmānuja seems to be referring here to three aspirants although previously he has mentioned four.

120 teṣām jñānī viśiṣyate, kutaḥ nityayukta ekabhaktir iti ca. tasya hi madekaprāpyasya mayā yogo nityaḥ. itarayos tu yāvatsvābhilāṣitaprāpti mayā yogaḥ. tathā jñānino mayi ekasmin eva bhaktiḥ itaratayos tu svābhilaṣite tatsādhanatvena mayi ca (RBhGBh 7.17).

121 kiñ ca priyo hi jñānino'tyartham aham atra atyrtaśabdo' bhidheyvavacanaḥ; jñānino'ham yathā priyas tathā mayā sarvajñena sarvaśaktinā api abhidhātum na śakyate ityarthaḥ; priyatvasya iyattārahitatvāt (RBhGBh 7.17).

122 See Soifer 1991 and Hacker 1959 on more on this narrative.

123 yathā jñāninām agresarasya prahlādasya—
sa tv āsaktamatiḥ kṛṣṇe damśyamāno mahoragaiḥ
na vivedātmano gātram tatsmṛtyāhlādasamsthitaḥ.
(VP 1.17.39)
iti saḥ api tathā eva mama priyaḥ (RBhGBh 7.17).

124 Biardeau 1975: 44.

125 RBhGBh 9.29.

126 Hacker 1959: 594.

127 Soifer 1991: 98.

128 VS #108.

Bibliography

Primary Sources

Abhyankar, V.S. (1916) *Śrī Bhāṣya of Rāmānujācarya*. Part I & II. Bombay Sanskrit and Prākṛt series.

Bhagavadgītābhāṣya of Rāmānuja with the Tātparyacandrikā of Vedānta Deśika. (1972) Ed. U.T. Virarāghavācārya. Madras: Ubhaya Vedānta Granthamala.

The Bhagavadgītā with Eleven Commentaries. (1935) Ed. Gajanana Shambhu Sadhale. 3 Vols. 2nd Edition. Bombay: Gujarati Printing Press.

Mahābhārata. (1971) Vols 1–5 Ed. R.N. Dandekar. Poona: Bhandarkar Oriental Research Institute.

Pathak, M.M. (Ed.) (1997) *The Critical Edition of the Viṣṇupurāṇa*. Vols I and II. Vadodara: Oriental Institute.

Śrībhāṣya of Rāmānuja with the Śrutaprakāśikā of Sudarśanasūri. (1967) Ed. U.T. Virarāghavācārya. Madras: Ubhaya Vedānta Granthamala.

Śrīviṣṇumahāpurāṇa. (1996) Ed. R.N. Sharma. Delhi: Nag Publishers, Reprint.

van Buitenen, J.A.B. (1956) *Rāmānuja's Vedārthasaṃgraha*. Poona: Deccan College Postgraduate and Research Institute.

Vedārthasaṃgraha of Rāmānuja with the Tātparyadīpikā of Sudarśanasūri. (1953) Ed. T.V.K.N. Sudarśanācārya. Śrīvaiṣṇava Sampradāya Granthamāla. Tirupathi: Śrī venkateśvara Oriental Institute.

Vālmīki Rāmāyaṇa. (1960–75) Vols 1–7. Ed. J.M. Mehta *et al*. Vadodara: Oriental Research Institute.

Secondary sources

Adluri, S. (2006) "Defining Śruti and Smṛti in Rāmānuja's Vedānta." *Journal of Vaishnava Studies*. 15.1: 193.

Alston, A.J. (1980) *Śaṃkara on the Creation: A Śaṃkara Source-book*. Vol. II. London: Shanti Sadan.

Alston, A.J. (1981) *Śaṃkara on the Soul: A Śaṃkara Source-book*. Vol. III. London: Shanti Sadan.

Bartley, C.J. (2002) *The Theology of Rāmānuja: Realism and Religion*. London: Routledge-Curzon.

Biardeau, Madeleine. (1975) "Narasiṁha, mythe et culte." In *Puruṣārtha: Récherches de Sciences Sociales sur d'Asie du Sud*. Paris: Centre d'Études de l'Inde et de l'Asie du Sud, pp. 31–48.

Burley, Mikel. (2005) *Classical Sāṃkhya and Yoga: An Indian Metaphysics of Experience*. London: Routledge-Curzon.

Cardona, George. (1981) "On Reasoning from Anvaya and Vyatireka in Early Advaita." *Studies in Indian Philosophy: A Memorial Volume in Honor of Pandit Sukhlalji Sanghvi*. Ahmedabad: L.D. Institute of Indology, pp. 79–104.

Carman, John B. (1974) *The Theology of Rāmānuja*. New Haven, CT: Yale University Press.

Carman, John B. and Vasudha Narayanan. (1989) *The Tamil Veda: Piḷḷāṉ's Interpretation of the Tiruvāymoḻi*. Chicago, IL: University of Chicago Press.

Champakalaksmi, R. (1981) *Vaiṣṇava Iconography in the Tamil Country*. New Delhi: Orient Longman.

Clooney, Francis X. (1988) "I Created Land and Sea: A Tamil Case of God Consciousness and its Śrīvaiṣṇava Interpretation." *Numen*. 35: 238–59.

Clooney, Francis X. (1992) "Binding the Text: Vedānta Philosophy and Commentary." In *Texts in Context*. Ed. Jeffrey R. Timm. Albany: State University of New York Press.

Clooney, Francis X. (1994) "From Anxiety to Bliss: Argument, Care, and Responsibility in the Vedānta Reading of Taittirīya 2.1–6a." In *Authority, Anxiety and Bliss: Essays in Vedic Interpretation*. Ed. Laurie L. Patton. Albany: State University of New York Press, pp. 139–70.

Clooney, Francis X. (2005) "From Person to Person: A Study of Tradition in the *Guruparamparāsāra* of Vedānta Deśika's *Śrīmat Rahasyatrayasāra*." In *Boundaries, Dynamics and Construction of Traditions in South Asia*. Ed. Federico Squarcini. Florence: Firenze University Press and Munshiram Manoharlal, pp. 203–24.

Dasgupta, Surendranath N. (1991) *A History of Indian Philosophy*. Vols I–III. Delhi: Motilal Banarsidass, Reprint.

Datta, K.S.R. (1978) "The Viṣṇupurāṇa and Advaita." *Purana*. 20.2: 193–96.

De Smet, R. (1953) *The Theological Method of Śaṅkara*. Dissertation. Rome: Pontifical Gregorian University.

Deussen, Paul. (1990) *The System of Vedānta According to Bādarāyaṇa's Brahmasūtras and Śaṅkara's Commentary thereon set forth as a Compendium of the Dogmatics of Brāhmanism from the Standpoint of Śaṅkara*. Delhi: Low Price Publications Reprint.

Edgerton, F. (1964) *The Bhagavadgītā*. New York: Harper and Row Publishers.

Farquhar, J.N. (1920) *An Outline of the Religious Literature of India*. Oxford: Oxford University Press.

Ganeri, Jonardon. (2010) "Sanskrit Philosophical Commentary." *Journal of the Indian Council of Philosophical Research*. 27: 180–207.

Goudriaan, Teun. (1994) "Rejection of Duality: On the Atman Conception in the Vishnu Purana." *Weiner Zeitschrift für die Kunde Süd-und Ostasiens und Archiv für indische Philosophie*, p. 38.

Grimes, John. A. (1990) *The Seven Great Untenables: Saptavidhānupapatti*. Delhi: Motilal Banarsidass.

Hacker, Paul. (1959) *Prahlada – Werden und Wandlugen einer Idealgestalt – Beiträge zur Geschichte des Hinduismus*. Vols I & II. Mainz-Wiesbaden: Akademie der Wissenschaften und der Literatur, Abhandlungen der Geistes-und Sozialwissenschaftlichen Klasse.

Hacker, Paul. (1965) "Relations of Early Advaitins to Vaiṣṇavism." *Weiner Zeitschrift für die Kunde Süd-und Ostasiens und Archiv für indische Philosophie*. 9: 147–54.

Halbfass, Wilhelm. (Ed.) (1995) *Philology and Confrontation: Paul Hacker on Traditional and Modern Vedānta*. Albany: State University of New York Press.

Halbfass, Wilhelm. (1991) *Tradition and Reflection: Explorations in Indian Thought*. Albany: State University of New York Press.

Hardy, F. (2001) *Viraha Bhakti: the Early History of Kṛṣṇa Devotion in South India*. New Delhi: Oxford University Press, Reprint.

Hill, W.D.P. (1953) *The Bhagavadgītā*. London: Oxford University Press.

Hirst, J.G. Suthren. (1993) "The Place of Bhakti in Śaṅkara's Vedānta." In *Love Divine: Studies in Bhakti and Devotional Mysticism*. Ed. Karel Werner. Surrey: Curzon Press.

Hirst, J.G. Suthren. (2005) *Śaṁkara's Advaita Vedānta; A Way of Teaching*. London: Routledge Curzon.

Hohenberger, Adam. (1960) *Rāmānuja, ein Philosoph indisher Gottesmystik: sein Lebensanschauung nach den wichtigsten Quellen*. Bonn: Selbstverlag des Orientalischen Seminars der Universität Bonn.

Hopkins, Steven P. (2002) *Singing the Body of God: The Hymns of Vedāntadeśika in Their South Indian Tradition*. New York: Oxford University Press.

Inden, R., Daud Ali and Jonathan Walters. (2000) *Querying the Medieval: Texts and the History of Practices in South Asia*. Oxford: Oxford University Press.

Jacob, G.A. (1891) *A Concordance to the Principal Upanishads and Bhagavadgita*. Bombay: Government Central Book Depot.

Lacombe, O. (1966) *Le Aboslu Selon le Vedānta*. Paris: Libraire Orientaliste Paul Geuthner.

Larson, Gerald J. (1979) *Classical Sāṃkhya: An Interpretation of its History and Meaning*. New Delhi: Motilal Banarsidass. Reprint, 1998.

Lester, R.C. (1976) *Rāmānuja on the Yoga*. Madras: Adyar Library and Research Center.

Lipner, Julius J. (1978) "The Christian and Vedāntic Theories of Originative Causality: A Study in Transcendence and Immanence." *Philosophy East and West*. 28.1.

Lipner, Julius J. (1986) *The Face of Truth: A Study of Meaning and Metaphysics in the Vedāntic Theology of Rāmānuja*. Albany: State University of New York Press.

Lott, E.J. (1976) *God and the Universe in the Vedāntic Theology of Rāmānuja*. Madras: Ramanuja Research Society.

Lott, E.J. (1980) *Vedantic Approaches to God*. New York: Barnes and Noble.

Malinar, Angelika. (2007) *The Bhagavadgītā: Doctrines and Contexts*. Cambridge: Cambridge University Press.

Malkovsky, Bradley J. (2001) *The Role of Divine Grace in the Soteriology of Sankaracharya*. Leiden: Brill.

Matchett, Freda. (2001) *Krsna: Lord or Avatara? The Relationship between Krsna and Vishnu*. Surrey: Curzon.

Mesquita, R. (1990) *Yāmunācāryas Philosophie der Erkenntnis: eine Studie Zu seiner Saṃvitsiddhi*. Wien: Verlag der Österreichische Akademie der Wissenschaften.

Menzies, Robert. A. (1991) *The Viṣṇu Purāṇa as Śruti*. M.A. Thesis. Department of Religion. University of Manitoba.

Mumme, Patricia. (1988) *The Śrīvaiṣṇava Theological Dispute: Maṇavāḷamāmuni and Vedānta Deśika*. Madras: New Era Publications.

Narasimhachary, M. (1998) *Contribution of Yāmunācārya to Viśiṣṭādvaita*. Hyderabad: Sri Jayalakshmi Publications.

Narayanan, V. (1987) *The Way and the Goal: Expressions of Devotion in the Early Śrī vaiṣṇava Tradition*. Washington, DC: Institute for Vaishnava Studies, Center for the Study of World Religions.

Narayanan, V. (1992) "Oral and Written Commentary on the Tiruvāymoḻi." In *Texts in Context: Traditional Hermeneutics in South Asia*. Ed. Jeffrey R. Timm. Albany: State University of New York Press.

Nayar, Nancy A. (1992) *Poetry as Theology: the Śrīvaiṣṇava Stotra in the Age of Rāmānuja*. Studies in Oriental Religions. Vol. 22. Wiesbaden: Otto Harrassowitz.

Neeval, Walter G. (1977) *Yāmuna's Vedānta and Pāñcarātra: Integrating the Classical and the Popular*. Missoula: Scholars Press.

Oberhammer, Gerhard. (1997) *Yādavaprakāśa: der vergessene Lehrer Rāmānujas*. Wien: Verlag der Osterreichische Akademie der Wissenschaften.

Oberhammer, Gerhard. (2000) *Zur Lehre von der Vibhūti Gottes*. Wien: Verlag der Osterreichische Akademie der Wissenschaften.

Olivelle, P. (1998) *The Early Upaniṣads*. New York: Oxford University Press.

Olivelle, P. (2004) "Manu and the Arthaśāstra: A Study in Śāstraic Intertextuality." *Journal of Indian Philosophy*. 32: 281–91.

Penner, H.H. (1965) "Cosmogony as Myth in the *Vishnu Purana*." *History of Religions*. 5. 2: 283–299.

Pollock, Sheldon. (1985) "The Theory of Practice and the Practice of Theory in Indian Intellectual History." *The Journal of the American Oriental Society*. 105.3: 499–519.

Pollock, Sheldon. (2011) "The Revelation of Tradition: śruti and smṛti and the Sanskrit Discourse of Power." In *Boundaries, Dynamics and Construction of Traditions in South Asia*. Ed. Federico Squarcini. London: Anthem Press, pp. 41–61.

Radhakrishnan, S.S. (1996) *The Principal Upaniṣads*. New Delhi: Harper Collins. Reprint.

Raghavan, V. (1975) "The Viṣṇupurāṇa and Advaita." *Adyar Library Bulletin*. 39: 294–99.

Rambachan, A. (1991) *Accomplishing the Accomplished: The Vedas as a Source of Valid Knowledge in Śaṅkara*. Honolulu: University of Hawaii Press.

Ram-Prasad, Chakravarthi. (2013) *Divine Self, Human Self: The Philosophy of Being in Two Gītā Commentaries*. London: Bloomsbury.

Ranganayaki, S.T. (1999) *Sri Visnucittiya of Srivisnucitta: A Study*. Ph.D. Dissertation. Madras University.

Rocher, L. (1986) *The Purāṇas. A History of Indian Literature*. Vol. II. Fasc. 3. Wiesbaden: Otto Harrassowitz.

Rocher, L. (1994) "Orality and Textuality in the Indian Context." *Sino-Platonic Papers*. 49: 1–28.

Salomon, Richard. (1986) "The Vishnu Purana as a Specimen of Vernacular Sanskrit." *Weiner Zeitschrift für die Kunde Süd-und Ostasiens und Archiv für indische Philosophie*. 30: 39–56.

Sampatkumaran, M.R. (1985) *The Gītābhāṣya of Rāmānuja*. Bombay: Anantacharya Indological Research Institute.

Sarasvati, S. (1989) *The Method of Vedānta: A Critical Account of the Advaita Tradition*. Translated by A.J. Alston. London: Kegan Paul International.

Sargeant, W. (1979) *The Bhagavadgītā*. New York: Knopf Doubleday Publishing Group.

Sheth, N. (1985) *The Divinity of Krsna*. New Delhi: Munshiram Manoharlal.

Smith, Jonathan Z. (1982) *Imagining Religion*. Chicago, IL: University of Chicago Press.

Soifer, Deborah A. (1991) *The Myths of Narasiṁha and Vāmana: Two Avatars in Cosmological Perspective*. Albany: State University of New York Press.

Sydnor, Jon P. (2008) "Rāmānuja's Philosophy of Divinity: From Brahman to Nārāyaṇa." *Journal of Vaishnava Studies*. 16.2:3–26.

Swami Adidevananda. (1949) *Yatīndramatadīpikā of Śrīnivāsadāsa*. Madras: Sri Ramakrishna Math.

Thibaut, George. (1996) *The Vedānta Sūtras with the Commentary by Rāmānuja*. Sacred Books of the East, Vol. 48. New Delhi: Motilal Banarsidass, Reprint.

van Buitenen, J.A.B. (1955) "The Śubhāśrayaprakaraṇa (VP 6.7) and the Meaning of Bhāvana." *The Adyar Library Bulletin*. 19: 3–19.

van Buitenen, J.A.B. (1971) *Yāmuna's Āgama Prāmāṇyam*. Madras: Ramanuja Research Society.

van Buitenen, J.A.B. (1974) *Rāmānuja on the Bhagavadgītā*. New Delhi: Motilal Banarsidass.

van Buitenen, J.A.B. (1981) *The Bhagavadgītā in the Mahābhārata*. Chicago, IL: University of Chicago Press.

Vaidya, C.V. (1921–26) *History of Medieval Hindu India*. Poona: Oriental Book-Supplying Agency.

Varenne, Jean. (1960) *La Mahā Nārāyaṇa Upaniṣad*. Vols I–II. Fasc. 13. Paris: Publications de l'Institut de Civilization Indienne.

Venkatachari, K.K.A. (1994) "Purāṇaratna." *Journal of the Oriental Institute*. 43: 3–4.

Wessler, Heinz W. (1995) *Zeit und Geschichte im Viṣṇu Purāṇa*. Bern: Peter Lang.

Wilson, H.H. (2003) *The Viṣṇupurāṇa Vols I & II*. Delhi: Nag Publishers, Reprint.

Zaehner, R.C. (1969) *The Bhagavadgītā*. London: Oxford University Press.

Index

Adjunct (upādhi) 22, 67, 70, 72, 81–82, 86, 96, 99, 103, 124–25, 127, 129, 135, 137
Advaita *see* nondualism
Āḻvār 6, 12 fn3
Amplification 3, 83; *see* corroboration
Ātman 14–24, 27, 36; *see* puruṣa and individual self
Attribute 10, 15, 21–24, 39, 42, 51, 54–55, 62 fn103, 66–68, 71, 77, 79, 102, 117, 129, 140
Attribute-less 10, 65, 69, 70–71, 73, 76, 80, 82, 84, 92, 103; *see* quality-less
Attributive consciousness 23–24, 86
Attributive nature 16, 17, 54, 79, 91
Attributive quality 15, 17
Auspicious object (śubhāśraya) 10, 41, 52, 55, 73, 81–82, 121–23
Avidyā 11, 22–23, 64–65, 67–68, 81, 89–90, 92–94, 96–100, 102, 104, 129–31, 142; *see* ignorance and karma

Bharata 10, 88, 130–32, 144 fn23

Causal state (kāraṇāvasthā) 25–26, 31, 34, 38, 51, 54, 57 fn31
Causality 11, 14, 25–26, 28, 30–34, 36–38, 54–55. 58 fn42 and 43, 69, 71–72, 95, 98, 114, 116
Co-ordinate Predication (sāmānādhikaraṇya) 57 fn31, 68, 79–80, 82–83, 105 fn11, 140
Concealment 22–23, 37, 54, 75, 79, 95, 96
Contraction 22–24, 79, 86
Corroboration 3–4, 17, 30, 54, 83, 126

Devotion (bhakti) 3, 6, 12 fn3, 15, 40, 50, 53, 76, 121–22, 135, 137–40, 142–43
Disposition 8, 90, 131
Divine form (divyarūpa) 10–11, 14–15, 37–55, 60 fn70 and 76, 64, 77, 82
Doctrine of Causality (satkāryavāda) 26, 69, 98, 114, 116
Dual characteristics (ubhayaliṅga) 68–73, 75, 103
Dual manifestation (ubhayavibhūti) 45–46, 51

Effected state of Brahman (kāryāvasthā) 25–26, 28, 31, 34, 39, 48, 54, 57 fn31, 76
Embodied self 21–24, 68, 90
Essential nature (svarūpa) 3, 9–11, 14–21, 22–26, 28, 31, 55, 58 fn42, 65, 67–85, 114–20
Eternal manifestation (nityavibhūti) 46, 76
Existence (sat) 39, 65, 67, 69, 93–94, 97–98, 104, 114–19, 135–36, 141

Field (kṣetra) 92–93, 113, 124, 126, 129–30, 132, 142, 147 fn83, 148 fn98
Field-knower (kṣetrajña) 83, 92, 124, 129–30, 132–33, 142
Form (vigraha) 37, 42, 45, 48, 76

Ignorance (avidyā) 11, 22–24, 64–68, 81, 89–99, 102, 104, 129–31, 142; *see* karma and avidyā
Illusion (māyā) 55, 95–96, 116, 124, 127–28, 134, 136–37, 142
Illusionist (māyāvin) 55, 95, 136
Incarnation 47–48, 75–76, 140
Individual self 9–11, 14–31, 33–36, 38, 54–55, 64–66, 68–69, 78–83, 85–93, 96–101, 103–4, 114, 116–26, 129–34, 138, 140–42; *see* puruṣa

Inter-textual 2, 113
Intra-textual 88, 91–93

Karma 8, 10, 19–20, 22–24, 28–29, 39, 54, 73, 79–81, 90–94, 96, 98–101, 104, 121, 132, 139
Keśidhvaja 10, 19, 122
Khāṇḍikya 10, 19, 122
Kṛṣṇa 113–16, 120–30, 134–42

Liberated self 21, 66, 89–92, 109 fn89
Liberation (mokṣa) 6, 10, 12, 15, 19–20, 83, 90, 101, 109 fn89, 134, 140, 141

Manifestation (vibhūti) 42, 68, 72, 76, 80, 82
Master (śeṣin) 73, 126, 138
Matter 6, 8–10, 14, 18, 20–21, 25–39, 47–49, 54–55, 68–69, 73–82, 85–86, 88, 91–92, 94–95, 98–101, 118–19, 122, 124–28, 131–34, 137–38, 141–42; *see* pradhāna and prakṛti
Meditation 10, 41, 55, 71, 73, 81–82, 90–91, 107 fn61 and 63, 120–23
Mode 27, 30–31, 128, 140
Mode-possessor 128, 140

Non-existence 94, 97–102, 104, 114–19, 126

Originative Causality 25–38

Plurality of selves 66, 81, 85–86, 88, 120, 129, 131
Power (śakti) 8–9, 14, 23, 37, 48, 54–55, 68, 80–81, 92, 104
Pradhāna 6, 8, 49, 79, 127–28; *see* matter and prakṛti
Prahlāda 136–37, 139–40, 142–43
Prakṛti 6, 8, 18–19, 27–31, 33, 37–39, 70, 76, 78–80, 82, 94–96, 99, 101, 122, 124, 127–28, 131–32, 134–38; *see* matter and pradhāna
Puruṣa 27–31, 33–36, 38, 43–44, 50, 78–80, 126–29, 134, 141–42; *see* individual self

Quality-less 68, 72, 81–82, 131, 142

Ṣāṃkhya 114–20
Śaṅkara *see* nondualism
Sat 94, 98, 104, 114–18, 135; *see* existence
Scripture 1–4, 8, 11, 12 fn4, 17, 20, 32–33, 39, 47, 51, 57 fn31, 65–67, 69–71, 74, 83, 85, 92–94, 102–3, 113, 134, 142
Scriptural harmony (samanvaya) 69–72, 83, 85, 91–93, 103, 109 fn89
Servant (śeṣa) 17, 73, 109 fn89, 126, 138, 140
Smṛti 28–30, 46–50, 72–74, 96–104
Soul-body 6, 8–9, 19, 26, 29–33, 35, 37–38, 57 fn31, 68–69, 72–74, 76–78, 83–84, 92, 98–99, 101–4, 105 fn18, 110 fn101, 116, 126, 131–34, 141
Sport (līlā) 30, 46, 68, 76
Śruti 15–18, 26–28, 43–46, 50–51, 69–72, 93–96, 133–34, 137
Svarūpa *see* essential nature

Universal from (viśvarūpa) 39, 48–49, 77
Unreality (mithyā) 93, 97, 130, 135

Viṣṇu Purāṇa 5–12, 18–24, 30–39, 48–54, 74–82, 84–93, 96–104, 117–19, 122–23, 127–28, 131–32, 136, 139–40

Yoga 3, 11, 40, 73, 81–83, 121–23, 141, 144 fn35